Dynamic Pluralism

A Revolution in Ethics
by Ken La Salle

Dynamic Pluralism
A Revolution in Ethics

By Ken La Salle

There is only one good, knowledge, and one evil, ignorance.

- Socrates

To Professors Ted Shigematsu and James Crippen Jr.

Without whom this book would not have been imaginable.

Table of Contents

An Introduction on Experts

It seems a strange way to begin a book on philosophy, especially a book on ethics, to challenge the role of experts in finding our way through such issues. After all, who else is there to go to when we have a question on ethics but the experts, people of authority who hold the answers when the rules of the universe or the rules of life require clarification? If we challenge the experts, aren't we challenging the order of the very same universe and our own lives? Aren't we creating a kind of mental anarchy? That may be one way of looking at it. All the same, though, the challenge must be made.

I realized exactly why one night as I was drifting off to sleep, questioning exactly what I was doing by creating such a challenge, when the following words floated across my drifting conscience; "Expertise is an illusion and authority only exists to be questioned. Tis DOUBT, my friend, that makes the world go elliptically..."

And I rose with a start. I had no idea where that had come from. All I could figure as I tried to put myself back to sleep was that all the research that had led me into this book was backing up like some poorly maintained mental septic tank. Doubt makes the worlds go elliptically? Surely, the world goes round in circles, right? Paul Anka, Madonna, and even Ashlee Simpson tend to agree: "Love makes the world go **round**."

But no. That's not right. And that realization had me waking up even further, despite my need for sleep. For it was Kepler in the 17th century who determined that planets travel in elliptical orbits and not circles.[1] No matter what the old songs might tell you, they haven't checked their science. Kepler challenged the experts of his time, which led all the way back to the seemingly unshakeable logic of Aristotle, with scientific observation and the courage to challenge what to that point had seemed unchallengeable. Theories about the universe had for too long rested on the authority of experts and it is that very authority Kepler swept aside. It is that very authority we must all sweep aside when questioning something like ethics.

Which is why this book begins with exactly such a challenge.

Someone once aptly put it that "An expert is someone who insists something cannot be done and then takes credit for it once it is." It is just such authoritarianism that the great Oliver Wendell Holmes cautioned against in *Over The Teacups* "Do not be bullied out of your common sense by the specialist." The educator Richard Feynman applied this same idea to the pursuit of science in *The Pleasure of Finding Things Out.*[2] "Science alone of all the subjects contains within itself the lesson of the danger of belief in the infallibility of the greatest teachers in the preceding generation ... Learn from science that you must doubt the experts. As a matter of fact, I can also define science another way: Science is the belief in the ignorance of experts."

As long as there have been people, there have been experts. Even since before Og told Grog that fire was great but that new wheel thing was just a passing fad, some have been right but most have been wrong. The key has always been to realize just when such expertise has outlived its shelf life, instead of relying on the authoritarian expert to tell us.

Sadly, the logic of Aristotle was not put completely aside by Kepler, nor by the many great minds who came before him. Not by Galileo, nor by Copernicus. In the case of Copernicus, his attempt to rebuke authority was taken out of his hands. Copernicus's publisher, George Rheticus, was editing a manuscript by Copernicus in 1543 when he was called away to the University of Leipzig to become professor of mathematics. Editing then went into the hands of Andreas Osiander, a firm Aristotelian believer that divine revelation was the sole source of truth and that the Bible did not describe the solar system as Copernicus did. It was Osiander who first changed the title of the Copernican work from *On the Revolution of Planets in the Sky* to one by which it is still known, *On the Revolution of the Heavenly Bodies*. He also inserted a preface stating that while the author described a sun-centered system, it was simply intended to make the work of astronomers easier and did not reflect what was actually happening in the sky. (Mental gynamstics are not the sole property of our time.) By the time Copernicus received a copy of the book with its new title and preface, he was on his deathbed and it was too late to do anything about it.[3]

There are still those who hold Aristotle as an authority. Authority, it would seem, is exactly where the problem lies.

A primary authority is that of religion, notably The Bible. The Bible has often been seen as an authority on many topics, the answer to many questions, both religious and practical. In some cases, it remains so.

Until only a couple of centuries ago, the biblical interpretation of history reigned. That meant the universe absolutely was created in six days. There was an actual Garden of Eden. Some who believed in what was called "Young Earth Creationism" established the age of the Earth, using biblical chronology, at approximately six thousand years. As James Burke explains it: "The Bible was also the definitive text of geological history. The flood was an event which accounted for the discovery of extinct organisms. The purpose of natural history was only to elaborate god's Grand Design. Taxonomy, the listing and naming of all parts of nature, was the principal aim of this endeavor. The patterns which these lists revealed would form god's original plan, unchanged since creation."[4]

The problem with positioning The Bible as an authority in matters non-religious is that it is so easily disproven. Such as the 6,000 year age of the Earth. Back in the 1960s, an archeologist by the name of James Mellaart first excavated the town of Çatal Hüyük in modern Turkey.[5] The town was over 9,000 years old and at the time of the "Young Earth" creation had over six thousand citizens.[6]

This happens every time you allow one thing, be it a person or a book or any other resource, to become your authority. It just gets easier and easier to topple. When Aristotle's scientific theories fell away, the next authority became Newton. His clockwork universe – obeying the law of gravity, with time and space absolute, and all matter moving in straight lines – was unquestionable.

Until, of course, it was questioned. And it was a Swiss patent clerk, not an academic, not an expert, who did it. He changed everything we thought about the universe and he, too, became the expert, the authority.

Another reason to begin a book on ethics with a warning about experts is because of just the kind of ethical track record experts have had over the years. A great example of this lies with the tobacco industry. We've all heard the story by now: Big tobacco wants to continue selling its highly toxic product despite mountains of evidence of the harm it causes to health and society – as well as ruining any chance of ever coming home from a party without stinking like an ashtray – so they hire their own "experts" to counter the... well, the truth.

The tobacco industry had enjoyed a long history in America and could safely be referred to as an institution. Tobacco originated in America and, by the time of the Revolutionary War, helped secure loans for the fledgling nation.[7] Tobacco giants Phillip Morris and R.J. Reynolds were founded and flourished in the 1800s. By the dawn of the 20th century, 3.5 billion cigarettes and 6 billion cigars were sold every year. Millions of soldiers were hooked with cheap or outright free smokes in every war of the 20th century, adding millions of customers from that point on.

Of course, by that time, pesky scientists were beginning to prove just what a health hazard tobacco presented. It was time to bring in the PR industry to save the day for tobacco and, as John Stauber and Sheldon Rampton describe in *Toxic Sludge is Good for You!*[8]: "One of the PR industry's first major clients was the tobacco industry. In the early twentieth century, the tobacco companies used PR's psychological marketing skills to first hook women and then children on their drug. Edward Bernays, Ivy Lee and John Hill all worked on PR for tobacco, pioneering techniques that today remain the PR industry's stock in trade: third party advocacy, subliminal message reinforcement, junk science, phony front groups, advocacy advertising, and buying favorable news reporting with advertising dollars."

Prior to World War I, smoking cigarettes was considered unrefined for women and effeminate for men, who either smoked cigars or stuck to tobacco of the chewing variety. The war brought cigarettes into vogue for men, and during the Roaring Twenties, the American Tobacco Company turned to PR to develop a vast new market –

American women – for sales of its Lucky Strike brand. The company first hired adman A.D. Lasker, who portrayed Lucky Strikes as a healthy cigarette by concocting surveys using spurious data to claim that doctors preferred Luckies as the "less irritating" brand. Lasker also developed an advertising campaign featuring female Metropolitan opera stars, their soprano voices somehow unaffected by smoking, giving testimonials such as "Cigarettes Are Kind To Your Throat" and "I Protect My Precious Voice With Lucky Strikes."[9]

To persuade women that cigarette smoking could help them stay beautiful, Bernays developed a campaign based on the slogan, "Reach for a Lucky Instead of a Sweet." The campaign played on women's worries about their weight and increased Lucky sales threefold in just twelve months. (The message, "cigarettes keep you thin," continues to reverberate in the brand name Virginia Slims.)[10]

Once it became acceptable for women to smoke, it was time for babies. I remember having candy cigarettes as a child and I can tell you they looked just like the real thing and also tasted like ass, so I was ready. Getting kids to smoke wasn't just a conspiracy theory for people suspicious about Joe Camel, either. An R.J. Reynolds official in 1973 while I was munching those chalky "candies" assessed, "Realistically, if our company is to survive and prosper, over the long term, we must get our share of the youth market …"[11]

In case you missed all the health issues the tobacco "experts" denied, the consensus has been simple: **It'll kill you**. Rather than run through all the ways tobacco will kill you – because no book has the space to be that comprehensive – I thought it might be better to see the tobacco industry's response in 1998. It was then that thousands of previously confidential internal tobacco industry documents consisting of some 40 million pages were made publicly accessible. These documents covered six leading tobacco companies: American Tobacco Company, British American Tobacco Company, Brown & Williamson Tobacco Corporation, Lorillard Tobacco Company, Philip Morris Incorporated, and RJ Reynolds Tobacco Company. It also included documentation from two tobacco industry organizations: The Council for Tobacco Research and The Tobacco Institute

According to the World Health Organization in their manual "The Tobacco Industry Documents"[12]: the documents present an unprecedented insight into tobacco strategies and tactics. Document analysis has been used in academic research; investigative journalism; international organizations' investigations; advocacy campaigns; and litigation and public inquiries.

The documents revealed decades of industry misconduct including: the extent of industry deception, e.g. denials of addiction and links between smoking and cancer; attempts to manipulate scientific research; industry attempts to create a "debate" on health impacts of smoking including attacks on epidemiology and epidemiologists; recruitment of young smokers as critical to the industry's ongoing viability; target marketing to women (particularly in Asia); industry involvement in cigarette smuggling, collusion, anti-competitive practices and price fixing; efforts to influence national tobacco control policy, and to undermine unfavorable tobacco initiatives; industry efforts to influence national legislation; and campaigns to circumvent tobacco advertising bans.

When the tobacco companies still couldn't keep people from getting educated on the matter of how their products would kill them, when they lost customers who were trying to save their own lives, they shifted tactics to creating dummy groups (front groups made of dummies…) that pushed a dummy political agenda. One such group is the now defunct "National Smokers Alliance," an organization of smokers who would stand up for "smoker's rights."[13] This group was developed by Burson-Marsteller PR with millions of dollars from Philip Morris as a state-of-the-art campaign using full-page newspaper ads, direct telemarketing, paid canvassers, free 800 numbers and newsletters to bring thousands of smokers into its ranks each week. By 1995 NSA claimed a membership of 3 million smokers.

Through a combination of high-tech direct marketing techniques and old fashioned "feet on the ground" community organizing, the NSA recruited smoking's victims into becoming its advocates. The National Smokers Alliance had their own folksy but strident newsletter, called *The NSA Voice*. The NSA paid hundreds of young activists to sign up members in bars and bowling alleys in cities around the country. They handed out free stickers to place in stores and restaurants, which read: "I am a smoker and have spent $____ in your establishment." NSA members who signed up another ten people at $10 each could win a free NSA t-shirt. The committed and informed pro-smoking advocate could also call a toll-free number to get the latest marching orders regarding which bureaucrats or politicians need nudging from Marlboro's masses. Burson-Marsteller's propagandists even coined a clever play on words to question the patriotism of anti-smokers by calling them "anti Americans". The NSA's newsletter advised, "If 'Anti' America is pushing a discriminatory smoking ban in your workplace, speak up," and "check the laws in your state with regard to protection of individual rights."[14]

This was an organization created to convince people that they were being patriotic by smoking, that smoking made them good people. It was an organization that told people they weren't any good if they weren't poisoning themselves. The more marginalized smokers felt by being pushed away from the rest of society, the more the NSA made them feel welcome and right for purchasing their poison.

These were the experts, the authorities people were trusting rather than thinking for themselves. These were the experts who lied year after year, decade after decade. These were the same tactics that would later be used to deceive people about the truth of climate change. And these are the same tactics that will continue to be used just as long as people blindly follow "the experts."

Sometimes it's not quite so easy to see when the experts are misleading you. Sometimes the issue isn't so obvious. Take Thomas Midgley, for example, a sure candidate for hell if such a place existed. In 1921, Midgley discovered the benefits of lead components in gasoline to prevent knocking in automobile engines. Then, in 1928, he developed chlorofluorocarbons (CFCs) – chemical bad Karma still chewing up our fragile ozone layer – as a "non-toxic refrigerant." It wasn't until 1974 when Mario Molina and F. Sherwood Rowland issued the first warnings against the damage to stratospheric ozone, for which they shared the Nobel Prize for Chemistry, that we had a hint at what nearly 50 years of damage was doing… what it continues to do. CFC industry "experts" tried to cast doubt on the science that was impinging on their profits. Oftentimes, that's what experts do best.

Sometimes expert, authoritarian rulings can appear harmless but the propagation of ignorance seldom is. I first heard about the theory of plate tectonics when I was a boy and it was still new enough that many of my peers referred to California as "floating on a bed of molten rock," which could slide into the ocean at any time. Al Gore in *An Inconvenient Truth* shares a plate tectonic story of his own: "my sixth grade teacher taught geography by pulling down a map of the world in front of a blackboard. One of my classmates raised his hand, pointed to the east coast of South America and the west coast of Africa and asked, 'Did they ever fit together?' And the teacher responded, 'Of course not! That's the most ridiculous thing I've ever heard!'

That sixth-grade teacher had an assumption in his mind that he didn't bother to question: Continents are so big, obviously they don't move.

As we now know, they did move. At one time they fit together, then moved apart millions of years ago. And they're still moving."[15]

The father of plate tectonics, Alfred Wegener saw something very similar. Then, in 1911, Wegener came across paleontological evidence that strengthened his views. Almost identical fossil snails had been found in Africa and Brazil and, in 1912, Wegener made public his continental drift theory. His hypothesis was met with derision and it would take fifty years of further discovery to confirm Wegener's basic thesis. Until then most geology "experts" thought Wegener was seeing things.[16]

Maintaining the status quo might not have killed as many as tobacco or CFCs, but it held science back and the only ones to benefit were the experts who believed the Earth to be static.

Experts Overthrown

It would be simple to say that the authority of experts could be shunned and long-accepted premises destroyed if the results were always in the negative column. Unfortunately, this is not so. Sometimes, experts pose valid arguments and help advance the collective human intellect.

Rather than solidify an argument for trusting in their authority, however, I'd say this goes further to ruin their credibility. In short, the problem with experts is that they're so unreliable.

You never know if you can count on them.

Orson Welles's documentary (some might say part mockumentary) *F for Fake* questions the verisimilitude of experts. How real are they? And how can they be trusted when even they cannot trust themselves. The example Welles provides is, in part, based on the story of the great art forger Elmyr De Hory and his friend, confidant, and betrayer Clifford Irving. Elmyr exposes how his forgeries hang in galleries around the world, undetected by the "experts" even as Clifford Irving learns the "trade" and presents his own forged biography of Howard Hughes, with every detail you'd expect from the real thing. In the end, no one can be trusted, no matter how trustworthy they may be or seem to be.

Experts are so often made into liars even when they're telling the truth.

Case in point: Thomas Malthus, whose most important contribution to mankind is still considered by many to be a lie.

Malthus wrote a book called *Essay on the Principle of Population* in 1798, during a time when French wars influenced grain prices to rise through the roof, bringing famine to Britain. Malthus argued that diminishing returns were bound to happen, that the best that could be expected from agriculture would be arithmetical gains, increasing as a multiple of 2, of 3, of 4, of 5 and so on, and providing just enough food to encourage populations to grow. Unfortunately, however, populations do not grow arithmetically. They grow geometrically, which means in multiples of 2, of 4, of 8, of 16 and so on. Production would not keep up with reproduction and Malthus encouraged such sacrilegious counter-measures as contraception, late marriage, and so on.[17]

Anyone who has kept up with politics since then can infer how well Malthus's ideas have fared. It didn't take long before Malthus was shown to be right, either. He found figures to immediately support his claims with the enormous population increase in the census of 1801. As immediate as those figures were then, they are even more dramatic now, with the world population more than doubling since the time I was born.[18]

Not only can agriculture not keep up, ecosystems are failing as a result, bringing further disaster. Not only was Malthus doubted but the "experts" who restricted reproduction rights (along with the education necessary to question their authority) employed (as some still employ) the term "Malthusian" derisively, as if to mean "crackpot". The ethical implications of ignoring a warning from two centuries ago are monumental.

This goes to show that experts must be doubted, even when they are questioning other experts. An immediate example of this is in the way communism and socialism have been so demonized in the United States that the ideas these terms are based upon are no longer even scrutinized. It's the terms themselves that are used by so-called "experts" in the media to discredit anything they might disagree with. Those who disagreed with President Obama's attempt to reform health care, called it communism. When the National Rifle Association wanted to strike fear in gun owners that their guns were going to be "taken away", they called that communism. Similarly, Republicans and those on the "political right" have fought every attempt at raising taxes on the wealthy by calling it communism.

The problem, of course, is when someone with a brain comes by, someone who knows that communism (as with socialism) is an economic system that eliminates privatization and advocates collectivization… which means that President Obama's plan that benefited private insurance companies could not be considered communism. Efforts to increase safety and protect people from getting shot by a gun are not necessarily economical and, therefore, not communist. And taxes can be levied no matter what system you support. Again, these experts are not trying to make a valid argument of any kind. They are simply using their authority to lie with impunity.

You've got to question them.

The Questioner. Florence Nightingale.

During the British cholera outbreak in 1851, hospital conditions were so appalling as to be unrecognizable in the modern sense. Patients usually slept on the fouled sheets of previous patients and filthy mattresses were never changed.[19] Florence Nightingale described the nurses of the time as little more than drunken "whores brought in from the streets" who continued to ply their trade in the hospital. Doctors were of little help, operating in filth and rarely washing, wearing blood-encrusted coats.

The Crimean War exceeded even these levels of the nightmarish. When Florence Nightingale and her personally-trained staff of 38 volunteer nurses arrived on October 21, 1854, they found the hospital a charnel house. The hospital had no furniture. Mattresses on the floors and the floors themselves were covered in human waste and blood. It's important to remember that this wasn't exceptional for the time. This was the expected state of medicine.

Nightingale took it on herself to change all of this. With public financing raised by the London *Times*, she helped provide the bare necessities – operating tables, clean sheets, and food just for starters – for some level of cleanliness, if not yet sterility, in army hospitals. She lobbied the chef of the Reform Club to go to Crimea and provide wholesome food for the sick. These simple measures among others Nightingale recommended and worked for brought the hospital's mortality rate from 44% to 2%.

Florence Nightingale kept the pressure on the military authorities until a sanitary commission was established. Then, thanks to her unceasing efforts, the Royal Army Medical Corps was established.[20] Nightingale's writing profoundly influenced Jean-Henri Dunant, a Swiss philanthropist, and it was their efforts that resulted in the first Geneva Convention in 1864, established for "the amelioration of the condition of wounded armies in the field." Nightingale's most enduring work, the International Red Cross, was established at this convention.

The authority of experts only exists for the perpetuation of the expert expressing authority. That is to say it hardly exists at all.

Consider an extreme example to illustrate this: The 18th century writer J.G. Herder, in an attempt to better understand the nature of German culture, borrowed an idea from German art historian Johann Winckelmann that cultural expression needs to be understood in an historical context. Herder's concept of man as part of nature, part of history, helped give birth to what would become known as Romanticism and was known as "historical outlook."[21]

Time is an invention and our place in it is as well. We not only invent the world around us but we also invent how we see it. And it's not always done by experts.

Consider the change from Roman to Arabic numerals in the west, sometime around the 10th century. Up until that time, multiplication and division were practically out of the question. Geometry could only be performed with cut pieces of parchment. One performed math problems like a child held back in a remedial class: with their fingers! But that wasn't all. On top of that, there was no zero. The number zero did not exist according to the experts of the time and, when it became hinted at, the experts wouldn't acknowledge it. They couldn't.

You can't wait on experts to tell you what to do or how to solve your problems. They're not capable. They turn out wrong. Even when they're right, things get confused. Look at it this way: finding the answer for yourself makes the times when they're right feel like a discovery!

That's the problem, of course. Finding the answers for yourself. We Americans have been trained, maybe inadvertently and maybe intentionally so, to expect some expert to provide our answers for us. This reliance has led to an anti-intellectualism that has caught on like wildfire. Presidential candidates sign pledges not to think for themselves. We cheer for those who flaunt their stupidity. And very few of us stop to ponder where that will lead.

Malcolm X once famously said "As long as you are convinced you have never done anything, you can never do anything." As long as you're certain there's an expert around the corner, waiting to provide convenient answers, you'll never look for the answers yourself or even wonder if you have the right question. In the end, the ethics this provides is a lazy form of ethics, a reality TV form of ethics where nothing is wrong as long as we're entertained by it. Nothing harms us if we can deny it loudly enough.

The fact is that real ethics, simple, understandable ethics, ethics you can rely on reside in no expert. As this book will show, ethics are part of a dynamic process that is always changing amidst a plurality and no expert can tell you what that is. You create ethics as a part of this plurality.

The purpose of this book is to provide a roadmap but it is the traveler on that road who decides his or her own actions. In the pages ahead, we'll create new experts of ourselves and become better people for it.

PART 1
How Do We Find Ethics?

Where do we look for ethics in a world where ethics have become so hard to find? In the first part of this book, I'd like to lay out a roadmap to ethics, using ideas from the past combined with common sense solutions we have right now to find the ethics that have proved so elusive.

Chapter 1
An Essay on Ethics

Your Introduction to Ethics

It starts out when we're children.

Someone expects us to know right from wrong.

They may not have exactly showed you the difference or even took the time to explain it but they were expecting you to know it and when you didn't they showed their disappointment in a number of ways. Then, slowly, you began to catch on. You learned to pay attention when someone was speaking, not to interrupt, and that you should share your toys.

This wasn't ethics, or anything approaching ethics. At best, this was a Robert Fulghum, *All I Ever Really Needed To Know I Learned In Kindergarten* kind of ethics, but it was good enough at the time. It served its purpose.

Then, the day came when you realized that wasn't quite enough. It may have come recently. It may have been a realization that has been pecking at the back of your skull as you wondered at it: *What are ethics, anyway?*

If you're anything like me, that realization came just before the dull thud of reality – that our society, and mine is the United States in the second decade of the twenty-first century, has no idea what ethics are and very possibly had none to begin with. It's a terrifying realization. Politicians are sucking on the teat of the rich while forcing the poor to pay more in taxes so the rich won't have to. Wars are waged for little more reason than justification for starting them. Food is grown to turn into fuel for those nations who can afford it while people starve. We sunder the planet, sometimes as dramatically as cracking a hole in the Gulf of Mexico. We ignore the devastation we've wrought on the earth with "reality TV" that shows an endless parade of bimbos who will do anything to show their genitals to the highest bidder, or in lieu of that just anyone. Lobbyists run the country. Crooks are exonerated as long as they're entertaining or wealthy enough. And unjust laws lead to the persecution of innocents, while we look for the next low-cal snack to shovel into our gullets and wonder why we're obese.

In the most cynical corner of my psyche, I think this probably isn't so different than in other times in our history and the future may see this as well. William Faulkner said, "The past is never dead. It's not even past." And I wonder if the same applies to every crime we allow to be committed by every corrupt politician, greedy businessman, media pusher, lobbyist and other prostitute, and every other lazy god-damned American. Will our sins perpetuate endlessly so it's just one thing after another? Sometimes, it sure seems that way.

Towards the end of the last century, a corrupt, right-wing politician named William Bennett published a book called *The Book of Virtues*, which was quickly a bestseller. It was the only book in a long time that came close to addressing the issue of ethics and it did so in a patronizingly authoritarian manner, spoon-feeding morality into the mouths of a public hungry for any kind of guidance they could get. His readers were looking to be addressed as children, hoping for the very sort of authoritarian guidance cautioned against in this book's *Introduction…* and he happily provided it.

The problem with that, though, is… that's not ethics. Political pundits scooping morality into the waiting, chirping mouths of a populace so starved for guidance that they'll listen to anyone, even a corrupt politician, can't be ethics. If it was, our ethics would change every four years or with the wavering ratings of Fox News. Ethics have to be greater than that and it seems to me that, buried somewhere under a steady diet of Happy Meals, we surely must know this. There are examples throughout our history, some very recent.

But if that isn't ethics, if the suckling guidance of political pundits isn't or if even the reassuring rules of kindergarten aren't… then what is? How can we identify ethical behavior? How do we know when we're being ethical or how to be ethical as situations arise? More importantly, how do we know when we're not being ethical?

Just two centuries ago, a relatively short time in the history of humanity, there existed the disturbing, downright revolting, sport of bull-baiting. The sport was simple. A bull was placed into a specially constructed ring and tied to an iron stake. The bull was enraged. Then, attack dogs were sent into the ring to tear the bull to shreds. Great sport, huh? As repellent as that may seem, the first bill to outlaw this "sport" failed to pass through the British Houses of Parliament in 1800. George Canning, who would later be England's Prime Minister, claimed that bull-baiting "inspired courage and produced a nobleness of sentiment and elevation of mind... Putting a stop to bull-baiting was legislating against the spirit and genius of almost every country and age."[22] But such legislation (the first of its kind in any country) was eventually passed in England in 1821, protecting both horses and cattle against ill treatment. This led to the establishment of the Society for the Prevention of Cruelty to Animals in 1824.

People understood that some things were unethical. They learned how to identify it and stop it, even to the point of legislating the end of such behavior. If people can identify that bull-baiting is unethical – just like dog-fighting or cock-fighting – then it seems reasonable to assume that they should be able to identify when their actions towards other people are also unethical.

How we do that and how we put that into practice is exactly what I intend to identify in this book.

A Warning About Ethics

They aren't easy.

I'll tell you that from the beginning.

Those assuming that they can be ethical while they do whatever they like, pursue monetary wealth above everything else, push cynicism, avoid empathy, behave like a contrarian and generally act like an ass should probably put this book down right about now. You're not going to get much out of it. That's just how it works. There are traps on the way to finding ethics and those are just a few.

A couple of other traps worth noting are selfishness and value rigidity.

For those unfamiliar with institutionalized selfishness, I suggest the works of Ayn Rand, which should be avoided no matter how much of an object lesson in selfishness they may represent. This is where ethics go to die. Rand preached self-value (ignoring the needs of others) and capitalism (more specifically greed) as a philosophy, which in the end turns into nothing more than a reactionary, childish wail of "Mine! Mine! Mine!" As we'll see, ethics are not an island and no person can have any sort of ethics without considering others. Selfishness is the refusal of ethics.

Value rigidity, on the other hand, is not seeing ethics when they're right before you. This book will contain quite a few references to history to help the reader avoid the trap of value rigidity. For such an historical reference to give you some idea of what I mean by value rigidity, let's return to Aristotle and the pig-headed insistence of certain experts to hold fast to his theories even after they were proven wrong. After Europeans first began sailing to the Western Hemisphere, they brought back an abundance of plants (chocolate, tobacco, pineapples) and animals (some that could never have boarded the Biblical Ark, another example of value rigidity). Aristotle had claimed that the farther south one travelled the drier it would be but these explorations proved that wrong. Added to this was proof that the Earth was not at the center of the universe and that the Sun and Moon were not the perfect spheres they were supposed to be and, yet, certain folk stuck by Aristotle's every word. Ethics, as we'll see, cannot suffer from this kind of rigidity.

One of the most recognizable exercises in ethics is the "Lifeboat" exercise, and I think this ties those two examples together rather well. Lifeboat exemplifies the danger of looking at things in the same old way and hoping to find something new. The Lifeboat exercise is simple. You are on a ship at sea and tragedy strikes – or it might have been an iceberg. One way or another, you find yourself in a lifeboat with several other passengers. These could include a young mother and her child, a navigator, an old man, and several other stereotypes meant to force you into making a difficult decision. There are only enough rations for you and your fellow passengers… minus one… but which one? Who do you kick off the boat? Who dies? (Insert evil laugh here)

Despite the possible fun of killing off shipwreck survivors, the Lifeboat game combines value rigidity and selfishness. You may think you have to stick with these rules and you can't off yourself or, at least, if you do people are going to wonder. The good news is you can spare your own life and you also don't have to stick to those silly rules.

Because the fact of the matter is that the primary problem with so-called "Lifeboat Ethics" presented in the game of Lifeboat is that IT NEVER HAPPENS. (Okay, to be fair, "never" in this case means "it happens so very rarely as to be statistically impossible".) I can assure you that 99.9999% of ethical dilemmas you will face in your life will not be of the Lifeboat variety. The other problem with Lifeboat is that it does not allow for other solutions. What if there was a way of extending rations? What if modern technology allowed for quick communication with rescue vessels? What if, and this is a big one, there's something you haven't thought of, yet. Why the rush to kill off the peg-leg welfare mother who voted for Bernie Sanders, I ask you?

Lifeboat comes with a twist, which is that it isn't so easy to kill off other people as we would like to think. (And, for those who find it easy, this may also raise some red flags.) When you arm yourself with selfishness and value rigidity, you also put down the tools that come in so handy in solving your problems, such as flexibility, creativity, empathy, and the like. Ayn Rand and those who insist we stick with the old way of thinking too often assume that ethics are easy, one-dimensional problems to be dealt with in simple, single-dimensional ways. And they're wrong.

We'll find a system of ethics that works but we'll do it creatively, compassionately, and with actual intelligence.

Why do we care about what ethics are, anyway?

It's a good question to eliminate before we go any further: What's the big deal? We get along just fine the way things are, don't we? Why ask difficult questions that are just going to give us all a headache?

Well, I won't deny the question is difficult but I gotta wonder who in the world would think we get along just fine the way things are. Poor folks starve as the rich get richer. We're destroying the very world we live on. Our nation's number one pastime is watching others fall flat on their face on YouTube. I can't imagine anyone calling that ethical.

One of the keystones to a working society, one that thrives, is in making sure we all follow the same rules. Having a common set of rules helps us function better as a group; it helps us know we're not completely crazy. It's how you know that if you gave an amount of money equaling the price of something to a store clerk, they'll give you that item and not rob you or cheat you. It's how you know you can live in your home without getting robbed most of the time; it's why robberies are the exception and not the rule. It's how you know how fast the cars on the freeway are going… ideally.

Having a universal standard just makes things easier to understand. Consider the metric system; it's a standard of measurement that is easy to understand, easy to convert, and applies to sciences across the board. It's pretty much the standard system of measurement for the entire world… except for the United States, where we're too cool for metrics… and by "cool", of course I mean "lazy."

For every member of society, there has to be a way of saying, "If you behave this way, things will work out." That was supposed to be ethics. That was the expectation that we would all be able to raise our kids with a system they could understand and obey and learn to live by. What we've ended up with instead is more along the lines of a dysfunctional cafeteria. "You can behave this way… or that way… or that way. Actually, we have no real idea how you're supposed to behave. Nobody does. You can rest assured, however, that if you step out of line we'll get you."

This is essentially what we've settled for, an incomprehensible set of rules that are so difficult to understand that to challenge the system and change it for the better has become almost impossible. We need to start from scratch. We need to make something new. Maybe what we create won't be perfect but it will be a system we can understand, that we can build upon, and that will change the world in ways we couldn't imagine.

According to the second law of thermodynamics, entropy increases over time, which is to say that things in the universe (including people) have a tendency to go with the flow. In fact, that's how most people live from day to day, by going with the flow. Standing up for something you believe in, behaving in an ethical manner, actually means not going with the flow. It means defying entropy. The second law of thermodynamics actually accounts for this; it's referred to as "putting energy back into the system."

You may not realize it but everything you do changes the world. It may not be a huge change. It may not even be noticeable by the naked eye but your every action changes things around you. (Yes, that's more science for you: Newton's Third Law.) Think about it. When you shop. When you work. Even when you party, you are changing the world. In a global economy, your every act creates change throughout the system. Food you buy at the store changes the way food is grown on the other side of the world. Work you do may be experienced in some way on the other side of an ocean. This is unique in most of humanity's history.

Now, what if you chose for each of those actions to be ethical actions? What if the change you created was ethical change? By choosing ethics, by committing to ethical behavior, and not just going with the flow you are putting energy back into the system. You change the world a little every day, no matter what you do. Why not choose to make that change for a better world?

As strange as it might seem, this can be one of the most revolutionary things you can do every day of your life.

The Latin phrase "status quo" or more specifically "status quo ante" literally means "the state of affairs that existed before." By going with the flow and maintaining the status quo, you are ensuring that nothing improves – that reality TV gets increasingly bad, that politics become increasingly corrupt, that the Earth turns further and further into a cesspool – you are guaranteeing entropy! Defying this, standing against this, turns ethics into an act of revolution!

George Orwell once said that: "During times of universal deceit, telling the truth becomes a revolutionary act." The interpretation of ethics in this book takes that idea a step further. The world needs revolution in a time of seemingly universal apathy and that revolution lies within you!

Too long have we put sports figures on a pedestal and made them heroes for our children. All far too many of them do is throw a ball around! Too long have we shrugged our shoulders at every political malfeasance, chalking it up to an increasingly corrupt system. We forgot that politicians work for us; they should be better than us! Too long have we allowed war and greed, assuming that this time after so many times before there will be some kind of payoff. There isn't; not for good people. Only for criminals. Too long have we used celebrities as both our goal and distraction. We don't need more celebrities. We have enough! We need decency, compassion, and empathy! More than ever, we need ethics.

This revolution will be unlike any other you may have encountered. Previous revolutions relied on political will and social movements but fell victim to time and changing attitudes. It is those elements, however, that will serve this revolution best because, as you will see, with time attitudes will change. There will be no martyrs. While there have been many martyrs over the centuries in other revolutions, the rate of exchange is often rather abysmal. For real revolution to be successful, we must have a revolution of individuals, a personal revolution, which will spread out with every ethical action we take.

I say again for those who still aren't sure: this will not be easy. It will require a new way of thinking, of accepting that "right" and "wrong" are not necessarily ethical distinctions. An ethical decision may be considered wrong by some and what some see as right may be unethical. It will require a new way of looking at ourselves. We perform unethical deeds every day - driving our cars, supporting wars that appear to be "just", ignoring those in need, and so on – and we will need to find a way to mitigate the unethical with the ethical, to find our way through. Most importantly, it will require a new kind of honesty. Because you cannot claim to love your children if you are creating a world that is killing them. You cannot claim to love your fellow man if your actions are hurting them.

Some might say ethics have been lost but I'm not entirely sure they were ever found, at least not in any solid, philosophical way. True, there have been many who displayed ethics in the past and I'll be spotlighting many of them here, both the famous and overlooked. I'll also highlight the infamous who have taken us down many dark rabbit holes of unethical sludge.

With every ethical choice, you will affect some kind of change in the world and you will move others towards ethics as well. This is the way it has to be. In a world where we have left tough choices, such as energy policy, the ending of war, and the welfare of mankind to whoever has the most money, we need a new kind of currency, a currency of ethics. The prevalence of laissez-faire capitalism hasn't helped anyone. We need to grow up. It's time to become adults.

This book will look at the world through the lens of ethics. It will cast a light on our history to show where we've gone wrong but, more importantly, what right behavior might help point the way. It will explain, without too much jargon, past philosophies in ethics, where they went wrong and where they were right. In addition, it will put to rest the confusion of ethics and morality and lay a clear and easy to understand path towards making ethics a part of your life.

This book will not be comprehensive. There are bound to be things I leave out, either intentionally or carelessly, but there will be enough to get my point across. My apologies for the western bent of this book; my experience is based in the United States and the focus will therefore reside there. This is not to say that the ethical theories herein should be avoided elsewhere. On the contrary, the ethics of Dynamic Pluralism are universal.

There may be some science involved to help us understand things along the way. There will be some history as well.

But, I promise: No math!

Chapter 2
Ethics and What We Have Been Told

When Henry David Thoreau eulogized John Brown, after his defeat at Harper's Ferry, he may have been summing up the goal of philosophers throughout history. "It seems as if no man had ever died in America before, for in order to die you must first have lived," Thoreau said. "These men, in teaching us how to die, have at the same time taught us how to live."

To live a meaningful life is to die with meaning and it is the duty of philosophers to show us just that way to die. I believe there is nothing that can show us a more meaningful way to live and die than a true understanding of ethics. With that in mind, I would like to spend this chapter discussing those philosophers who have shown us the way towards just such an understanding. Now, before you throw the book down and run screaming for some kind of distracting drug like social networking or basic cable, let me assure you that it's not as painful as you might think. We'll shoot through these fairly quickly and I'll be sure to stay away from all that philosophical jargon that... well, quite frankly, gets me running off to watch cartoons myself.

We'll review the main contributors but we'll stay away from nihilism and its cousin religion... for now. Let's dive right in with...

Early Philosophers and
What They Knew That You Don't

Philosophy was not owned by ancient Greece but an important step in its development began with the conflicting views of Heraclitus and Parmenides. Heraclitus was of the opinion that everything changes. You cannot step into the same river twice, due to the running water changing that river. All is in flux. Parmenides, on the other hand, took things more at face value. It is what it is and what is not, is not. The river is the river. To say that something goes from what is to what is not is silly. And, of course, they were both right. But they gave us something extremely important in the matter of ethics: perspective. We'll revisit the implications of perspective later but it is important to keep in mind that issues we still wrestle with today have been contemplated since the birth of philosophy.

Humanity has been contending with issues of ethics since very early in its history. Even the domestication of fire has been interpreted as an ethical act. Our earliest examples of Homo Erectus, discovered in China, were clearly associated with the remains of campfires, suggesting that our ancestors domesticated fire much more than one half million years ago.[23] More recent findings put the date closer to 1.6 million years.[24] And yet, this grand achievement has been mythologized as an act of theft. As misplaced as this is, it is significant that humanity has been seeing in the ethical spectrum since the beginning.

And trying to understand what it means.

Socrates identified from early on that ethics result from human conflict. In the dialogue of Euthyphro, Socrates encounters upright citizen and dutiful son, Euthyphro, on his way to court to charge his father with murdering a slave. But Socrates, who was a terrible busy-body who would pry into everyone's business, soon learned that Euthyphro wasn't really being a good citizen or a dutiful son (his father did not exactly kill the slave) and the question arises, "Are you doing this because it's right or because it's required?" Ethics, it would seem, happen when we're prodded into them.

While Socrates[25] was satisfied to stir the pot without needing to find an answer, Aristotle took a more comprehensive look at ethics. To be sure, Aristotle took a comprehensive look at everything and, as with most things, he wasn't always entirely accurate, just thorough.

For Aristotle, the most ethical thing was virtue and "the good." He explained this as the good life, or what he called "eudaimonia." Now, in case that isn't confusing enough, Aristotle suggested that the best way to reach eudaimonia was in doing the one unique and characteristic thing humans can do, which to him of course meant philosophy. I have to say, even I can see how that can be somewhat limiting. But according to Aristotle, there was no way around this because everything else could lead to the opposite of virtue, the opposite of ethics: vice. In fact, anything could lead to vice. You say you want to make money to help others? Well, making money can lead to greed, which is a vice. You say you want to live an honorable life? According to Aristotle, honor cedes our happiness to the will and whim of others. When we leave our happiness to others, we risk the capriciousness of human nature, which can be fickle… and lead to vice. Sorry. You say you just want life to be pleasurable? Well, pleasure can lead to all kinds of evil, vice-ridden pastimes that anyone in Las Vegas can tell you about. No dice; it's vice.

The problem, according to Aristotle, is that far too often virtue can lead to vice. You can care too much. You can love too much. You can be selfless too much. You can too much anything too much! Any perceived good can lead to evil. Aristotle's resolution for that he called the "Golden Mean," which is the line straight down the middle between the vice of vice and the vice of virtue. It lies between bravery and cowardice, between love and hate, between selfishness and squandering, and dedication to The Mean leads to eudaimonia.

Now, there are several problems with this, of course, beginning with the fact that it's just nonsense. Aristotle provides the example of the soldier who, being too brave, becomes foolish and wastes his life. The problem with that, though, is that bravery and foolishness are not necessarily related to one another and one does not necessarily lead to the other. While Aristotle believes that humanity is not capable of tempering its better impulses as well as its worse, leading to the corruption of virtue, he forgets that just because something could possibly happen does not mean it will happen. Virtue can lead to Vice but it does not need to, which kind of throws Aristotle's entire system of ethics right down the toilet.

As wrong as he may be, however, Aristotle does provide us with something unique that had not existed before: a guide. An ethical platform. A way of saying "This is the path to ethics." It was an impressive achievement because it was new and it was solid enough to last for several centuries.

There were still those who challenged him and we'll end with one of my favorites, one of the most misinterpreted philosophers of all time: Epicurus. Epicurus was a clear-thinking Greek who said such things as: "Do not spoil what you have by desiring what you have not; remember that what you now have was once among the things you only hoped for." He liked to gather his friends for a nice meal and some wine and some great conversation. He believed, "The art of living well and the art of dying well are one." The puritans of his time and of many times since then misinterpreted this as a philosophy of gluttony and hedonism and greed, of big, fat men shoveling cakes into their gob while lusting after half-naked women… or boys… Puritans of any time tend to overreact a bit.

The contribution to ethics that Epicurus gave us was the idea that we can be ethical and happy, that the two concepts are not mutually exclusive. It is this idea (and ideal) that we'll pursue in this book.

Results Matter

Many of those who study ethics, including many courses in ethics, divide the question of determining what is ethical into two schools of thought: Teleological and Deontological. This can be seen as results versus intentions, deeds versus thoughts. Deontological ethics put their focus on the ethics you carry inside of you and have in their corner such heavy-weights as Immanuel Kant. We'll deal with him later. For now, I'd like to concentrate on results.

That is, after all, how most people think of ethics. They consider a person's deeds; they are "consequentialists." "You did this and it was unethical." You see? It's easy to understand when something is right in front of you. "You were able to accomplish that and that was very ethical." We are raised to be results-oriented, for the most part, so this way of understanding ethics is just about the easiest.

The primary school of thought in this form of ethics – you've probably noticed by now that I've stopped calling it "Teleological" as I want to keep this book understandable and that's a tongue-twister, besides – is Utilitarianism. You would probably recognize Utilitarianism by the rule "the ends justify the means." Utilitarians look at what you do, not what you meant to do or intended to do, not how you do it or why. They look at the total at the bottom of the column. Q.E.D.

You might say Utilitarianism is the "Les Misérables" school of ethics. "Yes, I stole the loaf of bread. But my child was starving." And, really, how do you argue against that? (We'll see in a minute.) And, strangely, the U.S. justice system can also be seen as a Utilitarian institution. They call it "adversarial," where the goal of each party is to further their position: either finding the prosecuted guilty or getting their client off. Each party will very often do whatever it takes to get to this end. They will use slander, misrepresentation, obfuscation, and plain old lies to further their case. In an adversarial system, Utilitarian cost/benefit analyses put winning and not justice as the goal. Producing the evidence most favorable to a client is far from being, "The truth, the whole truth, and nothing but the truth." It is, however, the truth that they can get away with. The two lawyers produce the truth most favorable for their side and the truth that comes from these, the so-called "courtroom truth" may be false but it is true for the purposes of the justice system. Such phrases as "truth most favorable" and "courtroom truth" and "true for the purposes of" are in no way to be mistaken for TRUTH, but the Utilitarian is not considering TRUTH. TRUTH is a concept removed from the focus of Utilitarians: the end result.

Sound problematic? Well, it is.

Utilitarianism simply doesn't do a very good job at considering, well, anything else except the end result. So, you end up with a kind of Tom Sawyer ethic, "You asked for the fence to be painted. It was painted. You never specified HOW it should be painted." You end up with the ethics of the bad guy in a spy thriller, "I shall save the planet by wiping out all human life!" Simply put, you end up with something very spotty.

Not that some very smart people haven't been working on this for a long time, either.

Francis Hutcheson (1694 - 1746), Chair of Moral Philosophy at the University of Glasgow, is often seen as the first utilitarian. It was his belief that Utilitarianism would not lead to such ethical equivocations or shortcuts because we are each endowed with a "moral sense" in addition to our other senses. (The terms "moral" and "ethical" are often used synonymously, leading to quite a bit of confusion, which I shall address in the next chapter.) We should be able to sense when something is wrong.

Sure. Sure we can. Right? (Anyone who has made it past adolescence probably already knows that simply isn't true.)

Still, Hutcheson's thinking inspired an entire school of thought. Shortly after his passing, Jeremy Bentham (1748 – 1832), jurist, philosopher, and reformer, picked up his cause. His Utilitarianism followed the "greatest happiness" principle: We prefer pleasure over pain, therefore whatever creates the greatest happiness must be ethical. He even set up seven categories by which we can judge such happiness: Intensity, Duration, Certainty, Proximity, Fecundity, Purity, and Extent.

The nice thing about this is that it's so practical. It even has a way to work out just how ethical your behavior is! One problem does remain, of course: How you get there. If I may use an extreme example: The people in Nazi Germany were doing just fine until the Allies began really fighting back. The atrocities committed didn't matter to the many people who experienced the most pleasure. Another, more current example, is the way in which we are presently burning away all of our fossil fuels. Pleasure trips, inefficient factories, NASCAR – all seem just fine right now. How can it be unethical? (We'll get to that later.) In the end Bentham's "Why worry" Utilitarianism falls short due to its focus on pleasure.

Which brings us to John Stuart Mill (1806 – 1873), who suggested we avoid the inherent weaknesses in Utilitarianism quite simply: by following the rules others follow. There's a thought. We have laws and social mores and general rules of behavior all around us. There are laws against stealing. We are told by our parents not to be rude. If we just stopped to follow them, we wouldn't have to worry about… you know…

But wait. The rules don't really help us all that much in the long run. In fact, they often present the obstacle to change our society has to overcome in order to do the right thing. Consider the civil rights struggles of African Americans, Women, and Gay and Transgender Americans. Consider the movement to save the environment (and, in doing so, human society as a whole). Laws and rules only take us so far. We have to think beyond them if we're going to progress as a people.

Utilitarianism is an old idea but it is still around us every day in many forms. You see it at the grocery store when someone "samples" something. You see it at work with the guy who takes a pen (or a box of pens) home. In the end, however, it is clear that selfishness is not a form of ethics. Utilitarians have for a very long time tried to justify their actions. They say that, very often, selfish behavior can have altruistic consequences. A little selfishness often benefits those who satiate our selfish desires. That's true but it can easily apply to paying a prostitute.

There has to be more for a system of ethics to work. There has to be something to guide it. This is where Kant comes in.

Following Rules

The inherent flaw in Consequentialist ethics such as Utilitarianism, the lack of rules that guide you in life, is exactly the strength Deontologists provide. *Deon* comes from the Greek word meaning obligation. Deontological ethics are guided by obligation and not consequences. Their goal is to do the right thing no matter the outcome.

As strange as this may sound, we're surrounded by it every day. One of the schools of Deontology, called Divine Command Theory, says that we must obey god's commandments no matter the church or the time (as these things often change with time) or even the commandment. So, for the sake of demonstration, let's go back to Les Misérables and that loaf of bread. One of the Ten Commandments insists "Thou Shalt Not Steal." According to Divine Command Theory, there's no excuse to be made; if you stole, you are guilty.

And yet, Jean Valjean knew there was more to the ethical question of his stealing bread than breaking the law. Victor Hugo knew that. But Javert, the fanatical officer who hounds Jean Valjean for years, is a strict Deontologist and, if we were to take the law of the land in place of god's law, a strict Divine Command Theorist as well. There is no subverting the law, he might say. A crime is a crime.

Deontological ethics don't leave a lot of wiggle room, if any at all. In Les Misérables, Javert did not let the issue of time or redemption or anything else get in his way of upholding the law. And yet, he might argue, there is nothing necessarily wrong with that. If everyone who broke a law or commandment was held to it, you'd see a lot fewer people breaking the law. To a Deontologist, ethical behavior lies in doing the right thing no matter what happens.

When I first came to study ethics, I was very attracted to the Deontological theories of the German philosopher, Immanuel Kant (1724-1804). When I first realized where the problems lay in such theories, it felt like something of a betrayal to one of the greatest thinkers of all time.

Kant's masterwork, the *Critique of Pure Reason,* wasn't published until he was 57 years old, in 1781. Part of this was synthesis, taking Hume's idea that all we could know was what we individually perceived and Leibniz's view that the world could be known objectively to create Kant's unique viewpoint that objects might actually exist independently of the viewer but that they were influenced by the viewer's perspective. Since perspective was limited and unique to each person, each person perceives differently. Perspective is key here, not only to Kant but to the theory of Dynamic Pluralism spelled out in later chapters.

To detail this a bit more, you might say that we work, not with reality, but with our idea of it. According to Kant, we cannot know a "thing in itself," and if you think about it that really is the case. Be it your car or your shoes or your lover, you can't know everything about a thing; you can only know your perceptions about those things. That's not to say things don't exist but just that we can't get into someone else's head or understand anything completely; we're limited by those things our senses tell us. Instead of saying "the world is out there" (as Realists did) or "the world is all in our head" (as Idealists did), Kant put aside "either/or thinking and synthesized them into subjective reality.

When Kant approached Ethics, it was with the acceptance that rational beings (and, for some reason, he included humanity in that category) are going to make ethical judgments one way or the other. It is better, then, to do it with an objective, universal morality. (The questionable synonymy will be dealt with in the next chapter.) Kant begins with Reason and Will, which he saw as necessary faculties inside each of us, and applied each in the creation of what he called "Imperatives." Some Imperatives, such as "I'm thirsty so I'll get a drink of water," he called Hypothetical Imperatives. These were consequence-based and Kant was NOT a consequentialist. No, he wanted something more than that, something that would synthesize Reason and Will into a logical, universal law of Ethics. He called this the Categorical Imperative.

"Act only according to that maxim whereby you can, at the same time, will that it should become a universal law." That is the Categorical Imperative. Easy to understand, isn't it?

No, of course it isn't. That's why so many universities teach entire courses on the damned thing. It's telling you to act according to a maxim (a rule or law) that you'd apply universally. If it works for the rest of the world, it is ethical. Kant provides guidelines on how to do that. The maxim should not be contradictory. It should not make false promises or end one's life. There are other guidelines as well.

The bottom line is that when Will is guided by Reason this way, good comes about from acting out of duty and not inclination. To act out of inclination is to make your aim a certain outcome and consequence-based actions, Kant would insist, are not ethical. To Kant, acting with respect to moral/ethical law, out of a sense of duty, is ethical.

So, let's try out a few rules for size and see if this works. One rule that I particularly like comes from the United States of America's Declaration of Independence: "All men are created equal." (Or for the sake of not sounding so 18th century, "All persons are created equal.") I like this law. It says that no matter who you are or where you are or what your circumstance, all people are created equal. That's such a bold and leveling statement; it makes us all the same. So, I see everyone as the same and they see everyone as the same. It's really quite nice as far as a universal maxim goes.

… except when we consider that it's not true.

After all, some are born with disabilities. Some are born with disease. Some are born impoverished. Some are born ugly. Some are born Republican. Some are born Star Trek fans. The fact of the matter is we are not all created equal, and assuming this is far from a leveler of any kind, it is far from fair. There are people who need our help and others who can give help. The trouble is we still don't really understand the concept of all people being equal. It wasn't too long ago that a black and white couple couldn't walk down the street without fear, just as it is still considered unacceptable in some communities for a homosexual or transgender couple to walk down the street. As I write this, there are still people who cannot legally marry simply because of the person they love – law-abiding, consenting, of age, it just doesn't matter. And how about wealth disparity and the way we treat our poor? Do we even know what equality means?

No. No. No. This won't do.

For the next rule, let's go back to the source, to Kant. One of Kant's most groundbreaking ideas could be a universal maxim in itself. Referred to as the "Humanity Formula," it states "that we should never act in such a way that we treat Humanity, whether in ourselves or in others, as a means only but always as an end in itself."[26] This idea of respect, of not using people simply as tools for your machinations or things to step on to get what you want, could be followed universally. (And wouldn't it be nice if it was, considering all of the pious among us who routinely walk on those "beneath" themselves?) But what if it was? What does it mean to treat Humanity (that being the thing inside ourselves and others that makes us human) as an end in itself? Some might say this ties very neatly to our idea of the "Golden Rule": to do unto others as you would have them do unto you. It also parallels very nicely with the "Tat Tvam Asi" principle: Thou Art That. It is a way of acknowledging the humanity, godhead, divine, or whatever you want to call it in another person.

But even when we finally find this fundamental principle, a guiding maxim, there's still something missing. Because we are doing these things with no concept of consequence. In a practical sense, if we want real ethics that we can see, we haven't done it, yet. The strength of Consequentialist ethics turn out to be the downfall of Deontologist ethics, just as the strength of Deontology could be found in Consequentialist weaknesses.

Worse still, with the 20th century came an idea that brought new troubles to the establishment of any ethical groundwork and would sweep away everything that came before it.

After centuries of argument and discussion about what is ethical, how to understand ethics, and how to go about being ethical – some of which I have condensed up to this point – nobody really had an answer at all. It was all sort of, "Well, you can obey the law or you can not. You can say the ends justify the means or you can not." And, honestly, that's how things are. Most people, when faced with an ethical dilemma do what works for them at that moment. Sometimes, depending on the circumstances and repercussions, they'll obey the law. Other times, when they're running late and know they'll get chewed out by their boss if they're late one more time and they don't see a cop around who will catch them speeding anyway… won't.

The only position winning in any way was that of the Deontologists who looked down their noses at Consequentialists and Utilitarians with a smug kind of righteousness. After all, they had the law on their side.

And then, someone came along to ruin that. Because someone got the idea in their head about just how odd it is to have a maxim that all people would follow. When you get right down to it, after all, there are an awful lot of people and an awful lot of maxims. Odds are, people were beginning to see, that wasn't how the world really worked.

This all came about during the last half of the 19th century, at about the same time a man named Adolphe Quetelet (1796-1874) was making people see people in a very different way. Quetelet was a statistician with Belgium's statistical bureau who believed that if you could reproduce people mathematically then a new science of social physics would reveal natural laws governing human behavior.[27] He called this concept, the concept of the "average person." The "average person" would remove the element of guesswork from social planning, criminology, and social science. The idea is simple and remains with us today: Apply a general rule that describes the masses to each individual. Universality, which was ironically one of Kant's catchwords, meant assumptions about generalities and putting aside individual considerations.

When it came to ethics, a group of people began to see that ethics of the individual run into the same sorts of problems. Maxims for each individual applied universally don't work because of all the conflicts they create, as do general rules applied to everyone. There is no average – because rules change from place to place and from time to time. Rules are always going to change.

John Dewey (1859 – 1952) was one of the leaders of this new "Pragmatist" movement, so-called because of their wish to return ethics (among other things) to a pragmatic level. He saw how rules changed throughout his life, which spanned the years from the Civil War to the Cold War. He saw many wars come and go and many enemies as well. He saw the rights of people suppressed and affirmed. He saw technology create ethical issues never dreamt of by Kant. Dewey believed that so-called "traditional viewpoints" were simply not up to the transformations that happen in one's lifetime.

Ethics, the Pragmatists argued, must therefore be flexible and practical.[28] This was interpreted by some as too subjective and naïve and ethics got it in the knee caps. I doubt this was the Pragmatists' intent. I think they were trying to find a system that worked. But even when they tried to define rules, the very stand they took about how rules change made it unworkable. Still… they were right.

Ethics do need to be flexible and practical. This is just as right as when Kant said that ethics require some kind of rule and just as the Utilitarians correctly assert that consequences matter. As strange as it might sound, they were all right. The problem is that none of these ideas are mutually exclusive. It's just that nobody has found a way to come at these things from the correct angle or perspective.

Before we get to that, though, I'd like to take a few more minutes to analyze what happened to ethics after the Pragmatists. After everyone kind of threw up their hands and walked away from the table, the idea of ethics without ethics stepped in.

Anyone with some education in ethics will tell you that I've left out a few things up to this point and that's true. There are dozens of ethicists I haven't mentioned simply because it is what has made philosophy so boring to so many people for so long: more and more of the same. Rather than dull your senses with an endless list of theories and figures, I set this up as a central narrative that I believe portrays the history truthfully as well as laying a foundation for what is to come. That is: Consequentialists look at the outcome without focusing on how they got there, which can lead you down some shady alleyways. Deontologists came along righteously and held up the law, thus casting light into those shady alleyways… but then, since they neglected the outcome, the Pragmatists said, "Yeah, but you're wrong, too."

When I think about what the Pragmatists did, it doesn't surprise me. It might sound cynical that someone came along and shot down Immanuel Kant but that wasn't the cynical part because neither side of the ethical argument was working. Neither of the two main schools created a system of ethics people could really understand.

The Pragmatists created an ethical wasteland, which is not to say that they destroyed ethics but that they showed it for what it was: an empty promise. If ethical rules could change at the county line,[29] they weren't really ethics at all. What was left?

Along came a guy pretty famous for saying "God is dead": Friedrich Nietzsche (1844-1900). If you ever get a chance to sit down and read his work, go easy on yourself because he tends to be a bit inflammatory. Actually, that was kind of his point. His response to the façade of ethics was to lash out and call life a struggle and say people are going to mess you up! There's nothing right or wrong about it; it's just the way things are. He said, "'Exploitation' does not belong to a corrupt or imperfect and primitive society: it belongs to the essence of what lives, as a basic organic function; it is a consequence of the will to power, which is after all the will of life." He called the book he wrote that in *Beyond Good and Evil*. Ethics are an illusory by-product of the basic struggle of life and it's absurd to try and define it, is what he seemed to say.

From this was born a seemingly new way of looking at ethics and one that plays a huge part in Dynamic Pluralism. It was the idea that we each have a responsibility beyond a simple list of what is or is not ethical. We have a responsibility to ourselves, to living the most authentic life we can. This idea was eventually called Existentialism and it broke new ground in the understanding of ethics because it looked at something new. It looked at a relationship, a relationship we each have with our own lives. Our choices have consequences, the Existentialists told us, and we are each responsible for them. We cannot sit on the sidelines as some imagined the Pragmatists were saying (which they were not); we cannot be inactive. Even inactivity has consequences. We must accept the reality of our lives.

But how are we to do that? The answer, oddly enough, goes back to ethics and it is why Existentialism is sometimes classified as a form of ethics: Act Deontology. As you remember, Deontologists are about following the rules. Act Deontologists aren't about broad laws that set the rules for everyone. Rather, they believe that ethics should be judged on a case-by-case basis. In Existentialism, each case represents each person. As far as defining "What is ethics" once and for all, it doesn't quite do the job but, remember, Existentialism approaches ethics as a relationship. And this makes it essential.

There is another way of looking at the idea of ethics without ethics and I'll close this chapter with this alternate view. It's the schoolyard method. It's "bully's rules." It's much more than "might makes right". It's even more than Nietzsche's "will to power."

In the mid-20th century, Ayn Rand (1905–1982) introduced her new "philosophy," which she called "Objectivism." I refer to it in quotes because I have a hard time calling selfishness a philosophy and Objectivism was little more than that. Rand believed that selfishness was ethical and moving beyond selfishness, considering others for instance, was unethical.

It was her rationale, and the rationale of most Objectivists, that people don't want you to consider them. They want to be stepped on. In fact, it's an insult if you don't step on them! Objectivists claim that helping others is evil because, and I wish I was making this up, it leaves the individual to the whims of others. In other words, "Helping others helps others." And how could you dare do that?

Objectivism is what happens when you leave ethics to those without ethics. The vacuum that is created without a system of ethics, as it turns out, is easily filled without ethics. It's just like life. If you want something dead, let someone kill it.

But if you want something to thrive, you have to make a choice. You have to fill that void. It is my hope that Dynamic Pluralism fills the void left behind by the absence of a system of ethics so bully philosophies such as Objectivists can be left far, far behind us all.

But before we get to that, what do we mean when we use the word "ethics?" Is it synonymous with "morality," as so many have thought for so long? In the following, brief chapter, I'd like to address the issue of ethics versus morality and finally lay to rest that confusion once and for all.

Chapter 3
Ethics & Morality.
What They Are and What They Mean

Ethics and Morality: Synonymously Different

Before we discuss ethics as interpreted by Dynamic Pluralism, I think it's important to make very clear one thing ethics are not and, in this way, help lay a bit more foundation for the theory of Dynamic Pluralism to come.

For a very long time, a word synonymous with "ethics" – just check your thesaurus – has been "morals". I'm not exaggerating that, either. When I checked with Merriam Webster,[30] I found that the definition of ethics included "a set of moral principles," while the definition of morals included "principles of right and wrong behavior; ethical." This is known as a circular definition. It's also known as crap. You don't learn anything from it. "Ethics are morals and morals are ethics" tells us nothing at all about either of them.

And when you proceed to further definitions, things become no clearer. These include "principles of conduct," "a guiding philosophy," and "a standard of right behavior." These definitions tell us nothing because they are lazy and, if you ask me, seek to avoid the issue lest they get it wrong.

But I can almost forgive the heirs of Noah Webster (or so their website claims) because it's not the job of dictionaries to go after what should be a philosophical hardball like differentiating ethics from morality. What I cannot forgive is the institution of philosophy itself. For centuries, philosophers have been mixing their ethics with their morals, their chocolate with their peanut butter – philosophically speaking. Kant's theory of Deontological Ethics is historically referred to as his "Moral Philosophy."[31] This also applies to David Hume, whose *Enquiry Into Human Understanding* laid out his system of ethics.[32]

For too long, too many of us have been missing the point, allowing morality to masquerade as ethics, and never realizing we gain much more in distinguishing their differences than in lazily assuming they're the same.

Ethics and Morality: Two Sides of Different Coins

It's hiding right there, in plain sight, the answer to the riddle of ethics. The key to knowing what ethics are is in knowing what ethics are not. Ethics are not Morals.

To start with, if ethics and morals were the same, you could simply say "ethics" in place of "morals." That is, after all what any good synonym should be able to do. It's called the Rule of Substitution. So, in place of a "Morality Play" we would have a… Ethical Play? But that doesn't work. An ethical play would be a play that shows, to use one of the above definitions, "a standard of right behavior." Conversely, a Morality Play is very different. It's an actual subclass of theatrical works whose very intention is to portray the benefits of a godly – and that's a Christian god – life and the perils of life without Christianity, going back to the 15th century! In this context, "morality" is quite different from "ethics."

Let's try another one. Those of you who were around in the 1980s may remember a group of evangelical Christians who referred to themselves as the "Moral Majority." They were a single-issue political action group, not the first and certainly not the last, which used their religious views (and money, lots and lots of money) to influence political change. Again, you find terms like "morals" and "morality" tied with religion. What would this group have been like if they had been named the "Ethical Majority?" Quite different all together, I wager.

So, there's an important difference right away: Morals tend to be associated with religion of some sort. A moral Christian asks "What would Jesus do?" A moral Jew observes the Sabbath. A moral Muslin observes the Five Pillars of Islam. And so on. Immoral people disobey god's laws. Immorality is synonymous with sin,[33] which is breaking god's laws. Morals are the rules religion gives you to teach you how to behave.

But perhaps the most powerful expression of how we know morality is associated with religious rules comes when someone actually tries to use morality as a synonym for ethics. Take David Caton for instance, a certain "family values" crusader, who when speaking out against light rail – that is low-capacity, low-speed trains – claimed that light rail was immoral.[34] Immoral! Despite whatever reasons he may have had to oppose low-capacity, slow trains, we know that speaking of it as "immoral" is hyperbole at best. And his reasoning was not related to ethics. Once again, morality goes to religion.

And that puts ethics in a secular light by contrast. This is not to say that ethical people are not religious, but rather that ethical people are not always moral. In fact, it's actually possible to be immoral while being ethical or unethical while being moral. For instance, many religions consider abortion immoral but, if you consider an abortion (which as of this writing is still legal in the United States) a lawful act it is therefore perfectly ethical by Deontological standards as well as Utilitarian ones. It would be utterly immoral for a Christian to have any other gods before his or her Christian god but would that be unethical? No. As a matter of fact, none of the systems of ethics we've talked about, which cover the most widely accepted forms, talk about god.

There must be an explanation for ethics and morality, even if it's one we haven't quite understood. It's easy to see how even morality can slip into the same subset of ethics: Deontology and Consequentialist. There are those who believe morality is spelled out in the rules of religion and others who find a deeper meaning and express their morality, and their understanding of their religion, through their actions. But there's more to it than that.

I think we can start with the fact that morality, like ethics, is about more than a list of rules. When we learn about religion through morality plays or when some stand up for their faith and call it morality, it has little to do with handing down blocks of stone à la Charlton Heston dressed as Moses. I think it's more appropriate to say that morals help people to better understand their relationship with the higher power they are worshipping. "What would Jesus do," is not just an outdated, Christian tagline; it's a way for followers of Christ to better understand their idea of god. Moral Muslims don't just observe the Five Pillars of

Islam because it's a rule and there's more to the observation of the Sabbath by Jews than a mandated day off. Morals are a way of looking at our relationship with a higher power, if you chose that route, and understanding it a bit better.

Understanding morals as simply another way of saying, "God says to do this," limits it to the level of absurdity. God says, "Thou shalt not kill," and yet religious wars go on and on. Humanity wipes out species after species and yet there's very little moral outcry. Making morality about a list and not a relationship is a fundamental misinterpretation of the idea.

This is why morality tends to be specific to a group, because you've allied yourself with those who believe the same as you. This is also why morality tends to reflect on your relationship specifically and not just a general concept, because it's a way of understanding your place a little better.

But if morality delineates a relationship between a person and their higher power, just as existentialism outlines a relationship between a person and their own life, what kind of relationship does ethics formulate? And, once we know that, how will that knowledge help us determine a system of ethics that actually works?

Chapter 4
Dynamic Pluralism. Ethics Found

Sometimes seeing the world in a whole new way comes down to a simple change in perspective… and when that perspective changes, the results can be explosive.

I'll give you an example. At the dawn of the age of film, when moving pictures were still very new, "L'arrivée d'un train en gare de La Ciotat" premiered in January 1896. "L'arrivée d'un train en gare de La Ciotat" was a short film by Louis Lumière and the title translates to "Arrival of a train at La Ciotat." Legend has it that the French filmgoers were so new to the concept of film that as the train pulled into the station, at a nearly dead-on angle to the movie screen, the audience panicked! They thought a train was going to slam through the theater wall!

This may be just an exaggerated urban legend but the truth of it is not diminished. Too often, our concept of the world around us just doesn't keep up with the way things really are. We hold bizarre, often destructive ideas as truth or somehow beneficial until someone batters them down and changes the way we see things. The idea of Manifest Destiny, that we can simply take what we want when we want it, has only been reduced in power after centuries of asinine behavior. The KKK was once a powerful organization that taught hatred in broad daylight and it took decades of shame before we began to catch on to what an embarrassment they were. Sometimes those views are so powerful they're difficult to refute. Our nation once bought into the Horatio Alger myth of equal opportunity, that all you had to do to succeed in America was simply pull yourself up by your bootstraps. The myth, which continues to be perpetuated under updated names and branding despite being blatantly untrue, accused anyone who didn't pull themselves up by their bootstraps of laziness at best… and maybe even (gasp!) communism. They didn't explain what to do if you had no bootstraps or couldn't afford boots or shoes. You were on your own. This is very similar to the nonsense of Ayn Rand, which teaches selfishness as a philosophy. Often, it is difficult to see things as they really are.

Such is the case with ethics. For too long, we've accepted flawed approaches and half answers. That's how I first approached ethics. I considered myself a Kantian until I realized how difficult that really was and how often Utilitarian compromises slipped into every day behavior. Eventually, I began to see ethical systems for what they were: declarations of surrender. Every ethical system starts out with a bold statement and then… gives up. Utilitarians say they're about more than just the ends, except they're not really. Kant painted a vivid picture of strict Deontological logic… that ended up sounding a bit silly. Make a law that can apply universally. And then?? By the time the Pragmatists entered the story, I'm sure it was hard not to sound cynical. The ideas of the Pragmatists do not signal an end to ethics, just the same old surrender.

Each system was doomed to fail because of a significant lack of perspective. What you need is a train – and you need to slam it through a wall.

And that was my decision when I set out to write this book. To change ethics with a shift in perspective.

Let's begin with a question, then: What are you looking for in a system of ethics? There have been many systems of ethics in the past and each had its own list of ingredients. What do you want? When someone behaves ethically, what does that include? Go ahead. Make your list.

I'll warn you now that lists won't work. That's been one of the problems all along. Everybody had their list. Utilitarians listed outcomes. Deontologists listed laws. If lists worked, someone would have gotten it right by a simple process of elimination. But they don't work because situations change and when they do change adding to your list or changing it in some way is a temporary fix at best. Everything changes. So, throw out your list. I realized that the minute we try to create a list and call that list comprehensive, we've already lost. The minute you put a certain number of things in a box and call that box "ethics," you've excluded something else. Leaving out one thing is just as bad as leaving out everything.

Once I realized I couldn't create a conclusive list, I tried thinking of the question differently. "What about unethical behavior?" I asked myself. What's generally considered unethical behavior? Well, I consider when someone lies to me to be unethical. I'd call stealing from someone unethical behavior. Killing a person is pretty unethical, too.

I formed this new list not to be comprehensive but to analyze what traits each had in common and soon realized each item shared a very important quality: Every time behavior is unethical it somehow relates to someone else. And it occurred to me that ethics relate to actions between people. (As it turns out, you can also apply ethics to actions between people and animals as well.)

Just as morality expresses a relationship between you and whatever higher power(s) you might worship, ethics express a relationship between you and another living creature.

Now, the pieces begin to fall into place. As I've already shown, ethics need to be flexible and practical according to Immanuel Kant and also need to focus on consequences according to the Utilitarians. As it turns out ethics fulfill both requirements when seen from a relational point of view.

The Ethics of Dynamic Pluralism

As I mentioned previously, the world's population has doubled since I was born in 1965. At that time, the world's population was an astounding 3.5 billion people, far more people than we'd ever need to do just about anything you could think of: go to the moon, destroy the world with nuclear arms, you name it we could do it. As I write this in 2016, the world's population has reached nearly 7.5 billion people and doesn't look like it'll slow down any time soon.

The primary takeaway from a statistic like that should rightfully be shock but there's something else to consider. In a world where we have 38 people for every square mile of the planet's surface (including water, volcanoes, and Wal-Marts – you know, the uninhabitable zones), everyone is connected.[35]

As obvious as that is now, it has always been just as true. In the autumn of 1831, when cholera struck England, people had already known it was coming. They had known because they had tracked the disease as it spread from person to person, city to city, country to country. Though they were too late to do much about it, that did not change an undeniable fact. Human beings have been connected since long before the 21st century.

Now, it's more than disease we worry about. The exhaust that comes out of your car as you drive impacts the health of children hundreds of miles away. The water that many Americans drink from their taps travels hundreds of miles to get to them – and if they are dumb enough to drink bottled water the journey is longer by far, creating more car exhaust and waste that impacts the health of even more children. On a more pragmatic level, we can turn to the European financial crisis of 2011, which impacted the retirement accounts of older Americans. Anthony Valeri, a markets strategist for fixed income with LPL Financial, stated that a recession in Europe would likely bruise numerous U.S. stocks, especially bank stocks.[36] If the Eurozone broke up, retirement fund investments in stocks could decline 17 percent in value, he added. If the days of thinking that your actions only affected a select few around you ever existed, they are certainly over now. To believe that what you do does not impact millions of people around you is naïve at best, dangerous if taken to the extreme.

We are all connected.

Georg Wilhelm Friedrich Hegel (1770 – 1831) saw this from a slightly different point of view. To Hegel, we're not just connected. We are each a part of each other. In fact, we're a part of everything. While Kant said we cannot know a "thing in itself", only what our senses tell us, the "thing" is also known in our experience of it. And, like something out of quantum physics, we cannot experience something without it also experiencing us. There is no objective experience; everything is subjective. When you try to divide the experience, you tell only half the story. You cannot separate yourself from the experience any more than you can separate the experience from you.

So, we are all connected and that connection is so great as to be indistinguishable. This connection provides us with a new perspective for our new system of ethics. Remember, this new system should be results-focused while also being guided by rules. With that in mind, here is the definition of ethics as interpreted by Dynamic Pluralism:

Ethical Behavior describes a relationship between two individuals that is both fulfilling and fair to both parties.

That's it. Now, it might sound simple and after all that's the point of it, but the implications are far reaching as I'll show.

First, let me give you an example of how Dynamic Pluralism works with a short, mental exercise. Draw a circle around yourself. Now, look at it. This is your circle. It could represent anything. It could be your house, your town, your nation. It could be your world. The circle represents any finite space and you are standing in the center of that space. Ethics occur when you step outside that circle and encounter the circle of another individual. You now have a relationship. The factors that determine the success of that relationship, if it will be fair and fulfilling to both parties, are ethical factors.

The results are up to you. The rules are simple: Make this relationship work in a way that is fair and fulfilling to both parties. Why fair and fulfilling? Because if ethics are to start anywhere, it would need to start at "fair", where neither individual has an advantage. Sadly, though, fairness is not enough because of the way humanity so often manipulates the meanings of words. In too many cases, fairness has been manipulated to equal vindictiveness. Further, fairness is too often seen as a static state and, as I previously explained, an ethical revolution puts energy back into the system and doesn't settle for stasis or entropy. This is where fulfillment comes in. Your role as an ethical being is to be more than fair, to fulfill the other individual. Giving of yourself to the betterment of others and the world around you is what ethics is all about.

I call it Dynamic Pluralism because it includes two qualities that have not been included in previous ethical systems. First, it is Dynamic, meaning that it is flexible enough to change as events in our lives change and as our relationships change. Life is not static and events happen all the time but it is through this constant change that our actions within our relationships are defined as ethical or not ethical. Next, it is Pluralistic, meaning that there is more than one person involved. You know what you call ethics for one? Anything but ethics. Ethics only applies to multiple parties, specifically a relationship between two individuals.

(We'll get into larger numbers later.) Dynamic Pluralism makes ethics understandable in terms of how you treat others. If it works for both parties, it's ethical. If it doesn't, it's not. It's that simple.

Dynamic Pluralism fits Consequentialist ethics because it is result oriented. Your goal is to create a working relationship and that is defined by consequences. Dynamic Pluralism also fits Kant's system of ethics. Even though it moves away from the self, it maintains the ideal of judging the humanity of others "in and of itself," which as I showed above is subjective and not objective. And moving away from the self is important here. No longer should you consider "your ethics" because "your ethics" do not exist. The ethics of Dynamic Pluralism are seen in a relationship and, therefore, are seen as a shared thing. You can talk about ethical outcomes and ethical relationships but references to one person's ethics no longer exist.

Dynamic Pluralism meets the requirements of philosophical systems of ethics but how does it measure up against the actual rules of life? This is even more important because I think most people live without any consideration of Deontology or Consequentialism; they're just trying to follow the rules of life. One of those rules is the Golden Rule, which most of us learn from a very early age. Most of us don't follow it but we know it. It is: Do unto others as you would have them do unto you. And it's a good rule, no doubt about that. They're all good rules.

I'll list them here in case you don't know them:[37]

The Golden Rule	Do unto others as you would have them do unto you.
The Silver Rule	Do not do unto others what you would not have them do unto you.
The Brazen (Brass) Rule	Do unto others as they do unto you.
The Iron Rule	Do unto others as you like, before they do it unto you.
The Tit-for-Tat Rule	Cooperate with others first, then do unto them as they do unto you.

As I said, these are all good rules that have worked for plenty of people in the past. Most religions push the Golden Rule as the best and most people follow one or another to a degree. So, why create a new rule? Why have Dynamic Pluralism as a system of ethics?

Well, let's start out by agreeing that the Iron Rule (Do unto others as you like, before they do it unto you) just wouldn't work if we all followed it. If we all followed the Iron Rule, we would never have made it past the Iron Age. The Brass Rule as well (Do unto others as they do unto you) can make it a bit difficult to get along. I mean, if you treat people only as they treat you there'd never be compromise or a system of fairness.

The Silver Rule may sound like it's written backwards (Do not do unto others what you would not have them do unto you) but what it boils down to is not treating people poorly if you don't want to be treated poorly. It's a karma kind of ethics; what goes around comes around. The Golden Rule, the one most try to follow (Do unto others as you would have them do unto you), sounds reasonable. The problem with these two rules is their inflexibility. It just doesn't make sense to always be nice to people because some people are not nice. Part of life is learning when to be nice and when to be wary. If you keep being nice or if you keep watching your ass, you can't exactly adjust to the situations life presents. I think this is why most people have difficulty with the Golden Rule.

The rule most like Dynamic Pluralism is the Tit-for-Tat Rule (Cooperate with others first, then do unto them as they do unto you). Where it differs is that Dynamic Pluralism acknowledges that sometimes you have to suck it up and be a mensch.[38] Sometimes you end up having to be the one who makes peace, when you say "This person may not be treating me right but giving that treatment back in kind is going to get us nowhere."

Ethics under Dynamic Pluralism requires us to change and be flexible so we can make our relationships with others work. When our relationships are fair and fulfilling, they are ethical. Right and wrong are no longer defined for us. There is no authoritarian dharma to tell us the natural order of things. It is up to us to create ethical outcomes in our lives and to see what that means: fair and fulfilling relationships.

And this is what makes Dynamic Pluralism so revolutionary. Because you're going to have to deal with people no matter what you believe. Tuning your behavior to each individual on a case by case basis changes the whole ballgame. You don't behave with indiscriminate selfishness. You don't apply one rule universally with no consideration of how it's being applied. You engage in each relationship with the goal of making each one fair and fulfilling.

As I mentioned before, you have an effect on the world no matter what you do so why not make the world a more ethical place? The ethics of Dynamic Pluralism are revolutionary because they change how you see the world, how you treat the world, how you live in the world. No longer can you ignore others as you veil them behind some archaic rule. People who are selfish are probably going to turn out to be selfish anyway but engaging with others might help you create a world that is less selfish.

And this is a new kind of revolution. There are no leaders or followers. There is you and the other individual. Don't look for experts. You're the expert! Previous revolutions have left behind the memories of martyrs. Revolutionaries have often been put to death – more often than not. While this has certainly helped the human race progress, the rate of exchange on martyrs has been abysmal. In this revolution there is no fighting or dying; there is you and another individual creating a working relationship that is fair and fulfilling.

This creates an entirely new kind of meaning as well, for those who look for it. To borrow a phrase from Nietzsche, Dynamic Pluralism makes us the "meaning makers." Meaning is created in your relationships and in your life. You don't need anyone to tell you what ethics are; you're finding it yourself!

As I'll explain, Dynamic Pluralism describes a new way of seeing not just ethics, but morality and justice as well. Each expresses a relationship and you're place in it. How is this expressed?

Ethical Behavior, as suggested by Dynamic Pluralism, describes a relationship between two individuals that is fulfilling and fair to both parties.

Moral Behavior, as suggested by Dynamic Pluralism, describes a relationship between an individual and that individual's higher power that is fulfilling and fair to both parties[39].

Just Behavior, as suggested by Dynamic Pluralism, describes a relationship between an individual and a society that is fulfilling and fair to both parties.

In the course of this book, I'll show how each of these work.

Now that I've defined the ethics of Dynamic Pluralism, it's time to look at what that means. What are its implications? And how will Dynamic Pluralism create an ethical revolution?

Dynamic Pluralism, a history of revolution

For those wondering how I came up with the idea of Dynamic Pluralism, I have to say that actually I didn't. Dynamic Pluralism is quite an old idea; it's been around for a while. All I'm doing it putting a name on it and assembling it in (what I hope is) a cohesive system of ethical behavior.

Throughout this book, I will present for you examples of people who have used the ethics of Dynamic Pluralism, even if that's not what they called it. Each is a terrific example of just how Dynamic Pluralism can revolutionize the world and make it a better place. I call them Heroes of Dynamic Pluralism.

Florence Nightingale, the first hero I mentioned, changed the face of modern medicine but that fact is not remembered to this day as revolutionary simply because she was a good nurse. Her change was born of a deep commitment to ethics, of looking at each person individually and seeing the humanity each of them possessed. Every patient she treated had a relationship with her and she dealt with each one individually. What does that mean? It means she didn't say, "Get rid of nurses; they're ineffectual tramps." She didn't excuse the lack of healthy food for patients based on the situation that existed. She didn't come in with standard rules and ignore the people there. That's what the experts in the medical field were doing at the time; that's why they failed to see the problem before them. Florence Nightingale trained new nurses. She petitioned the chef at London's Reform Club. She engaged with each person individually and understood their needs and their gifts.

That's what Dynamic Pluralism is all about.

Other examples abound: Ghandi's revolution in India. Nelson Mandela's bravery in the face of apartheid in South Africa. Reverend Martin Luther King's leadership in the United States. Every revolutionary change has been sparked by individual change. Slavery, civil rights, women getting the vote – one might say they were sparked politically (Civil War, Civil Rights laws, etc.) or by an organized group of people (civil rights or women's marches) but before any of that happened people had to take a revolutionary stance in their own lives. They had to look at each other as individuals and understand they held a relationship with these people and that the status quo just could not stand.

Dynamic Pluralism is often used in special cases until a goal is met. Then, once that special case is in some way ameliorated, dynamic, pluralistic ideals are pushed aside in favor of expedience and laziness. Too often, we don't witness the changing power of ethics because, as previously stated, ethics are difficult. As a result, we forget the power such ethics exhibit over time.

I will present many examples of this in later chapters but, for now, let's start with one you can see every day. That example lies in a single word and that word, which I am hesitant to use here even as an example, is "nigger." When I was a child, I heard it all around, mostly spoken by white people about black people. And it was never, ever a good thing. Eventually, though, a message was communicated by one person to another and another person to another, hundreds upon thousands upon millions of times. That message was, "Don't call people that." Eventually, most people got the message. The word was mostly dropped from our common lexicon. This happened because people spoke, they engaged others. They may as well have been saying, "It's not fair for you to call us that. You're not helping make this relationship any more fulfilling."

Now, I'm not saying racism has ended in America and I'm not saying the act of calling someone a "nigger" has not been replaced with a pocketful of other injustices. But it's a road on the way there. It's a start. It worked.

And it continues to work. It works in the efforts of groups like the Center for Public Integrity, which reports diligently on the status of individuals for good or for ill. It works in such individuals as Jack Ryan, a true hero of Dynamic Pluralism who stood up as an FBI agent for the cause of peace and was crushed for it. Ethics come with a price, as Jack

Ryan's story in Chapter 7 will show. But the cost of turning away from ethics and rejecting Dynamic Pluralism is even greater.

There are more examples of people who ignore others' humanity than I can mention but one that comes immediately to mind is that of Timothy McVeigh, the notorious terrorist of Oklahoma City. McVeigh wanted to strike out against what he saw as an unjust government and, forgetting that the government is made of people, forgetting that those who work in government offices are people, detonated a truck bomb in front of the Alfred P. Murrah Building in Oklahoma City on April 19, 1995. His act killed 168 people and wounded over 800 more men, women, and children (as there was a daycare center on the premises).

The revolution of Dynamic Pluralism is a revolution against the McVeighs of the world and against so many others mentioned in these pages who ignore the humanity in each of us and, in doing as they wished anyway, provide clear examples of what is unethical.

The Meaning of Dynamic Pluralism

Having defined Dynamic Pluralism, what does it actually mean? What happens when you accept the goal of making all of your relationships fair and fulfilling? And is that even possible?

Dynamic Pluralism is a big phrase for a simple idea. It means that ethics are dynamic. They change with every situation you're in and with every person you encounter. It also means that ethics are pluralistic. The same set of rules cannot apply to everyone because everyone is different. The only way you can apply one universal ethical rule is to make that rule that ethics change with each relationship you involve yourself in. Treating each relationship you're in so that it is fair and fulfilling is what it means to be ethical.

In my own life, I have plenty of relationships.
- I have a relationship with my wife.
- I have a relationship with my mother.
- I have a relationship with my siblings.
- I have a relationship with the publisher of a monthly column I write.
- I have a relationship with other people on the freeway when I drive.

- The food I purchase gives me a relationship to the clerk at the store, the folks in shipping, and even with the people at the farm where the food is grown (providing I'm eating healthy and this food wasn't the product of some factory accident).
- The electricity I use to write this gives me a relationship to others who depend on the energy, to those who work in making and distributing it, and to those whose lives are affected by the pollution it creates.

As I said, I have plenty of relationships. There are many I intentionally left out and there are even more than that, besides. And it's important that I consider them all. But is that even possible? Isn't it slightly hypocritical to think so?

Of course, there will be those who believe this to be the case. Just as individuals so often push to be treated as individuals, the herd mentality of the group often tries to pull in those individuals who try to break free. Their most compelling argument in this case is that you cannot decide things like ethics for yourself, that it is the group mind that creates standards of behavior. It was this very mindset that created puritanism, that sinking fear that somebody somewhere else is having a good time. The hive mind in each of us reminds us that we need the group to set rules for us and, consequently, we end up settling for the committee mentality.

A perfect example of this resides in one of the least ethical things we do, which is to lie. As a group, we've decided that lying is unethical because it is telling an untruth – but that's about as effective a definition of truth and untruth as defining ethics as morality and morality as ethics. The reason lies are unethical is not because they're untruths. This is not to say lies are not untruths but that the reason for them being unethical rests in a very different definition. Lies are unethical because (to use the lingo of Dynamic Pluralism) liars cheat us out of fair and fulfilling relationships. Liars succumb to their insecurity and dodge having an authentic relationship with us, which cheats us out of what it would be like to experience a fair and fulfilling experience, to experience ethics. That's why it's wrong to lie, and each of us determines for ourselves just how that feels and how we interpret it. Some lies are worse than others, like a killer lying to escape justice. Some lies make us feel good, like telling someone their cooking is superb even if it's otherwise. No group can decide our experience for us, no matter how they might try.

One of the most pervasive memes of the past few years has been the idea of the false equivalence. It works like this: "You can't be any more ethical than me unless you're perfect. Nobody is perfect; therefore you can't be more ethical than me." I remember hearing this accusation used against Al Gore's *Live Earth* concert: "While the organisers' commitment to save the planet is genuine, the very process of putting on such a vast event... is surely an exercise in hypocrisy on a grand scale."[40] In other words, you have to be perfect otherwise you're just as corrupt as everyone else. In the case of all the relationships I listed above, the false equivalence would suggest that Dynamic Pluralism cannot be possible because there's no way to be ethical to everyone everywhere. But there's more to it than that, and to turn to the false equivalence is just cynical. For whatever good *Live Earth* did or whatever good any imperfect individual does, treating that good as pointless just because it's imperfect certainly doesn't help anyone. As we'll see, one of the strengths of Dynamic Pluralism is in recognizing when we're not ethical as well as when we are.

False equivalencies are just lies by another name and some startling examples from recent years immediately come to mind. The outrageous lies of the George W. Bush administration that Iraqi "weapons of mass destruction"[41] started the U.S. war with Iraq, is a clear one. The lie of anti-intellectualism[42] has also become common in the past decades, that somehow smart people are not to be trusted, equating intelligence with dishonesty. An equivocation like that was told by a recent Presidential nominee, "We need a leader, not a reader."[43] Really? That would seem to doom us to ignorance. As if that wasn't enough, I could also mention the shameful lies told by representatives of the United States in its recent and disgraceful flirtation with torture.[44]

(You may notice that most of my examples are not recent ones. That is to show that our problems with ethics are in no way recent manifestations. A glance at your favorite news source will undoubtedly display even more absurd rejections of ethics.)

One of the reasons lies work so well – and they must to have been bred so deeply within us – is that they rely on generalizations and ignorance. Would any of us have believed the lie of "weapons of mass destruction" if people, and in this case I'm focusing on the news media, had questioned the lie? When Colin Powell was before the United Nations showing photographs of nothing and claiming weapons were being hidden there, what would have happened if more of us had thought "he's not sounding very fair and what he's asking wouldn't be very fulfilling." And when people warn us that intelligence leads to dishonesty, how long would that lie last if questioned? Or when we are made accessories to torture, how long would that last if we questioned the ethics of it?

Once you change ethics from a list of behaviors (a list that's easy for any creative liar to circumvent) to a relationship, that changes how you see a lie. The ethics of Dynamic Pluralism help us to see how such actions are neither fair nor fulfilling to our relationship. It may not register immediately but there would be no going back, no lame excuses, once the truth was out.

It's not as if unethical behavior would disappear the minute people chose Dynamic Pluralism and began to see ethics in every relationship they had. Unethical behavior is inescapable. It is ingrained in the DNA of our societal mythology. Consider the fact that it was Cain the killer, and not his more peace-loving brother and victim Abel, that western myth tells us began our "civilization". Surely, that speaks volumes as to who we are. And though our crimes against each other are dehumanizing – if not just all crimes across the board – the act of treating people as individuals, comprehending their needs, and not treating them with some arbitrary rule applied indiscriminately is the opposite of dehumanizing. It is humanizing.

Dynamic Pluralism is not a method for ending all unethical behavior, however. It is, on the other hand, a method for understanding it. To expect a world where everyone lived with the purest form of ethics, in harmony, is unreasonable just because of who we are, which is not a value judgment but simply a fact of life. Part of living is acknowledging that we sometimes do the wrong thing.

There are at least three reasons why unethical behavior won't magically stop the minute people behave ethically. I'll start that list with the good old "oops." Because we make mistakes. Even the most well-intended person can do something that can be misinterpreted and sometimes their lack of action can be seen the wrong way, too. Making mistakes doesn't end with Dynamic Pluralism. The next reason for unethical behavior isn't quite so easy to understand. The simple fact that we are all connected means that we have a relationship, no matter how distant, with every other person in the world. Ethical acts over here may have unethical implications over there. Part of living involves taking and it can be either food or fuel or anything else but an ethical person has to accept that fact as a part of life. When you take, you take from others, no matter how ethical you try to be. Finally, and perhaps the worst of all, ethical behavior is not always possible because what is ethical and what is right are not always the same thing. And they never will be. Ethics are relative and subjective. Right and wrong, far too often, are a lot less so. Abortion is a terrific example of this. There are going to be instances of unwanted pregnancy, where it would be horribly unethical based on either health reasons or economic circumstance or a hundred other reasons to have the baby and based ultimately on the judgment of the mother (and no one else) the pregnancy is aborted. Does that make killing right, though? No. Sometimes ethical choices supersede issues of right and wrong. Another example is if you have to kill another person in self-defense. There are few things less fair and fulfilling than a person trying to kill you so defending yourself against that is surely ethical… but killing is wrong. Stealing bread to feed your starving children is another dilemma. As is driving over the speed limit to get to work (so you can keep your job and buy the bread to feed your children).

Dynamic Pluralism makes no promises about ridding the world of unethical behavior, but it does present a very clear method for mitigating the unethical. We already have a tool for that mitigation built inside of each of us. It is what we commonly refer to as a conscience.

There is also an argument that can be made for an increase in ethical behavior with Dynamic Pluralism. Once you begin understanding the implications of your behavior, you may be more open to creative solutions to dilemmas. Perhaps, in the examples above, you're more careful about preventing unwanted pregnancies or you learn to stop violence with non-violent methods. Mitigation is not just the act of creating excuses but also of finding resolutions. Once we see just how our behaviors affect others, there's a good chance we'll decrease those behaviors that hurt others.

Another argument that is even more powerful for the spread of ethical behavior with Dynamic Pluralism comes with the very old concept of apperceptive mass. This concept was introduced by Johann Friedrich Herbart (1776-1841) and was meant to explain the totality of experience with which an individual understands the world.[45] Herbart suggested that each experience modified a person and that the accumulation of those modifications created a new person. If this could work for general experience, surely the totality with which an individual understands ethical behavior has an equally-compelling apperceptive mass. Ethics, then, build on ethics. As you grow to understand another person, your ability to behave ethically towards that person increases. As you grow to understand the world around you, your ability to behave ethically in the context of that world also increases.

And it doesn't end there. The ethics of Dynamic Pluralism is cumulative. With every new person who behaves ethically, there is an apperceptive mass in the human community, showing just how powerful ethics can be. Dynamic Pluralism does not suggest that practice makes perfect. There is no perfection. Like our present understanding of the speed of light, the faster we near such perfection the faster it escapes our grasp. All the same, there is value to be found in the attempt.

Ethics create ethics. If Socrates was right about ethics resulting from conflict and I believe that he was, we share our ethics through every interaction we have. Conflict is not just about violence; it happens in every relationship. Knowing where you stand in the world and your place in the world, which the ethics of Dynamic Pluralism and being aware of your relationships with others helps you find, can be as fulfilling for you as for those with whom you relate. This centering of yourself, putting yourself in perspective with the world around you, can be thought of as an axis mundi, your ethical center. As the world dashes about around you, you understand your place. As the whirlpool of life, referred to by some as Samsara, whips around outside of you, you find the center of that storm. You find the eye within an ethical hurricane.

As the fulfillment of ethics emits from you with every relationship you have, you spread ethics to others around you. And that's what it means to be ethical.

The Ethics of Santa Claus

or The Santa Claus Effect

Many times when people discuss ethics, the questions break down to pragmatic, down-to-earth issues… such as "Is it ethical to tell your child about Santa Claus?"

For those not familiar with this line of reason, it goes something like this: Santa Claus does not exist and yet people tell their children he does exist. They are, in fact, lying to their children. It's unethical to lie, therefore it may also be unethical to tell your child about Santa Claus.

Of course, this issue goes even further than that because we're talking about more than just St. Nick. We're also referring to, however obliquely, whether it is ethical to live in ignorance. Take Thomas Midgley, for example, the discoverer of CFCs (referenced previously). Did he find out just how harmful they would be before he profited off of them? If not, the best you can say about him was that he lived in ignorance and profited off of avoiding the truth.

The question seems to ask, is it better to encourage ignorance?

A recent article on WebMD addressed this very issue, asking "Telling your kids that Santa Claus is real is a lie, but does it actually hurt them?"[46] One respondent replied, "I will never teach my children about the myth of Santa, because he is not the reason we celebrate Christmas." This person makes a very good point. Actually, that raises something perverse about the whole Santa Claus thing. If you think about it, the half of the world that does not celebrate the birth of Christ (the titular favorite on why folks engage in Christmas) has no reason for believing and thereby propagating the myth of Santa.[47] Those who do celebrate Christmas – Christians, retailers, and Claymation animators – have a vested interest in NOT spreading the Santa Claus myth. It seems baffling to me that people still do it!

And why don't they stop? The author of a New York Times article on coming clean about the Santa lie (and wouldn't people who lied end up with coal in their stocking anyway?) obviously had nothing to hide. "When my daughter raised the issue with me this Christmas, I told her the truth. Santa is real as long as you believe in him."[48] Um… no. That's wrong. Believing in something does not make it so. If that was the case, we'd all live in much nicer homes. Pastor Marc Driscoll had a different take in The Washington Post. According to him, "Saint Nick was a wonderful man who loved and served Jesus faithfully."[49] And I suppose we honor this service by lying to our kids. But I think the best indication of our ethics amidst this colossal lie was made clear in a recent online poll, in which 58.88% of those surveyed said they lied to their kids and let them figure it out.[50]

After all, lies are ethical as long as nobody finds out, aren't they? No. Of course, not.

The problem with letting your kids believe in Santa Claus – that some old fat guy living on a mostly melted North Pole (or – worst case scenario – in a boat) watches them and gives them presents if they're good (with parallels to religion, which, by the way, are just spooky) – go back to the reason lies are wrong in the first place. Rather than sharing your love with your child and letting them know that you love them, you are foisting some bizarre surrogate – one who doesn't even exist – in your place! You are cheating your child, with whom you share a very profound relationship, out of a fair and fulfilling relationship with you.

Now, listen. Let me come clean here. I'm not exactly a fan of the jolly, old elf. I think my problem with the whole Santa Claus thing began in my childhood. I was raised in a poor household and there's nothing more ludicrous to someone who doesn't have enough food to eat than the idea of a fat man coming down your chimney (which, in our house, did not exist) and handing out free stuff.

I'm not what you'd call a fan. And I don't think letting your kid believe that Santa Claus is better at providing love than their own parents is ethical.

But does that mean the whole Santa Claus thing is unethical? No.

Because there's a difference between lying to someone who doesn't know any better and sharing a fun tradition, a lark, a game. If people want to play "Santa", there's nothing unethical about that as long as it preserves fairness and fulfillment in their relationships. If you come clean with your children and let them enjoy Santa anyway, with the understanding that it's separate from the gifts you share, there's nothing wrong with that. That's fair. And it can be fulfilling.

In cases where the line gets blurred over what's ethical and what's not, it's always important to honestly consider your relationship. And if you're being fair. And if the relationship you're engaged in is fulfilling.

Ho. Ho. Ho.

Ethics & Morality Revisited

Now that we've established the rules of ethics under Dynamic Pluralism, along with what those rules mean, I'd like to turn back for a moment to the subject of morality. In a society in which morality and ethics are seen as synonymous, it's perfectly natural for the question to arise: Which is more important, morality or ethics?

Comparisons like this are bound to be natural. Without a working system of ethics or an understanding of what morality is, it's easy to twist the two. Having just addressed the issue of Santa Claus, I'm reminded about how the retail morality of "I want" has superseded any spiritual morality. In a capitalist state, "I want" has almost become a commandment: Thou Shalt Want. Another indicator of just how far from ethics and morality we've strayed can be seen in the way humanity brings wholesale destruction to the world. Don't the commandments, which include references to never killing, apply when we wipe out one entire species after another? And so, I think it's important to clarify and address what some may perceive as the conflict between ethics and morality.

As an atheist myself, I won't claim to speak with any authority to what someone's idea of a higher power may intend with morality. I'll just try to keep it simple and stick with one moral concept that can be applied fairly universally: The Golden Rule. As already mentioned, the Golden Rule states: Do unto others as you would have them do unto you

This concept, as I say, is fairly universal. You can find it in Christianity:

> Judge not, that ye be not judged.
> Matthew 7:1

In Judaism:

> What is hateful to you, do not do to your fellow man. This is the entire Law; all the rest is commentary.
> Talmud, Shabbat 3id

In Islam:

> No one of you is a believer until he desires for his brother that which he desires for himself.
> Sunnah

This concept is also prevalent in belief systems from the East. In Confucianism:

> Do not do to others what you would not like yourself. Then there will be no resentment against you, either in the family or in the state.
> Analects 12:2

In Buddhism:

> Hurt not others in ways that you yourself would find hurtful.
> Udana-Varga 5,1

In Hinduism:

> This is the sum of duty; do naught onto others what you would not have them do unto you.
> Mahabharata 5,1517

In Taoism:

> Regard your neighbor's gain as your gain, and your neighbor's loss as your own loss.
> Tai Shang Kan Yin P'ien

This concept is so universal; it even goes back to Zoroastrianism, which used to number in followers as one of the most popular belief systems in the world:

> That nature alone is good which refrains from doing
> another whatsoever is not good for itself.
> Dadisten-I-dinik, 94,5

If we can agree that the Golden Rule is a moral rule, which I believe I've shown, then I can see ethics and morality getting along just fine. Why? The Golden Rule does not work unless both parties are employing it, which is why the ethics of Dynamic Pluralism moves pragmatically to one side. One of the sad realities of life is that, quite often, both sides aren't using the same rule. If both sides are moral and thereby using the Golden Rule, however, it then fits within the rules of Dynamic Pluralism that this will lead to a fair and fulfilling relationship. No harm. No foul.

But what if both parties are not using the Golden Rule? What happens then? Does it become immoral to realize you might be getting screwed and stop acting in a way that is fair or fulfilling? I can't image that would be the case. Let me show you how ethics and morality would agree in this event.

Let's say you were the one not using the Golden Rule, while the other party was. You were screwing them. Well, that's obviously not in agreement with ethics and, according to the universality of the rule shown above, you wouldn't be acting morally either. Q.E.D.

Now, let's say you were the nice person using the Golden Rule and getting the shaft from the other person in the relationship. You must make a decision to put morality (The Golden Rule) aside and rely on ethics. At this point, the conflict is with another individual and not with your higher power, meaning that ethics would supersede. Dynamic Pluralism tells you that you can stand up for yourself to create a more fair and fulfilling relationship. Is that immoral?

If your morality, your religion, says you have to be abused in order to be moral then you are going to find yourself disassociated from your fellow man to maintain your morals. This does not just apply to the sap being taken advantage of, either. There are other examples of morality trumping ethics to devastating consequences. Consider religious fanatics of any religion who bomb buildings and kill people to uphold their sense of morality. In the end, your life amongst other people is ruined in one way or another. I would say that when morality steps on ethics, it makes it a whole lot harder for you to live with the fellow beings you know are there over the rules provided by a higher being you suspect is there. If that's a situation you find yourself in, I would strongly advise questioning the authoritarian figure that hands you your morality.

Otherwise, morality and ethics can live side by side. And that's the way it should be. Morality maintains your relationship with your idea of a higher power. Ethics maintains your relationship with other individuals, be they people or animals.

But there's another level to Dynamic Pluralism, of understanding our relationships. Having discussed how we relate to our idea of a higher power as well as how we relate to individuals, the next section will address how we relate with groups of people as well as how they relate to us. Next, I would like to discuss Justice.

Ethics and Justice

If ethics defines a relationship between two individuals, what defines a relationship between groups of individuals? After all, we all have relationships with groups. I have a relationship with the federal government, for instance. I also have relationships with the state government, with the city I live in, with the grocery store at which I shop, and on and on. Something must explain my responsibility towards them and, just as importantly, theirs with me.

As I come to realize that ethics works on layers of scale (self, others, and groups), I also realize that there is one name for this relationship: Justice. After all, we commonly refer to laws set by groups as just or unjust, treatment of workers by corporations as just or unjust, and on and on. In the context of Dynamic Pluralism, Justice and Ethics are synonymous in so far as they describe the same responsibility towards fair and fulfilling relationships, the essential difference between the two being one of scale.

As it turns out, the dictionary definition of justice is also just as lacking as that of ethics. Merriam Webster defines justice in this way: "the maintenance or administration of what is just especially by the impartial adjustment of conflicting claims or the assignment of merited rewards or punishments."[51] Taking this apart, you'll find that the definition begins by saying that justice is "the maintenance or administration of what is just." As I've previously commented, defining a word with itself tells us nothing.

Things become more interesting as we look deeper into the definition. The definition continues by saying that justice is "just" when it impartially adjusts conflicting claims and assigns punishments/rewards. Impartiality implies fairness and the "assignment of merited rewards or punishments" implies fulfillment. The dictionary's definition appears to have Dynamic Pluralism build right into it. This confirmation of Dynamic Pluralism appears to be further supported in another definition: "the administration of law." As laws are set by groups of people and not individuals (at least, in the democracies of our time), this provides further support for the idea that justice is ethics on a larger scale.

Justice is commonly seen in our society as a way to redress claims. It typically falls into four groups: distributive, procedural, restorative, and retributive. Each type refers to correcting a wrong done. Distributive justice concerns members of a society getting their "fair share." Procedural justice is concerned with ensuring "fair treatment." Restorative justice defines "fair redress" or payment. Lastly, retributive justice typically appeals to the notion of "fair punishment." Each refers to fairness and fulfillment in the relationship between the party wronged and the party who did the wrong.

What these four types of justice do not do – and, in fact, our current concept of justice as a whole does not do – is consider that justice is not simply a relationship that redresses wrongdoing. It is a relationship that can prevent wrongdoing. Just as ethics cannot only apply after we've been unethical, the relationship of justice must begin and end with all interactions involving groups of individuals prior to any wrongdoing.

A common and popular idea or meme in our society tells us that an ethical people are also a just people. One state creates and supports the other. This can be explained with the concept of apperceptive mass introduced previously and can be proven by looking at the converse: what happens to a group or society that is composed of unethical individuals? Simply put, they create governing bodies and groups that are unjust, that create unjust laws and treat individuals unjustly. This means the answer to injustice lies in the ethics of Dynamic Pluralism. The more we create relationships that are ethical, the greater our chances are of creating a society that is just.

Rather than seeing justice as simply a way for those who create laws (those who rule) to redress wrongs, a more proactive approach would be to create a system of justice that inhibits injustice. The two ways to do this would be through social justice, which would include social and political policy, and economic justice, which would include our economic system.

Most of our ideas of social justice stem from the English philosopher, Thomas Hobbes (1588 – 1679), who believed the best way to live a long and fruitful life would be to sign a contract with your sovereign (or political leader) to protect you from death at another's hands. It might sound as though those were far more dangerous times but we actually do that same thing today, which is why we pay taxes to fund police departments and fire departments and the like. (Those behind the recent move to privatize these services would like you to forget all about Hobbes and your taxes and pay no attention to the man behind the curtain.) After Hobbes, John Locke (1632 – 1704) expanded on this idea of a "social contract" to include such revolutionary ideas as that the government should keep things in order, not abuse its power, and the like. Just societies did not deprive people of their property and prevented tyranny through the separation of powers. The list goes on and on.

Sadly, just as the monied interests in power try to void the social contract through rescinding the protection Hobbes advocated, they are also hacking away at such things as the rights to property and separation of powers Locke suggested were integral parts of the social contract. Without justice, contracts hold little validity.

The result is a society in which we don't understand how the ethics of our relationships affect the justice of our society and the social contract has eroded down to little more than "Do as we say or we'll put you in jail... or worse." Our society is unjust when it no longer acknowledges the relationship between the government and its people. And that means all of the people, because justice for some is just as ineffective as justice for none.

We are lied to by our leaders on a regular basis and, for the most part, we accept it because the consequences of realizing the injustice of our system are far too frightening. We are lied to about our food, from what goes in our children's school lunches to what goes in our sweeteners. We are lied to about our rights, from the threats to habeas corpus to the idea of a living wage. We are lied to about the dangers of climate change, from what caused it to what we can do about it. When there's no relationship between a government and its people, there's no relationship with the truth, either.

A good example of this is the demise of the Fairness Doctrine. The Fairness Doctrine was introduced by the Federal Communications Commission in 1949 and charged broadcasters (which at the time meant radio and television) with two basic requirements: to discuss matters of public interest and to air contrasting views regarding those matters. In other words: to fulfill and be fair. And this makes a lot of sense because most people had and have a relationship with television and radio through shows and personalities that meets a certain basic need. All the FCC said to do was to be ethical.

The constitutionality of the Fairness Doctrine was challenged in 1969 before the Supreme Court of the United States in Red Lion Broadcasting Co. v. FCC. The court ruled unanimously in favor of ethics. Score one for the good guys.

But the opponents of ethical behavior won eventually when the FCC itself (loaded up with assholes)[52] tore up the Fairness Doctrine. After that, the opponents of ethics swooped in like vultures. As Howard Zinn describes it: "By the 1990s, 'talk radio' had perhaps 20 million listeners, treated to daily tirades from right-wing talk show 'hosts,' with left-wing guests uninvited."[53] Fairness was officially defeated, and that was over 20 years ago. Any sign of fairness in media since then has sadly become harder to detect.

So, how can Dynamic Pluralism renew our understanding of social justice? Knowing that justice is a relationship between a government and its people (and vice versa), we can see how this relationship becomes unfair and unfulfilled when the government ceases to serve its people, when it rescinds rights (even when they claim it's in our "best interests"), and when it gropes for more and more power.

Some say that the best way to reform the system is to get involved and work with it and I can't say I agree. It sounds like beating crime by joining a syndicate or ending wars by dropping more bombs. But you don't do that. The best way to reform a system of justice, which in this case is a social system, is to create members of that system who understand what justice looks like, who understand that like ethics it is based on a relationship that should be fair and fulfilling. If the society is corrupt, so are the members of that society. Spreading ethics amongst people spreads justice within a society.

This takes us to the issue of economic justice which, I'll be honest with you about, is not a pretty story. And let's not look to our friend, John Locke, for an answer, either. Locke felt that money created the ability to accumulate everything you could without running into the issue of "spoilage." As strange as that might sound, it was his only real argument against abhorrent consumption (which I say only because the phrase "conspicuous consumption" became meaningless only a decade after its invention). Locke didn't understand the "spoilage" that happens to a society whose greed insists on "McMansions" and Hummers and sandwiches that use chicken as the bread. We live in a society that demands its daily greed, where the American Dream of the house with the white, picket fence and 2.5 kids has become the million dollar house with no yard, stacked flat up against the neighbor's equally abominable house, with an video screen in every face and the newest phone/car/take your pick in every pot.

We are told over and over that we live in an "ownership" society, never realizing what such ownership does to us. When you stop and think about it, it's clear that ownership reduces value. Think about how a car loses value the minute you drive it off the lot.[54] Consider the phrase "the grass is greener" and realize that the greener grass is not in your hands. As the things we have lose value, we are taught to want what we do not have and undervalue those things we do have. How can we learn to treat others fairly and fulfillingly when our economic system tells us to focus away from what's right in front of us and crave what's next?

How can we use ethics to create a fair and fulfilling system of economic justice? For an economic system to be just, according to Dynamic Pluralism, it must be fair and fulfilling to those within the system. Let's look at the two major economic systems of our time and see how this might apply.

Socialism is not foreign to the United States. Its proponents have been a constant force for change, even when they are overpowered by the wealth of capitalists. All the same, when socialists have spoken out it has been with compassion for their fellow man. The root ideal of Socialism (as well as its older sibling, Communism) has been to strengthen the Proletariat, who are the workers, the common man. This means most people.

If you want to understand Socialism's fight against Capitalism, you need go no further than the Workingman's Party of Illinois July 4, 1876 Declaration of Independence.[55]

> The present system has enabled capitalists to make laws in their own interests to the injury and oppression of the workers.
>
> It has made the name Democracy, for which our forefathers fought and died, a mockery and a shadow, by giving to property an unproportionate amount of representation and control over Legislation.
>
> It has enabled capitalists... to secure government aid, inland grants and money loans, to selfish railroad corporations, who, by monopolizing the means of transportation are enabled to swindle both the producer and the consumer...

And so the system continues to this day. You don't have to be a Socialist to believe it, either. The greatest advocates of the way capitalism concentrates wealth in the hands of capitalists are the capitalists themselves. They like getting all that money! (If you're unsure about your status as a capitalist, you might want to keep in mind the words of a professor I knew who said, "If you don't have any capital, you're not a capitalist.")

So, Socialists defy Capitalists for the sake of the working class, the Proletariat who does all of the work and should share in the reward, it would seem. They advocate such virtues as sharing, not being selfish, and state ownership of the means of production, which is to say businesses and farms and the like. There's just one problem, of course. It doesn't always work. You'll hear people say the problem is inherent in the system but, in actuality, the system is great. The problem with Socialism, the reason it never works for long when it does work, is the people. People become selfish and greedy and, to bring this back to the topic at hand, unethical.

What would happen if the ethics of Dynamic Pluralism were spread within a Socialist system, in which each person worked towards fair and fulfilling relationships with each other and in which the system's aim was fair and fulfilling relationships with its people? That would be interesting to see.

Our present economic system, the one the U.S. has employed since its conception, is Capitalism. That's the system the Workingman's Party was so incensed about. Why? Because Capitalism, for whatever virtues it might have, is just about the most inane economical system mankind has created. Its central premise is greed, which works very well for making money but not well at all for other things a system of economic justice must do, such as ensuring fairness, perpetuating the health of the system, and so on. Greed feasts on greed and whenever our country has seen Capitalism feast on itself, such as just before the Great Depression of the 20th Century, it has been ingredients of Socialism added to the soup (such as social security and welfare) that have ended the feeding.

Capitalism has brought us such things as hand sanitizer, the liquid alternative to washing so popular in the last decades. Hand sanitizers actually do very little with regards to sanitizing. Mostly, they provide a false sense of security and create a lot of garbage. But we're convinced to buy more hand sanitizer through capitalism's favorite son, advertising. Advertising has made us believe that we're not making things dirtier, we're killing germs... but we're not.[56]

One of Capitalism's greatest problems is that it is very wasteful. Capitalism has discouraged strides to help prevent climate change such as when the mass-transit street cars in Los Angeles were destroyed to make way for more individually-owned cars.[57] Our capitalist system perpetuates this waste with the damage privatization has done to the remaining forms of mass transit to keep more automobiles on the street[58] as well as the difficulties communities have been encountering trying to repurpose roads for bikes or pedestrians against the lobbying dollars of automobile advocates.[59] When you consider a method of restricting waste developed in a capitalist system, such as the move to digital music formats that save on shipping costs as well as on the materials needed to physically distribute music, those methods are not exclusive to capitalism and could easily have evolved in socialist systems. They are not an argument for the efficiency of capitalism.

Capitalism's corruption is entire, sadly. It's not just about automobile manufacturers saying, "I want the roads for my cars and nothing else." With greed being the primary motivator, Capitalists have been able to corrupt the very idea that anything could be shared. Aside from the police and fire departments I've already mentioned, "Privatization" (the idea that anything commonly held should be owned by one party) goes to absurd lengths. The concept of "The Commons", that being the idea that there are some things a society shares – common resources, common responsibilities – has been utterly corrupted.

As if it's not bad enough that our government has sold the resources our society needs to thrive (electricity, water, and other utilities) to private parties, the facilities we employ with the supposed intent of rehabilitating those in our society who break our laws are also sold off. The intent of incarceration no longer becomes rehabilitation but storage. Our prisons are truly storage units for the homeless. With prisons run by private industry, prisoners can no longer rely on the sympathy they might receive from a just society but are at the mercy of the profit motive, which insists on driving down costs (such as food, water, and other necessities) while maximizing profits. And though the prisons are sold off by cash-strapped governments trying to save a buck, the results are often just the opposite. As a CNNMoney article noted in 2010,[60] "an internal Arizona Department of Corrections report found that, in 2009, those savings narrowed to around $2.75 per inmate per day, and in certain instances, private facilities were found to cost even more per day than public ones." Fortunately for them, the lobbyists and other crooks who profited off the deal were by that time long gone.

If Capitalism is so wasteful and unethical, you may find yourself asking, why haven't we learned? Because our ethics have not been sufficient to teach us. We haven't had a system of ethics through which to interpret economic justice. Capitalism puts greed before relationships so you can't see (you're not taught to see) how your actions are affecting others.

Let me give you an example using storage units and homeless people. According to a National Coalition for the Homeless estimate, the United States held about 3.5 million homeless persons in 2009 with 1.35 million of those being children.[61] With that many homeless, you might think that the demand for housing of homeless persons would be rather high. Capitalism is rumored to run according to the law of supply and demand, with demand increasing supply, so you might also think that housing for the homeless would have been a priority. Right?

Sadly, something else was also a priority and that was other people's greed. Some Americans had acquired too much junk and couldn't store it all in their homes – those people not being the homeless, of course. These folk demanded places to store their junk, housing for unnecessary things if you will.

So, who won in the battle between demand for human housing and the demand for junk housing? It was no contest. According to the Self Storage Organization (Your Not-for-Profit Trade Organization of the Self Storage Industry), there were approximately 50,000 self storage facilities in the United States by the end of 2009. These facilities could hold upwards of a hundred or more individual storage spaces. How did the homeless do by comparison? Well, as of this writing in 2016, ShelterListings.org still only has about 4,000 shelters for the homeless nationwide.[62] We would rather put a roof over the heads of our junk than that of our fellow man.

This isn't because we're bad people. It's because we have a bad system and, together, we fail to recognize how our ethics affect the world around us. This is why, day after day and year after year, we fail to do anything about the poor and hungry who live right next door or, worse still, out on the street. We are taught that greed is the most important thing and many of us go to absurd lengths to meet that greed. We play the lottery or gamble or work at jobs that hurt others – I'm specifically thinking about the fossil fuel industry here but there are many others. Then, once that greed is met we find out through stories repeated in the news how lives fall apart and things don't work out. The Capitalist promise of greed remains unfulfilled.

Capitalism doesn't just desensitize us to other people. Sometimes it turns us against them outright. In the last few decades, a common argument heard by American politicians as well as the American people has been against illegal immigrants crossing the border "to take our jobs." Again, this is the greed motive undermining our own humanity. This is, of course, a lie as many immigrants take work Americans won't do. One recent study, in fact, found that immigrants add value to the economy rather than take it away.[63]

When I was a boy, I would often hear another lie told to turn people against each other. It was a lie devised by those who opposed the welfare system, a common foil for those who would rather you not pay attention to corporate welfare or government programs that waste far more money, such as "Defense". This lie was the lie about the welfare queen who drove a Cadillac, which in my childhood were fabulously expensive cars. The idea was to make you believe that welfare benefits were so plush and easily manipulated that nobody would ever want to work as a result. In reality, of course, welfare benefits are meager and help the neediest of us barely get by. But those who spread the lies don't care about the people they're hurting – and to point out that they're unethical seems redundant at this point – all they care about is undermining the system. They want that money. This is what Capitalism, untempered by ethics, does to us.

Obviously, it is not within the scope of this book to fully explore the ethics of economic or social justice. New systems based on ethics can and should be developed in a different forum. It is my belief that seeing just how much ethical (and unethical) behavior effects how we live helps us understand just how important the ethics of Dynamic Pluralism can be in our lives.

I began to realize something was wrong with our ethics from a very early age. Even if I couldn't put it into words, the way people acted as though their actions had no consequences beyond themselves (or even sometimes including themselves) struck me as kind of odd. I know where that began, too. It began with Proposition 13.

Proposition 13 was a ballot initiative put before the California voters in 1978. I was in the 6th grade then. When I asked a teacher why she was wearing a "No on 13" button, she explained to me how schools were (and still are) funded primarily through property taxes and how Prop 13 would drastically lower those taxes. You see, the folks who supported Prop 13, and the folks who eventually approved it, felt their greed was more important than their children. They would rather have had the money than see it go towards their kid's education. That was the bottom line.

Eventually, Prop 13-like initiatives passed around the country. People were far more interested in money than in their children in every part of the nation.

That's when I began to think, "There's something very wrong with people."

Later, of course, when folks complained about the quality of their schools and how they were so underfunded they certainly weren't irate enough to raise taxes again – because in America raising taxes and paying your fair share is a sin right up there with needing to get your car smogged. They still wanted that money and the hell with the kids.

My teacher also told me, by the way, that she could have been fired for wearing that button. Her belief in education and commitment towards her students could have caused her serious economic harm while others legally stole money from education for their own greedy hands.

Just as ethical people create just societies, you can be sure that unethical people will do their damndest to make things just as unjust as they can.

As this chapter has shown, Dynamic Pluralism takes many forms in our lives. Each of its forms – existentialism, ethics, morality, and justice – serves a different purpose and brings meaning to the relationships we form.

As a quick recap, here is each form and what you should remember about them:

Existentialism: This expresses your relationship with yourself and your own life, and in order for it to be fair and fulfilling it must be honest and authentic.

Ethics: This expresses your relationship with another individual, which must be fair and fulfilling in order for it to be considered ethical.

Morals: This expresses your relationship with your idea of a higher power. It is up to you to determine if that relationship is fair and fulfilling to know if it is a healthy one.

Justice: This expresses your relationship with groups of individuals and theirs with you. Societies that behave fairly and fulfill the needs of their members are just societies.

With these ground rules now laid out, I will use the following chapters to provide some examples of ethical behavior, just behavior, and the opposite in recent history and current events. While things might appear a little bleak, it's only through understanding history that we'll strive to create ethics in our lives.

PART 2
How Do We Know Ethics?

If we define ethics as a fair and fulfilling relationship with another, the opposite of ethics would be selfishness and greed.

In the following chapters, I'd like to show you just where such selfishness and greed has taken us. These chapters should answer any doubts you may have as to why we need to focus on ethics, where humankind with our strong sense of self-righteousness has gotten without a functioning system of ethics. Here is a new look at what a world without ethics has brought us.

Chapter 5
Ethics and Labor

This is what ethics and labor looks like

This is a story about Bob Bing, a man who has no apples. Of course, the apples are a metaphor and could refer to money or jobs… or even apples. This short passage explains the disaster that happens when we forget the simple rules of life with regards to ethics and labor.

…and is in no way meant to disparage The Apple Company or any of its fine products…

One day, Bob went to find a job picking apples. Bob was a skilled apple picker and knew it would make a great career if someone would give him the chance.

BOB
Hello. I'd like to pick your apples, please.

Orchard Owner
You would? Well, I do have a lot of apples that need picking. What would you like in return for that?

BOB
Oh, I don't know. A living wage would be nice. Enough time off to raise my family, help in my community, and cultivate a rich personal life. Insurance in case I get sick or injured. An opportunity to share in the wealth created with all of these apples. That would be nice.

Orchard Owner
Well, I don't see anything wrong with that.

BOB
Terrific!

Orchard Owner

Of course, by "share the wealth" you probably mean a cut of some kind...

BOB

Only what's fair when it comes to the value I put into the orchard by picking the apples and helping them get to market.

Orchard Owner

Sure, but the problem is those are my apples you're picking and you don't have any right to them I don't let you have. When it comes right down to it, you could be charged with stealing my apples if I didn't reclaim them right away. Anyway, I'm already going to pay you out of any money I make. If I give you a generous salary, I can't afford to give you a cut of the profits on top of that. You see that, don't you?

BOB

... No. I hadn't looked at it that way. What about my other requests?

Orchard Owner

Oh, those should be no problem at all.

BOB

That's good.

Orchard Owner

We have a complete insurance plan for all of our employees. Your premiums are offered at a lowered rate because you're part of a larger pool now that you're an employee. Those will be taken out of your paycheck.

BOB

Wait. I have to pay for my insurance?

Orchard Owner

Of course. I can't pay for your insurance along with everything else. I already pay you a handsome salary; I can't afford all of your other benefits besides. You said you wanted insurance. You didn't say you didn't want to pay.

BOB
Oh. Well, I suppose as long as you're paying a living wage –

Orchard Owner
We'll pay you what we see fit. You'll start at nothing and have plenty
of room for growth.

BOB
Nothing? How's that a living wage?

Orchard Owner
I haven't killed you, have I?

BOB
No.

Orchard Owner
You bet I haven't. That's against the law. I even put nets on the sides of
the orchard in case you want to jump to your death.

BOB
I see. Well, I suppose as long as you're providing time off –

Orchard Owner
Time off? You want time off? You haven't even started, yet!

BOB
You know, if all of your employees got together and asked for these
things, I bet you'd change your tune.

Orchard Owner
No. I'd change my employees. Or I'd grow my apples in a country with
a more motivated population, one that doesn't need so much. And that would
be your fault in the end because you're far too corrupted by greed, which is
evident by all of your demands. I can always find someone more desperate than
you. You're fired.

BOB
Fired? Do I get a severance package?

Orchard Owner

I suppose I'll let you pick some of my apples, but you have to pay for each one you pick.

The Tragedy of the Commons

It might seem a bit strange to begin a chapter on the role of ethics and labor with a discussion about the tragedy of the commons but when you're talking about greed and selfishness you really need to go that far back. Most people these days aren't even familiar with the term "the commons" so let's take a minute to discuss what that means.

"The commons" were once considered in a very real way those things that were common or, in other words, those things that were shared. Our society takes so much pride in ownership and in not sharing anything, it might sound strange and you might have some difficulty conceptualizing it. The only way we use the term "the commons" these days is when we refer to some common area, such as a common square or assembly area at a university. Actually, that's also how it started. Centuries ago, farmers would use common grazing areas for their livestock and common watering holes. "Commons" were resources that everyone shared and held an equal responsibility for, as in making sure they were preserved.

Author James W. Loewen provides a great example of how commons worked.[64] "Imagine a colonial New England town in which each household kept a cow. Every morning, a family member would take the cow to the common town pasture, where it would join other cows and graze all day under the supervision of a cowherd paid by the town. An affluent family might benefit from buying a second cow; any excess milk and butter they could sell to cowless sailors and merchants. Expansion of this sort could go on only for a finite period, however, before the common pasture was hopelessly overgrazed. What was in the short-term interest of the individual family was not in the long-term interest of the community."

Then, during the 18th century, attitudes began to change. Fields were fenced off and privatized. Animals were grazed on private land. Those who owned the land reaped the benefits of such privatization while the poor, those who relied on the commons the most, suffered the greatest. The world began to resemble the world we inhabit where, more and more, those who owned the resources reaped the rewards.

Those who didn't own the resources, which we can also refer to as "capital", were forced to labor for those who did. You might say this state of affairs has existed all along but by capitalizing on the resources that once were common, the owners were elevated into new positions of power beyond the political. They simply took what had once belonged to all and made others pay for it in their drive for more, in their greed. This didn't just apply to simple things such as places to graze animals or a common watering hole. The privatization of commons grew with time. Public resources such as electricity and rail travel became privatized. Public roads became privatized. Resources beneath the ground became a Frankenstein monster of public privatization to the point where private natural gas companies can now destroy private property owned by others to get at the public resource.[65]

Now, as private corporations encompass the globe, the issue of the commons is far more complex than before. James W. Loewen goes on to explain one level of complexity: "If we compare contemporary oil companies with cowholding colonial families, we see that new forms of governmental regulations, analogous to the relegated use of the commons, may be necessary to assure that there will be a commons – in this case, an oil pool – for our children." In a global economy or society, corporations are not the only thing that is global. So, too, are the resources held within the very globe we live on and in. If we are truly a part of our world, and what else could we be, then the resources we use must be global as well. (Some fine examples of the way these commons are abused are suggested by the over fishing of the seas and over logging of the forests.)

When it comes to matters of labor, we need to recognize how global corporations see labor itself as a kind of commons. Corporations have the ability to shift from one corner of the globe to the other, searching for cheaper labor. From an ethical viewpoint, their policy is to look beyond the individuals and see only their output. Their goal is to minimize cost and maximize profit, neither of which have anything to do with people. We cannot rely on corporations to treat us with fairness or engage in a fulfilling relationship. As long as corporations see human beings as a resource, a common, and not as individuals, they are by necessity unethical.

Why have we bought into this? Why have we allowed this system to exist? Why do we see libraries closing their doors and schools (and prisons) becoming privatized? Why do we even allow the debate over privatizing such common services as police and fire departments? Despite what William Simon, Secretary of the Treasury under both Presidents Nixon and Ford said in the fall of 1976, that we "have been taught to distrust the very word profit and the profit motive that makes our prosperity possible, to somehow feel this system, that has done more to alleviate human suffering and privation than any other, is somehow cynical, selfish, and amoral," we have not been armed with the correct context with which to process these teachings. It all may seem distrustful but without knowing why, without understanding how putting profits ahead of the relationship you have with people is unethical, there's nothing you can do about it.

Without understanding your ethical responsibility towards others, any number of lies can be sold to you and you'll be helpless before them. The lies aren't soft, either. The lies are compelling. The lies began with a revolution.

An Industrial Revolution

You might say the Industrial Revolution was sparked by a rat. This is not to say that the goals of the Revolution were underhanded; things were not organized well enough for there to be goals. Indeed, the goal of each person involved in moving the Revolution forward was probably no more than self-preservation, ambition, and gain. But certainly, the goal was not ethics. Clearly, the ethics of Dynamic Pluralism as described in this book were not understood at that time. This is not to impugn the characters of anyone I mention but to highlight how easy it is for ethics to slip from your fingers when ethics are not your goal. By the end of the Industrial Revolution, laborers were not treated with ethics and would be forced to wage war for a modicum of ethical treatment. Ethics were not understood and, therefore, were not fulfilled.

When I say the Revolution was sparked by a rat, I mean a rat in the literal sense. When, in the summer of 1347, a merchant ship brought black rats to the Sicilian port of Messina there was no way of knowing that a way of life would forever be changed. In just a couple of decades, half the population of Europe would be dead, most of them in cities where the black rats multiplied and spread.[66]

The Black Death spread into the country as well. With no one to tend the farms, land went uncultivated and livestock died in the thousands. In some parts of Europe more than half the land went to waste. In the agrarian economies of the time, the devastation was absolute. Some who survived the plague starved. Lawlessness prevailed. Many of the time believed the world was at an end.

It would take a century for the effects of those twenty years to pass and populations would take three centuries to return to pre-plague levels. Those who survived, however, found a world ripe for the taking. The dead had left behind all their wealth and many in Europe found themselves suddenly very rich. Those who weren't rich, the laborers, found work in demand and jobs easy to find. But the old order of things was forever changed and political might was soon overshadowed by the might of industry and invention.

Consider rum for just a moment. In the early 18th century when rising grain prices made hard liquor harder to come by, the distillation of molasses called rum provided a new market for hard liquor. Industry was creating new markets that stretched around the globe. Molasses, for instance, travelled to Europe to create rum. Those empty ships travelled to Africa for slave labor which was then brought to America where more molasses would then be picked up. This emphasis on wealth – hardly new but certainly exemplified – displayed just how easily ethics could be overlooked for the grace of a coin. After all, those same ships that carried slaves to America had previously carried goods to Africa and those longshoremen who loaded those ships may not have known they were perpetuating an unethical "triangle" trade. Of course, they were helping put slaves on the ships even as they loaded trinkets, guns, and ammunition bound for Africa.

While only a mere 207 gallons of rum were imported to England in 1698, the amount imported in 1775 exceeded two million gallons. Importing sugar, in the form of molasses, made it a luxury in 1750 and a necessity by the 19th century. Laborers who helped import the sugar and process it and refine it found extra cash to spend on sweet tea. As the British diet grew less bland and more calorie-rich, millions of Africans faced a life of hell in the resulting slave trade.

Africans were enslaved for the very same reason laborers in Europe and elsewhere were worked so hard: labor was needed. To spur the Revolution around them that made Europe (and soon the United States of America) richer and richer, more labor was constantly required. Those who could make more with less were eventually the winners and, so, labor saving devices were created.

In the textile industry, labor was maximized by the use of John Kay's flying shuttle, which in 1760 doubled the output of material. A decade later came James Hargreave's spinning jenny. By 1779, Samuel Crompton's mule mechanized the industrial output of cotton, quadrupling it by 1800. We are taught about such inventions in grade school but nobody considers what happened to the laborers who were put out of work by such inventions and I'm sure few considered it then.

On the other side of the ocean, labor was at an even greater premium. In the United States, more slaves were brought in year after year, sometimes adding to the slave population but oftentimes replacing men, women, and children who were literally worked to death. (Let's stop a minute and consider the ethical implications of that.) When an Act prohibiting the importation of slaves into America was passed in 1807, free human labor became harder to come by.

The invention of the cotton gin was originally meant to help supplant the labor of slaves, to get more work out of human mules. Eli Whitney was invited to the Mulberry Plantation in Savannah, Georgia, where he first heard about the issues of removing seeds from cotton, and believed he could design a machine to deal with such a problem. The cotton gin was patented the next year, 1794. (That's right. With more than a decade of slave importation to go, slave owners still needed more labor out of their slaves.) By the time the Act prohibiting the importation of slaves was passed, the cotton gin had increased cotton exports to over 66 million pounds from just 190,000 pounds in 1791.

There were many who believed such an output impossible without slave labor and fought a war to retain what was, at best, an unethical way of life. Fortunately for us, they lost that war. And while there were many who griped about the destruction of the South, cotton exports were back to pre-war levels by 1880. The status quo can and should be challenged at every turn despite those who would fight to protect it, especially when matters of ethics are at stake. If no other lesson could be taken from the Civil War, we have this to take.

This is not to say that progress always improved things, as in the Civil War, or that it was always necessarily ethical, as was the case for those workers stripped of jobs by machines. We should simply remember that ethics end when we refuse to regard our relationships with others.

Being replaced by a machine is a concept we commonly attribute to the 20th century and later but there were plenty of folks in the 18th and 19th centuries who suffered a similar fate. They found a figurehead in the person of General Ned Ludd, the leader of a riot of weavers in 1811, marching against the looms that were replacing them. The Ludd led rioters moved into the village of Arnold, outside of Nottingham, England, and smashed sixty of the looms. Pamphlets and proclamations appeared thereafter, written by the man whose name became synonymous with those standing up against being replaced by faceless machines: Luddites.

If being replaced by machines was the only unethical outcome of the Industrial Revolution, it probably wouldn't serve as a very good example. But you can add on top of that:

> **Income Disparity**, which increased capitalist's wealth faster than that of laborers;
>
> **Urbanization** that crowded laborers into cities where living conditions grew increasingly filthy – streets filled with trash, people packed into slums;
>
> **Abominable Working Conditions** that included 12-16 hour days, no sick time or vacation, and no accountability on the part of management;

Worse For Women who had to work just as much and keep a
home and take care of children on top of that;
Child Labor that worked equally long hours with no hope of an
education, perpetuating the cycle into further
generations; and
David Ricardo's "Iron Law of Wages," which espoused
paying workers only enough to survive and no
more, blaming the condition of the laborers'
lives on the laborers themselves.

The accepted standard of living for most people, in other words, was squalor. There was no hope of escaping it; this was your life. And it's important to remember this because there are still plenty of places in the world where this is very common.

What you might not know about corporations

I often hear people talk about how immoral corporations are because they turn the green earth to ash, starve children, and the like. Now, keeping in mind that morality is defined in this book as a relationship between one and their concept of a higher power, I'd say this is an empty term. Saying a corporation is immoral has no more meaning than saying an amoeba is a bad tipper.

But I'll improve on this assertion and insist that corporations are worse than immoral; they are unethical.

In fact, I'll up the ante and state that corporations cannot be anything but unethical. They are unethical by their very definition!

Just look at how "corporation" is defined:[67] a body formed and authorized by law to act as a single person although constituted by one or more persons and legally endowed with various rights and duties including the capacity of succession. Now, let's take that apart. Is a corporation a person? Despite what the United States Supreme Court might think, no. It can only act as a person – and that's where the problem with ethics comes in.

Remember, Dynamic Pluralism defines ethics as a relationship between two individuals, which must be fair and fulfilling in order for it to be considered ethical. Corporations, not being people, cannot have relationships. Just think about it. When you interact with a corporation, what do you interact with? A product? A person representing the corporation? Sure, but you never actually have a relationship with the corporation.

When businesses are small and run by one person or a couple of persons, it's easy to relate to them. You can speak with the owner, for instance. But in the case of corporations, it is literally impossible to speak with the owner because whoever runs the company is beholden to shareholders or investors and on and on. And even in those rare instances when someone does take responsibility, there are often so many employees, partners, and business relationships in between that it becomes impossible to find where the buck actually stops.

And how do corporations relate to you? Again, through their products or advertising or services; they come in contact with you but they can no more relate to you than a boulder or the ocean or the air. These things can also come in contact with you but you wouldn't say you are having a relationship with them in any way.

Ending our delusion that corporations can be treated like people, just because the dictionary says they're authorized to "act like people", would help us go a long way towards understanding our relationships in the world and understanding ethics.

Ethics and the Rise of Unions

On May 1, 1886, thousands of people in Chicago began demonstrations on behalf of an eight-hour workday. The marchers' slogan was, "Eight hours for work, eight hours for rest, eight hours for what we will."[68] Within just three days, confrontations between protesters and police along with Pinkerton security guards at Haymarket Square concluded with the death of eleven protestors with over a hundred more injured.

Once again in Chicago, a city that would eventually have an earned reputation, on Memorial Day in 1937, Chicago police shot and killed ten unarmed demonstrators. In the weeks that followed, more workers would be gunned down by police. What were the demonstrators trying to do? They were trying to stand up for their rights. For this, one policeman is said to have shouted, "Get off the field or I'll put a bullet in your back." For this, a Coroner's Jury declared the slayings to be "justifiable homicide."

As laborers grew more disgusted by their mistreatment at the hands of the new system born from the Industrial Revolution, more and more decided they'd had enough. They may have been met with bullets as a result of their movement to assemble, their movements to organize, but that didn't matter. They could take that because the alternative was far worse.

A perfect example of the alternative to organizing, letting the owners have their way, can be summed up in two words: Triangle Shirtwaist.

Very near closing time on March 25, 1911, a fire began in a rag bin at the Triangle Shirtwaist Company. It swept through the eighth, ninth, and tenth floors, which were above the seventh floor limit the New York City fire chief claimed his ladders could reach. The law at the time restricted doors from being locked during working hours but at Triangle Shirtwaist doors were routinely locked to keep track of employees. And so, people were locked in, trapped inside the fire, burned to death at their worktables, or jammed against exit doors that could not be opened.[69] Some, as the *New York World* reported, attempted a third option:

> ... screaming men and women and boys and girls crowded out on the many window ledges and threw themselves into the streets far below. They jumped with their clothing ablaze. The hair of some of the girls streamed up aflame as they leaped. Thud after thud sounded on the pavements. It is a ghastly fact that on both the Greene Street and Washington Place sides of the building there grew mounds of the dead and dying...
>
> From opposite windows spectators saw again and again pitiable companionships formed in the instant of death – girls who placed their arms around each other as they leaped.

When it was over, 146 Triangle workers, mostly women, were burned or crushed to death.

According to a 1914 Commission on Industrial Relations dialogue between Commissioner Harris Weinstock of the Commission on Industrial Relations and President John Osgood, head of a Colorado coal company controlled by the Rockefellers:[70]

Weinstock: If a worker loses his life, are his dependents
           compensated in any way?
Osgood: Not necessarily. In some cases they are and in some cases
           not.
W: If he is crippled for life is there any compensation?
O: No sir, there is none…
W: Then the whole burden is thrown directly upon their shoulders.
O: Yes, sir.
W: The industry bears none of it?
O: No, the industry bears none of it.

Clearly, laborers were going to die one way or another. The time had come for the workers in the United States to stand up. Consider for a moment the social contract we discussed back in Chapter 4. For justice to prevail, the social contract must consist of more than, "Do as we say or we'll put you in jail." Attacks against labor, on the part of businesses and the US government, have included measures far worse than incarceration. Justice was no longer an issue. Ethics were not a part of the equation businesses or the government recognized.

Keep in mind this was entirely new stuff. Indeed, it was revolutionary on par with the one industry had experienced. It's no wonder people equate the rights of labor with socialism; most of the early unionizers were socialists. They had to be! Can you imagine being a capitalist standing up for the rights of workers? It was the capitalists who were killing the workers and only the socialists who were in the workers' corner.

And so, I bring you again the opening lines of the Declaration of Independence for the Workingman's Party of Illinois delivered on July 4, 1876:

"The present system has enabled capitalists to make laws in
        their own interests to the injury and oppression of the
        workers.

One year later, as the country entered another year of economic Depression and the summer heat made New York City sick with dank, infested water, the *New York Times* used these words to describe the living conditions of workers:[71] "… already the cry of the dying children begins to be heard… Soon, to judge from the past, there will be a thousand deaths of infants per week in the city." That first week in July, in Baltimore, where all liquid sewage ran through the streets, 139 babies died.

At a time when people were forced to endure such injustices, even the most rational request can be made to sound extreme. If you don't believe that, just look at the news of the day where requests for workers' rights are still ignored or even worse lambasted.

New York Mayoral candidate Henry George summed up the reasonable expectations of the workers quite well in 1886. His Independent Party platform made these simple demands

1. that property qualifications be abolished for members of juries.
2. that Grand Jurors be chosen from the lower-class as well as from the upperclass, which dominated Grand Juries.
3. that the police not interfere with peaceful meetings.
4. that the sanitary inspection of buildings be enforced.
5. that contract labor be abolished in public works.
6. that there be equal pay for equal work for women[72].
7. that the streetcars be owned by the municipal government.

Other inspiring figures rose from the worker's movement to motivate good men and women to consider their fellow human being. One such person, Eugene V. Debs, orator and organizer, once said of the purpose of organizing labor and standing up for individual rights: "It seems to me that if it were not for resistance to degrading conditions, the tendency of our whole civilization would be downward; after a while we would reach the point where there would be no resistance, and slavery would come."

Of course, Debs was a Socialist. When faced with the selfish brutality of capitalism, of course an alternative is sought. Debs spoke on his decision to be a Socialist this way: "The issue is Socialism versus Capitalism. I am for Socialism because I am for humanity. We have been cursed with the reign of gold long enough. Money constitutes no proper basis for civilization. The time has come to regenerate society - we are on the eve of universal change."

I wish that were so. After all, standing up for the rights of individuals, recognizing the responsibility we have with every relationship we are a part of is what it means to be ethical. It means to treat people not as cattle, whether they are workers or strangers you see on television. Do not disregard; that is the lesson of ethics.

In the end, the benefits secured by the heroes of labor and the unions that were created changed the perception of labor and helped even those without a union. Aside from being treated with a bit more human dignity, the benefits unions have brought are many.

- With the representation unions provided them, union workers saw wages increase and a whole new middle class was created.
- This same representation helped reduce income disparity through most of the 20th century.
- Unionized workers saw the creation of such benefits as paid leave, health insurance, and pensions. The strength of unions helped those benefits perpetuate to non-unionized workers as well.
- An increase in job satisfaction equaled an increase in productivity.
- Finally, because unionization resulted from a recognition of individual rights and helped create an employer/employee relationship that was more fair and fulfilling, this relationship was a two-way street. Unions and business worked together for many years to build a stronger economy.

Where people led the government soon followed and as workers stood up for their rights and unionized the federal government also took action. In 1938, the Fair Labor Standards Act establishing a 40-hour work week and a national minimum wage was passed. The Minimum Wage was a national attempt at recognizing the value of human labor, if only at a minimum. The value of this action was inestimable.

- Working poor families found their struggle to make ends meet, to simply afford food and shelter, eased and national poverty was reduced. Quite simply, the nation as a whole was enriched. Detractors of minimum wage laws will tell you how much they cost the richest Americans but seldom tell you how much they help the poorest. By definition, the richest are more able to afford it.
- Communities found fewer of its citizens relying on social service agencies for assistance. Minimum wage helped build local tax bases and reduced the spending of local taxes on social assistance programs.

- Businesses saw benefits in reduced absenteeism, less turnover, and better morale among employees, as well as reduced recruiting and training costs for employers, all of which contributed to higher productivity.
- The nation as a whole benefited. The minimum wage law reduced the gap in incomes between the poor and the wealthy in America, which strengthened democratic values such as the freedoms to vote, speak out on public issues, and enjoy a stable and open society.

You may be thinking, "This all sounds great. So, what's the problem?" The problem, of course, is that while ethical changes were being made to our society while the relationships between society and individuals and businesses and individuals were becoming more fair and fulfilling, you can never underestimate the ability of a group of greedy assholes to ruin it for everyone else.

A New Economy

As a young man, I first encountered the United States' war against Vietnam through grainy footage on the evening news. Weapons exploded. Buildings exploded. People exploded. But the war didn't make much sense to me until I was a teenager and, discussing the war with a Navy veteran, first heard the phrase "fighting for Shell Oil." I didn't really know how to interpret it. I had been told, and this was the standard story our history books all held, that the United States had gone into Vietnam to stop Communism – just as we were later told our armies occupied countries to stop Terrorism.

When someone tells you they are going to war to stop an "ism", they are lying.

My Navy veteran friend said he had fought for the Shell Oil Company because of the expansive oil reserves American companies wanted off the Vietnamese coast.[73] Later, we would wage war in Kuwait and Iraq and across the globe for oil and labor and profits. Once unions moved in to help make things fair in America, it seemed, corporations moved out to take over the rest of the world.

But don't worry. They came back to the US.

More on that later. First, let's return to Vietnam. By the end of that war, a Harris poll reported that 65% of Americans opposed military aid[74] abroad because they felt it promoted dictatorships. And why shouldn't they? The United States in the 20th century had become very good at putting dictators into power across the globe. Here's a short list:[75]

General Jorge Rafael Videla, President of ARGENTINA
Colonel Hugo Banzer, President of BOLIVIA
General Humberto Branco, President of BRAZIL
Sir Hassanal Bolkiah, the Sultan of BRUNEI
General Augusto Pinochet, President of CHILE
Fulgencio Batista, President of CUBA
Rafael Leonidas Trujillo, President of the DOMINICAN REPUBLIC
Maximiliano Hernandez Martinez, General of EL SALVADOR
Alfredo Cristiani, President of EL SALVADOR
Halie Selassie, Emperor of ETHIOPIA
General Sitiveni Rabuka, Commander, Armed Forces of FIJI
George Papadopoulos, Prime Minister of GREECE
General Efrain Rios Mont, President of GUATEMALA
Vinicio Cerezo, President of GUATEMALA
François & Jean Claude Duvalier, Presidents-for-Life of HAITI
Roberto Suazo Cordova, President of HONDURAS
General Suharto, President of INDONESIA
Mohammad Reza Pahlevi, Shah of IRAN
General Samuel Doe, President of LIBERIA
Hussan II, King of MOROCCO
Anastasio Somoza, Sr. And Jr., Presidents of NICARAGUA
Mohammed Zia Ul-Haq, President of PAKISTAN
General Manuel Noriega, Chief of Defense forces, PANAMA
Alfredo Stroessner, President-for-Life of PARAGUAY
Ferdinand Marcos, President of the PHILIPPINES
Antonio De Oliveira Salazar, Prime Minister of PORTUGAL
Ian Smith, Prime Minister of RHODESIA
P. W. Botha, President of SOUTH AFRICA
Park Chung Hee, President of SOUTH KOREA
Ngo Dinh Diem, President of SOUTH VIETNAM
Chiang Kai-Shek, President of TAIWAN
Turgut Ozal, Prime Minister of TURKEY
Mobutu Sese Seko, President of ZAIRE[76]

The practice was simple. The United States determined it was more cost effective to put brutal dictators into power who could be bought off by US interests than to allow the citizens of Iran or Taiwan or Panama (or whatever country) the rights the US so zealously paid lip-service to. You want to talk about ethics? What we're talking about is systemic injustice perpetrated against entire nations, which may be why some people have a beef against the US. I'm just saying.

With the support of the United States military, new multi-national corporations took what they wanted wherever they wanted. In Chile, International Telephone and Telegraph decided they wanted Salvador Allende out. United Carbide wanted a piece of India and United Fruit wanted Guatemala, so they took it. Perhaps the United States was guided by the false assumption that multinationals had the best interests of the US economy at heart, if you'll pardon me a little ironic anthropomorphizing. Of course, they did not. Corporations are not guided by a heart or a head or a soul or a spirit but simply by a ledger. Multinational corporations wanted more money and the US politicians, who were bought and paid for year after year until finally nobody could deny it with a straight face, did their bidding.

The resulting policy could at best be referred to as mercantilism but that just boils down to strong-armed bullying. It boils down to a cold ignorance of ethics and a deliberate avoidance of justice as big business laughed its way all the way to the banks they owned. When imperialism results from corporations and not countries, the profits are funneled not to a country but to investors. Corporations seen as people in the United States practice Imperialist tactics while being permitted to supersede the rights of individual citizens while rarely being held to the rule of law our nation was founded on.

And, as I said, big business found its way back to the unions it had once been forced to acknowledge. As the 20th century closed, the attitude of big business and the politicians it bought was that they allowed unions to exist and they would treat unions however they pleased. Even as President Jimmy Carter praised the OSHA (Occupational Safety and Health Administration) program for protecting American workers, he conceded to big business with what would later be termed "deregulation." The idea was that businesses, which had run just fine up until this point, were overburdened by "needless" regulation that protected the American people. As Howard Zinn points out,

"Environmental regulation became more and more a victim of 'cost-benefit' analysis, in which regulations protecting the health and safety of the public became secondary to how costly this would be for business."[77]

During the Reagan and first Bush administrations, corporate profit held sway over any concern for the American people. More and more, regulations became "voluntary" and the political pressure to destroy unions, disregard the American people, abolish the middle class, and ignore ethics became so undeniable that by the second decade of the 21st century both major political parties had mostly conceded defeat.

Ethics and the Demise of Unions

Something you don't often hear about unions is how there were originally embraced with the idea that they would help stabilize labor and help the economy flourish. There was once a time in our history when the idea of fair working conditions and fulfilling work was considered a good one.

The Wagner Act, establishing the National Labor Relations Board legitimizing the powers of unions, passed in 1935 and immediately challenged Republic Steel.[78] In 1937, a strike at Republic Steel had resulted in the death of ten strikers when Republic representatives called the police on them. Autopsies on the victims of this Memorial Day Massacre, showed that the bullets had hit the workers in the back as they were running away. When Republic balked at the idea of being challenged, the Supreme Court sided with the Wagner Act, stating that the federal government had the right to regulate interstate commerce.

Unions might not have been loved by corporations but they were a stabilizing force. As CIO leader, John L. Lewis was quoted to say, "A CIO contract is adequate protection against sit-downs, lie-downs, or any other kind of strike."

Still, there were plenty of folks who – despite stabilization or organization, despite fairness or fulfillment – decided to defeat unions no matter the cost. One such person was Walt Disney. When hundreds of Disney animators went on strike in 1941, Disney fired the strikers, hired private security to beat them up, worked with an organized crime figure from Chicago to rig a settlement, and put out a full-page ad in Variety magazine that accused the unionists of being Communists.[79]

Eric Schlosser recounts the aftermath in *Fast Food Nation*: "The strike finally ended when Disney acceded to the union's demands. The experience left him feeling embittered. Convinced that Communist agents had been responsible for his troubles, Disney subsequently appeared as a friendly witness before the House Un-American Activities Committee, served as a secret informer for the FBI, and strongly supported the Hollywood blacklist. During the height of labor tension at his studio, Disney had made a speech to a group of employees, arguing that the solution to their problems rested not with a labor union, but with a good day's work. 'Don't forget this,' Disney told them, 'it's the law of the universe that the strong shall survive and the weak must fall by the way, and I don't give a damn what idealistic plan is cooked up, nothing can change that.'"

From anti-Semitism to anti-labor sentiments, Walt Disney, despite the impression you may have of him from the many animated films bearing his name, was something of a son-of-a-bitch. Of course, he may have been right about the law of the universe. Maybe it is true that the strong shall survive. But humanity has the option of being ethical and of making each of their relationships fair and fulfilling. It's either that or live as animals.

The forces against unionization and fair labor policies have found many ways to weaken the rights of workers. Sometimes, they let us turn against each other, something that would be prevented with an understanding of ethics. They make us fear those who would "take our jobs." I'm not talking about the jobs that get shipped overseas to save a buck, either. I'm talking about the jobs we're told those less fortunate are stealing. Those jobs include picking produce and cleaning toilets and many other things desperate immigrants who cross into the United States will do that so few of our citizens will do. We're made to fear immigrants who have very little power and wherewithal, while being assured that the powerful who run the corporations are not to be feared. Have you ever noticed the amount of energy that is put into stopping those less fortunate from "stealing our jobs" while so little energy is put into keeping jobs from being shipped overseas?

Lies are often the best weapons for those who oppose the rights of workers, or the rights of anyone for that matter. That should serve as a tip-off. Anyone who lies to you is not interested in engaging in a fair and fulfilling relationship. These liars hide behind lying names, such as the Anti-OSHA group, *Alliance for Workplace Safety*. They use such names to make you believe they're interested in preserving safety, when their real interest is in neglecting it or worse. Other such groups include *Focus on the Family* (not interested in helping families at all), the *Labor Relations Institute* (actually against labor's rights), and the so-called *Right to Work* legislation that has been so popular of late amongst crooked politicians. Right to Work legislation coaches its message in the language of worker's rights when its real intent is to demolish the rights of workers.

Those who criticize unions can't fight them on their merits. Instead of attacking the concept of unionizing, they try and make you believe that unions are wrong by citing specific examples, the details of which sound like something from an urban legend, "I knew a guy once…"

They'll tell you "Unions are corrupt and are only interested in pocketing your union dues." "Unions will take dues out of your paycheck, and you will be worse off than you are now." "Unions are outsiders. They will create an atmosphere of conflict between management and worker." "The union is powerless to affect anything, they cannot win you any improvements." "Your employer is your friend, talk to them about your concerns, you don't need a union to represent you." Assuming all of this is true, how is it unions have gained the benefits mentioned previously in this chapter? How is it unionized employees are better off? How is it that when you look around the world at workers who have no rights to collective bargaining, who have to stand alone against the corrupted might of the rich, they are so much worse off? How is it that as the strength of unions wanes we find ourselves growing poorer and poorer, both ethically and materially?

What happens when the rights of workers are stripped away? You can find entire books on that. But let me provide you with one example because it's not always as obvious as you might think. The safety of mines for mineral extraction has had many defenders in the United

States. After all, many US miners risk their lives daily extracting a long list of minerals, not least of these being coal. Mine safety legislation began in 1891 with the first federal statute governing mine safety in the US.[80] After a decade in which coal mine fatalities exceeded 2,000 persons each year, Congress established the Bureau of Mines, which was given inspection authority in 1941. Congress formulated the first code of mine safety regulations in 1947. The Federal Coal Mine Safety Act of 1952 aimed to increase mine safety. This was followed by the Federal Metal and Nonmetallic Mine Safety Act of 1966 and the Federal Coal Mine Health and Safety Act of 1969. If that wasn't enough, the Secretary of the Interior created the Mining Enforcement and Safety Administration (MESA) in 1973 and Congress passed the Federal Mine Safety and Health Act of 1977. To top off this impressive list of safety and enforcement legislation, Congress passed the Mine Improvement and New Emergency Response Act (the MINER Act) in 2006.

You'd think that after all this legislation mines would be the safest places in the world to work. And yet, every year, we hear about 50-60 miners who die in cave-ins here and there and there and there.[81] The news often catches heartless comments from mine owners who can't spare a dime of their shareholder's money to help their workers.

Why does this happen? Basically, it comes down to money. As corporate influences persuade legislators to cut budgets for enforcement agencies, safety legislation becomes useless. When the possibility of enforcement or the levying of fines becomes an issue, wealthy multi-nationals can grease the wheels of government to keep that from happening. When it does happen, the fines are laughably small. In the end, miners are cheaper to kill than keep alive.

One of the driving ideas behind Dynamic Pluralism is to start a revolution in ethics within you. Ethics can't start from the top down, because those on top find it too easy to shove aside ethics with a pile of money. But the more we use ethics every day, the more ethics will move its way upwards. It's inevitable.

In the meantime, those on top find it easier and cheaper to pay people not to be ethical and the lives of workers move farther and farther from anything resembling fair or fulfilling.

In the case of OSHA, for instance, a lack of funding (and what the more cynical might call a lack of giving a shit) has resulted in "voluntary compliance." In the meatpacking industry, this means that injury logs are kept by the company and you'd be amazed at how pristine their records are. After all, what company wouldn't report injuries that might result in OSHA fines or worse? (Actually, who are we kidding? Sarcasm aside, "worse" stopped being a reality long ago.)

OSHA's voluntary compliance policy didn't help provide a more fair and fulfilling environment for workers; it only reduced the number of injuries reported and encouraged companies, in the words of a subsequent congressional investigation, "to understate injuries, to falsify records, and to cover up accidents."[82] At the IBP beef plant in Dakota City, Nebraska, for example, the company kept two sets of injury logs: one of them recording every injury and illness at the slaughterhouse, the other provided to visiting OSHA inspectors and researchers from the Bureau of Labor Statistics. During a three-month period in 1985, the first log recorded 1,800 injuries and illnesses at the plant. The OSHA log recorded only 160 - a discrepancy of more than 1,000 percent. Was IBP unusual? Is it unusual in a society without an understanding of ethics to lie, cheat and steal? The answer, of course, is no.

And when ethics are ignored and workers are overlooked, it's not long before it spreads to you and me and everyone else. In the case of poultry plants, waste products including the sawdust and old newspapers used as litter are also being fed to cattle.[83] A study published in *Preventative Medicine* noted that in Arkansas alone, about 3 million pounds of chicken manure were fed to cattle in 1994. According to Dr. Neal Barnard, who heads the Physicians Committee for Responsible Medicine, chicken manure may contain dangerous bacteria such as Salmonelle and Campylobacter, parasites such as tapeworms and giardia lamblia, antibiotic residues, arsenic, and heavy metals. If you think that ended in 1994, run a search on the Internet with the term "feeding chicken litter." I found recommendations from the University of Missouri, the FDA, and North Carolina State University – and those were in just the top five results! Enjoy that steak!

There are many ways of looking at this. You could say it depends on who you trust, the guy with the money or the lazy, shifty-eyed, (insert your racial epithet here) worker. You could also say it shows a lack of initiative on the part of the government. You could shift blame to the consumer who purchases products from companies who perpetuate poor treatment and on and on… When it comes down to it, though, none of those answers work. Ethics don't start with the other guy. Ethics can only start with you.

Those who stand against labor won't tell you any of this. They won't give you an honest answer. They won't just come out and say, "We're against fair treatment. We oppose a worker's right to stand up for himself. We think it's wrong that people can band together and oppose our money with the only means at their disposal: their labor." They don't say those things because they know how they'll sound. They know people would wise up. So, instead, they pay millions to PR firms and ad agencies to "massage" and "wordsmith" their messaging, to make people believe that day is night and right is wrong.

In the next chapter, I'll take a look at the ethics of advertising, where "lying" is just another word for "ethics."

Chapter 6
Ethics and Advertising

This is what ethics and advertising looks like

This is a story about Bob Bing, a man who has no apples. Of course, the apples are a metaphor and could refer to money or jobs... or even apples. This short passage explains the disaster that happens when we forget the simple rules of life with regards to ethics and advertising.

...and is in no way meant to disparage The Apple Company or any of its fine products...

One day, Bob went to his favorite apple stand to buy some apples. Bob was especially hungry and looked forward to eating several of the little beauties.

BOB
Hello. I'd like to buy an apple, please.

Store Keeper
Excellent, sir. What kind?

BOB
Any kind is fine.

Store Keeper
We have these new Super Fancy Jumbo Deluxe apples.

BOB
... aren't they just apples?

Store Keeper
Yes, that's just the branding the advertising people put on them. I expect it'll make the apples sell better.

BOB
Very well. I'll take three Super Fancy Jumbo Deluxe apples, then.

Store Keeper
Would you like it with candy?

BOB
A candied apple? No thanks. I just want an apple.

Store Keeper
They're very sexy those candied apples. Look at the poster we have for them with a half-naked woman. I expect you'll be having lots of sex if you buy one of those.

BOB
I don't want sex. I just want an apple.

Store Keeper
Fine by me. Here you go.

BOB
Hold on. These apples are far more expensive than they used to be.

Store Keeper
Well, they're high quality aren't they? Just look at the label –

BOB
That's another thing. Since when did apples need labels?

Store Keeper
Look at it. See there? These apples have no preservatives.

BOB
They shouldn't have preservatives. They're apples.

Store Keeper
And you can be sure with the Super Fancy Jumbo Deluxe brand, you'll never have to worry about it.

BOB

I shouldn't have to anyway. And look at this – the label says "No orange residue."

Store Keeper

Yes, don't you hate that on those lesser apples.

BOB

But, it shouldn't have an orange residue, should it? It's an apple, after all.

Store Keeper

It's the Super Fancy Jumbo Deluxe guarantee! Look what else it gives you. "Now, with extra wax."

BOB

I don't want extra wax. I just want an apple.

Store Keeper

The wax preserves the luster and beauty of the apple so it lasts longer as you eat it.

BOB

I don't want it to last longer. I just want to eat it. Besides, what's this other sticker mean?

Store Keeper

Which one? The one that says "iFruit?"

BOB

No, the one next to it.

Store Keeper

Ah. "Now with extra protein."

BOB

What's that about? Since when did apples contain protein, anyway?

Store Keeper
Those lesser apples don't, but the Super Fancy Jumbo Deluxe apples do!

BOB
It means it has worms, doesn't it? You're selling me a wormy apple!

Store Keeper
We don't say "wormy apple," sir. We like to think of any added protein as a feature.

The Birth of Advertising

While modern advertising techniques go back just over a hundred years or so, at least one of the methods reaches back thousands of years. For that, we return to our old friend, Aristotle, and what he referred to as Rhetoric.

Aristotle saw rhetoric as many advertisers of today might see it, as an art. This was based on the idea that, unlike science, art is influenced by (and just as well influences) the unknowable, conflicting interests of society, where truth and untruth remain murky and require concepts such as "maybe," "probably," and even "probably not."[84]

I'm going back to Aristotle and rhetoric because rhetoric has long been classified as the art of communication and persuasion. Aristotle understood that this art could be used to mislead as well as enlighten. You've seen it yourself, I'm sure, when a particularly persuasive speaker sways someone into doing something they perhaps ought not to do. For this reason, Aristotle believed that wise members of society should be fluent in rhetoric so that they may effectively counter the rhetoric of the unwise.

This isn't exactly how things turned out, of course. Some might say that history is one long story of the unwise constantly persuading the masses to do all sorts of stupid things including though not ending with line dancing, religions that require the shaking of snakes, listening to talk radio, all the other religions, and any food item whose name begins with "World's Biggest."

Rhetoric has swayed people throughout history, far too frequently for the worst. But before we discuss when advertising really began, we'll need to make a couple more pit stops.

Our next stop is in Belguim, 1826, where we return once again to Adolphe Quetelet. Quetelet, you may remember, developed the science of social physics, which reduced individuals to numbers. His concept of the "average person" is something we're very familiar with today. If it wasn't for this idea, advertising would not exist as we know it. It was advertising's combination of rhetoric with social physics that has made it the force that it is today.

The origins of advertising and public relations go back to about the same place and about the same time, which is the Wilson administration during World War I. Two men named Edward Bernays and George Creel both worked in Wilson's Committee on Public Information; Creel led it. Another gentleman by the name of Ivy Lee was in there, too. Between the three of them, they changed the world.

For the better? Absolutely not. Advertising utilizes rhetoric, social physics, psychology, popular culture, and even a Ouija board if it must to fashion a lie into something that looks like the truth. The more a lie can look like the truth the more it is considered a win for public relations. (The terms advertising and public relations are practically synonymous.) In terms of ethics, for creating relationships that are fair and fulfilling, nothing could be further from the mark. Public Relations is the art of appearing ethical while being anything but.

The founders of advertising and public relations honed their craft in war, molding public opinion for the victory of America in World War I. They created the term "war to end all wars." The Committee on Public Information enrolled 75,000 civic leaders as "Four-Minute Men" to deliver war messages to people in churches, theaters and civic groups. Ivy Lee's publicity program for the Red Cross helped it grow from 486,000 to 20 million members and raise $400 million by the time the war ended. The Creel Committee also used the time-tested tactic of feeding wartime hysteria with fantastic atrocity stories depicting the Germans as beasts and Huns.[85]

Those efforts were not entirely altruistic. Advertising and public relations went on sale to the highest bidder just as soon as the war was over and quickly ended up in the hands of wealthy corporations. Aristotle's warning about rhetoric, however accurate, went ignored.

The public relation's industry served anti-labor money; they served crooked politics money. They served whatever master brought them the most money. This included the tobacco industry and entire books have been written about the absence of ethics in tobacco advertising and PR. The history is clear and simple: Those who do not understand ethics or choose to ignore them will sell you anything with any lie they can create to make a buck.

Bernays wrote the book on advertising and public relations. He called it *Propaganda*. He began his book with these words:

> The conscious and intelligent manipulation of the organized habits and opinions of the masses is an important element in democratic society. Those who manipulate this unseen mechanism of society constitute an invisible government which is the true ruling power of our country.
>
> We are governed, our minds are molded, our tastes formed, our ideas suggested, largely by men we have never heard of. This is a logical result of the way in which our democratic society is organized. Vast numbers of human beings must cooperate in this manner if they are to live together as a smoothly functioning society.

Is it, as Bernays calls it, "logical?" Perhaps. But advertising, public relations, or as Bernays calls it "Propaganda," should never be seen as ethical.

They say that you can judge someone by the company they keep. And you can judge the words of a man by the men they inspire. Bernays' writings, *Propaganda* as well as the later published *Crystallizing Public Opinion,* later ended up in the library of one Joseph Goebbels. As Reich Minister of Propaganda in Hitler's Germany, Goebbels used the theories Bernays and Creel and Lee laid out to their ultimate, logical conclusion. (And you thought it was just a funny coincidence that PRopaganda begins with a PR...)

Having mentioned Hitler, this might be a good time to mention an idea often attributed to him: *The Big Lie*. The idea behind The Big Lie is that if you tell a lie often enough and loudly enough people will believe that it is true. Sometimes, in Hitler's case for instance, this can be used to devastating effect. Other times, it's used to provide cover for other lies. More and more, however, it is used for everything: to sell soda, to sell candidates, to make you buy just about anything.

Some of our strongest held beliefs echo the idea that if we just believe something enough it has to be true. This explains climate change deniers, "birthers" during President Obama's administration, and other crackpots. It explains the success of such books at "The Secret," which claimed its "secret" to be that belief equals ability. They call it the "law of attraction." If you just believe hard enough, it must be so.

But that is sheer nonsense.

We can blame much of this neo-metaphysical claptrap on an early 20th century writer named Claude Bristol. His work, *The Magic of Believing*, did what so many after him did (just like Deepak Chopra and Rhonda Byrne), which was to steal a lot of silly new-age-y nonsense from other sources and string it together into a compelling narrative. That didn't make it any more true, of course. And such quotes as "every great thing starts with a thought and is powered into realization by a belief" told innocent believers that their ability to believe anything they were told would bring great things, just as so many other charlatans had done and would continue to do. Granted, Bristol sold a great many books but that says more about the ability of people to believe lies than the truth of Bristol's message.

As P.T. Barnum was famous for saying, "There's a sucker born every minute." (Although with the birthrate per minute at 280, according to the Population Reference Bureau's "2016 World Population Data Sheet", Barnum's original figure may require adjusting.)[86] This quote came from a man who began his career in 1836 by buying an old Negro slave woman named Joice Heth and exhibiting her to the public as "George Washington's childhood nursemaid."

Joice Heth claimed to be 160 years old. Barnum kept the public wondering if she was for real with a clever series of forged letters to the editors of New York newspapers. Written by Barnum himself and signed with various fake names, some of the letters went so far as to denounce Barnum as a fraud. Joice Heth was discussed in news reports and editorial columns, and the public turned out in droves to see for themselves. Barnum collected as much as $1500 per week from New Yorkers who came to see the pipe-smoking old Negro woman.[87]

When Joice Heth died, doctors performed an autopsy and estimated her true age at around eighty. Barnum handled the situation like the PR pro that he was. He said he was shocked, deeply shocked, at the way this woman had deceived him.[88]

Barnum's manipulation of the press, once considered fantastic, quickly became a standard practice. Why leave it to amateurs, after all? By the end of the 19th century, it was common for newspapers to "insert at a higher cost almost any advertisement disguised as a bit of news. Sometimes these paid reading notices of advertisers were distinguished by star or dagger, but more frequently there was no sign to indicate to the readers that the account had been bought and paid for and was not a regular news item."[89]

And when your propaganda can be hidden within a newspaper for adults to read, why not a book for children to read? Many people are outraged by the amount of advertising (corporate propaganda) presented to children these days but in the late 19th century an entire generation grew up with the lies Horatio Alger told about the American Society. Many of these lies are still with us today.

Alger's most famous lie was similar to Bristol's lie that belief in something makes it real. For Alger, it became known as picking one's self up by their bootstraps. The term "bootstrap" has been nearly lost to us but the dictionary defines it as "a loop at the back of a boot, used to pull it on." Alger meant it as a metaphor to mean you can do anything if you believe enough. (As a digression, though, just think what it would take to pick yourself up by a loop on the back of your boot. It would be impossible. This shows how completely Americans bought into this lie.) Alger's lie has been handed down, generation after generation, to mean that no one should ever have to help out, that people who need help are just taking advantage of you, that our connection to one another is a lie. The Horatio Alger "bootstrap" propaganda is a lot like that of Ayn Rand mentioned earlier in the book, and we know how foolish that is.

What Advertising Has Done To Us

We Americans have become incredibly adept at believing any lie presented to us. From the society that once preached "Don't believe everything you read in the papers," we've turned into a bunch of people who believe "reality TV" is real! We can be sold anything, from poisons to pound cake – and we'll love it, too!

One easy place to start exposing the lack of ethics in advertising would be the tobacco industry. So much has already been documented about the lies they tell consumers, you could fill a library.[90] The reason tobacco makes such a good place to start is because the techniques of lying and lying and lying and, when all else fails, lying that Big Tobacco applied throughout the 20th century and still applies today also apply to all advertising and public relations.

One of the most effective tools has long been to sell a product or idea by having a trusted figure, such as a scientist or a doctor, endorse it.[91] Actors in white lab coats are common on television and on the Internet, especially as the advertising budgets for medications increase. Also, by using "third party" experts, PR firms can mask dubious claims with the suggestion of respectability. Such experts are easily found, especially with the Internet's neutrality towards ethics. Services like Profnet supply "experts" paid on the part of advertisers to speak on behalf of those advertisers. This might not be a problem if we had a fourth estate, a public press capable of weeding through the claims – more on that later – but Profnet also provides such "expert" advise to consultants, meeting planners, and bloggers.[92] Keeping in mind that meeting planners are often admin assistants (our latest revision of the title "Secretary") and consultants are corporate pariah... That leaves it up to bloggers to protect us from propaganda, who could be giggling 14 year olds. It's no wonder we're brainwashed!

Even the trusted "non-profit agencies" get a piece of the propaganda action. The American Council on Science and Health

(ACSH) is an industry front group for any number of goods and services from chemicals to environmental issues, from food to disease, from terrorism to tobacco. The assumption is that they are anti-terrorism, disease, and tobacco... I'll leave that in the reader's hands. According to their own website, the ACSH was created "to add reason and balance to debates about public health issues and to bring common sense views to the public." Considering that the ACSH is on record, through their head Elizabeth Whelan, praising the nutritional value of fast food while receiving funding from Oscar Mayer, Frito Lay, Land O'Lakes, Coca-Cola, Pepsi, NutraSweet and the National Soft Drink Association, I have to assume they are either unclear as to what "reason and balance" are or that in creating a relationship with the consumer that is both unfair and unfulfilling, they are patently unethical.

This isn't unique. This is how food is marketed. They create high fructose corn syrup, which is toxic, and rather than do the ethical thing they simply change the name, knowing that most people won't know any better. They raise disease-ridden livestock shot full of antibiotics and hormones and, when people begin to find out, claim that simple irradiation will undo all of that harm with no risk to the consumer. Advertising is the art of selling you a lie, which is why liars rely so much on public relations.

The PR industry has made a killing on the denial of climate change because, as I've shown, the goal isn't the truth. The truth is far too risky because it might cost too much to the industries perpetuating global warming. The goal, instead, is profit. So it was when 12 journalists were paid to act as PR guinea pigs for DuPont pesticides, as reported in the February 1995 issue of the newsletter Environment Writer. DuPont lured journalists with invitations promising: "This learning endeavor will be used to help DuPont establish new policies regarding pesticides: their use and information important to consumers, the government, farmers and the press..."[93] In the end, DuPont was looking for nothing more than more efficient methods for manipulation.

Profit was also the motivation behind PR firm Hill & Knowlton's environmental coalition "Partners for Sun Protection Awareness," which was a front for drug transnational Schering-Plough.[94] You may know them for their Coppertone™ line of sun lotions. Rather than stand against the thinning of the ozone layer, Schering-Plough's coalition did little more than advertise the use of its lotions, urging people to "liberally apply sunscreen… to all exposed parts of the body before going outdoors."[95] If you consider how much damage chemical pollutants have caused our environment, this amounts to little more than a coalition that will sink your ship so they can make a killing on life jacket sales.

And you can't mention making a killing without mentioning war in the same breath. And war propaganda has a history going back to Attila the Hun. Vincent Kavalosku writes "Before ordinary human beings can begin the organized killing known as 'war,' they must first 'kill' their opponents psychologically. This is the ritual – as old as civilization itself – known as 'becoming enemies.' The 'enemy' is described by our leaders as 'not like us,' almost inhuman. They are evil. They are cruel. They are intent on destroying us and all that we love. There is only one thing the 'enemy' understands – violence. This 'logic of the enemy image' leads to one inescapable conclusion: the enemy must be killed. Indeed, destroying the enemy is an heroic act, an act of salvation and purification."[96] Any war you ever supported was sold to you just the same way you've been sold bread or cheese. The killing and maiming of human beings, some innocent and some not so, has been processed and packaged by public relations experts scientifically with cold, precise logic. You have been sold hate. You have been sold the most profane wrong doings.

And you bought it.

In case you're wondering if advertising is ethical, keep that in mind.

The Buck Stops Where?

Keep in mind that the liars who work in advertising and public relations won't tell you they're lying. Not a chance.

They'll even go out of their way to make you think they're not liars, by disguising themselves. Sometimes, they'll even disguise themselves as the very thing they're lying about. Take the American Council on Science and Health, for instance, a group far more interested in snacks than science or health. Such groups are often referred to as "astroturf" groups, which is a reference to fake, plastic grass. You get none of the virtues of grass with astroturf and you get none of the virtues of ethics with astroturf groups. Some other groups famous for their astroturfing include:

- *Focus on the Family*, a group that stands in support of families so long as they fall within Focus' strictly defined terms. In other cases, if you're gay or not Christian or fall outside of their narrow view, let's just say you're out of focus.
- *The British Columbia Forest Alliance*, a group that is allied against forests in British Columbia.
- *The Christian Coalition*, a group that is Christian just as long as you believe that the teachings of Jesus Christ included hate.
- *FreedomWorks*, which believes wholeheartedly that freedom works – just not for you.
- *The Family Research Council*, which purports to stand in defense of families but instead pushes an ultra-right-wing agenda against those with different sexual orientation, different faiths, and even those who would vote differently than they command.
- *The Save Our Species Alliance*, which apparently is for saving whatever one species they have in mind but killing off the rest.

Mind you, these are only a few. If you wiped these out tomorrow, they would be replaced with twice as many. There are going to be people in the world who believe it is their job to lie to you, who refuse to measure up to even the merest version of modern ethics let alone Dynamic Pluralism, and who don't care one bit.

Traditionally, it has been the role of our public press – the fourth estate – to warn us about these people. Journalists have for a long time fulfilled the role of those who speak out against those who would do harm. Thomas Jefferson is often quoted as saying, "Our liberty cannot be guarded but by the freedom of the press, nor that be limited without danger of losing it." In other words, a robust and free press is crucial in protecting us from those who would cause us the greatest harm and that is the harm that we are convinced to do unto ourselves.

So, what happened?

The press Jefferson understood, that of the newspaper, died a slow and painful death as paper was supplanted with pixels. Newsprint couldn't keep up with a rapidly changing society and we were left with TV news and the Internet to fill the void.

The problem with TV news is an obvious one: The news is broadcast on a channel and that channel is owned by a corporation, oftentimes by a multinational that owns scores of corporations and entities, brands and affiliations. TV news is beholden to profit, preventing it from ever being able to do its job. Consider the choices you have. First, there's Fox News – okay, so I was kidding with that one. Fox News is no more News than it is a Fox. It's a joke so old and moldy that even Canada knew better.[97] There are still other channels, of course, but they also run afoul of their corporate servitude. They need to keep up their ratings so they do what they can to avoid offending any guests they know will bring in ratings. These include politicians, celebrities, public figures and… before you know it, it means they can't tell the truth for fear of offending someone. You end up with a watchdog without teeth or claws or ears or a snout.

The other TV option is local news. I decided to study my local news options for a week to see what I would find. Here it is:

a) Advertising. Most stories on local news are transparent advertising to bring in money.

b) Banter. Everything else was chit-chat. Apparently, they wanted me to recognize that the models reading the news were regular people just like you and me, and not empty-headed boobs who can't just tell me what the weather's going to be or what happened in local sports. Lastly, there was…

c) Crime. Local news programs know you'll watch if they give you a reason to watch and be afraid. (This encourages older viewers, usually afraid of a rapidly changing world, to stay tuned.)

And that's it. That's TV news.

Sadly, on the Internet, you run into the same kind of problem but without the same reason for it existing: Vapid, lazily written stories too afraid to make a point lest they lose readership and that possible "click-thru" income for the 400 ads that are blasting for my attention.

Clearly, the buck is not going to stop with a robust, free press. It can only stop with you.

How Do We Defend Ourselves Against Lies?

Every day, we are faced with hundreds – possibly thousands – of ads. The consumer watchdog Media Smarts placed the number at 5,000 every day.[98] Even if only 10% of the ads you see are lies, that's still hundreds of lies you are bombarded with daily. How are we to defend ourselves?

There are groups, of course, that have been formed to help defend people from lies. The aforementioned Media Smarts endeavors to educate people on the role of media and the pitfalls therein.[99] In addition, Business Ethics magazine helps expose businesses with unfair practices.[100] Too, there is the well-respected Center for Public Integrity, an organization dedicated to journalistic investigation in the public's interest.[101] The problem with these and similar groups, however well intentioned, is that none are nearly as big as any of the corporate run media or the public relations industry or the marketing and advertising efforts on behalf of all the corporations and multi-nationals. Against the combined might of those who would lie for a profit, watchdog groups are essentially helpless on their own.

When I was a boy, there existed in this country a thing called The Fairness Doctrine. The Fairness Doctrine was the government's way of ensuring that issues were allowed equal time when discussed on airwaves that – at that time, at least – were considered public property. So, if you wanted to spew hatred towards blacks or Latinos or Democrats that was fine just so long as you allowed someone equal time to speak against that hate. It wasn't much of an insurance towards fairness but it was all we had.

And then, that was taken from us. It was taken away by greedy corporate interests and hatemongers who realized the best way to stir up a radical fan base is to not allow dissent. About this time, AM "talk radio" became populated with hateful imbeciles like the Rush Limbaughs of the world, who garnered a huge audience filled with equally hateful and equally stupid listeners.

Fairness was kicked to the curb.

In the end, the ethics of advertising and public relations, just like the ethics of hate-mongers on the radio, are absent because our own ethics are absent. Because we haven't understood what ethics are, we haven't been able to recognize when ethics have been absent. When a PR man told us that smoking made us look cool, no one thought to consider how what he was doing was neither fair nor fulfilling. When advertisers sold us gas-guzzlers, processed foods, and beef raised on chicken shit, we weren't equipped to question the ethics of it. This applies to our politicians, our talk radio hosts, and any of those astroturf groups as well.

It's advertising's job to make you believe lies. Ethics help you see the danger in that. Because if they can sell you a car that helps kill the planet, or a politician who brags about killing through state-run executions,[102] you're just a small step away from being sold a war.

In the following chapter, I'll look at ethics and war and try to reconcile how we see both.

Chapter 7
Ethics and War

This is a story about Bob Bing, a man who has no apples. Of course, the apples are a metaphor and could refer to money or jobs... or even apples. This short passage explains the disaster that happens when we forget the simple rules of life with regards to ethics and war.

...and is in no way meant to disparage The Apple Company or any of its fine products...

One day, Bob was hungry for some apples but couldn't find any apples, anywhere!

BOB
What happened to all the apples?

General
It's those apple-stealing nations what took 'em! That's right. Next thing, they'll be coming for your daughter, coming for your investment income!

BOB
I'm sorry, but what was that about the apples?

General
Stolen! Your sovereign apples stolen by godless heathens – appleless, too, I reckon. It's time to put together an army and get those apples back!

BOB
Couldn't we just grow more?

General

Not if you want to remain the most feared fighting force in the world, you can't. Nope. It's time to kill them all! They're a threat to everything you believe in!

BOB

I thought they were just hungry.

General

Hungry people are the worst threat there is – and the most terrifying. Why, if you don't kill them, or sign your kids up to kill them (that's your kids, not mine), they'll just come back and eat more apples, and maybe eat your head!

BOB

What if we just helped them grow apples?

General

Quick! Give me more money so I can build more bombs before they eat your head!

BOB

I assure you, my head looks nothing like an apple.

General

We'll bomb them back to stone and then torture their leaders – not because we want to but because we have to – to stop any future apple stealing or god knows what!

BOB

You think maybe you're getting a bit excessive?

General

(pointing at BOB) Enemy sympathizer! Quick! Water board him!

Let's agree on one thing from the outset: War is unethical. You might want to believe you have a just war. You might be able to convince yourself you have a necessary war. But there must be no circumstances under which you can convince yourself that it is ethical to kill other people. The antithesis of "fair and fulfilling" would have to be any of the arrays of death humanity has created in its pursuit of war.

So, here's hoping we can agree on that.

If only the argument ended there, this would be a very short chapter, indeed. Sadly, however, there's so much more to war than simple killing, maiming, pillaging, plundering, raping, and desecrating. Things can get rather ugly, too. There's something in us that tilts towards destruction. When nations find themselves unable to agree, far too often the voices suggesting compromise are drowned out by the choruses crying for war. It is those choruses I'd like to discuss in this chapter. For if all there was to war was a bunch of people killing each other, eventually we'd run out of people. And we haven't.

It isn't just the killing that makes war unethical but the impulse to war itself. "Fair and fulfilling" means you don't think of reasons to take what belongs to someone else, which is what war is when you get right down to it. From the Messenian Wars in Ancient Greece all the way up to the American wars in the Middle East in the early part of this century, war is all too often the way we say, "Hey, I rather like that. I think I'll take it."

It didn't take long for America to get into the business of making war. As George Carlin once famously put it: "We really gave the Indians a fast trip across the continent, you notice that? They were having a little cookout in Massachusetts—buncha boats came up... 'Hey, ya mind moving over, guys? Bring in the stuff. Would you move it over, man. Bring in the stuff.'" The Native Americans weren't even our enemies when the first immigrants we call "Our Forefathers" arrived but they had something we wanted, which was all of the land that eventually became the continental United States. Think of that. The United States began by stealing the United States! I'd say that took considerable blindness to the concept of ethics.

Of course, the first settlers were helped by the diseases brought over by the European fishermen, trappers, explorers, and venture capitalists that came before them. Whether you argue that the initial plagues brought to America by the Europeans were intentional or not,[103] they were no less effective. By 1620, up to 96% of the inhabitants of coastal New England were wiped out.[104] Robert Cushman, a British eyewitness, recorded a death rate unknown to all previous human experience stating that only "the twentieth person is scarce left alive."

Those Indians who remained we killed. Those we didn't kill, we forced into centuries of broken promises, shuffling them off with the buffalo. Those who still believed us, as strange as that might sound, we enlisted in our wars. Native Americans fought in the Seven Years War, the Revolutionary War, the War of 1812, the Mexican/American War, the Civil War, and on and on even to present day.

Now, you may be left thinking of Native Americans as about as gullible as the white man is evil – or, at the very least, historically unethical – but there's another message here as well. Those who were alive on September 12, 2001 might remember a world drawn together in the aftermath of the fall of the Twin Towers. You might remember how the world spoke seemingly as one in support of the United States. But what you might not remember is just how fast our mutual support, our connectedness, our sense of community was rapidly turned into a call for war. And it wasn't even a call for war against those who had attacked us, with so many accounts pointing to Saudi Arabia and Afghanistan. No, it was a call to war against Iraq, a nation that had nothing at all to do with the attacks on September 11. (In fairness, no single nation was responsible for the attacks on September 11, so far as we know. Any call to war would have been just as stupid.) But I think this shows the power war has over us, the sway it commands. It tells us any option to brutality is weakness and any alternative is small.

This is how a group of people as abused and devastated as the Native Americans could find themselves on our side. This is also how we find ourselves year after year, from one generation to the next, stockpiling weapons of war, ignoring their one inevitable end.

I remember being a boy in the 1970s, watching the remnants of the Cold War threat die off even as stockpiles of nuclear weapons grew and grew. The Cold War hadn't ended but it no longer made for good politics – People were actually suggesting we get rid of our nuclear arsenals! So, we kept building and building more and more bombs even as fewer in the "mainstream" mentioned it. We just accepted our doom. It reminds me a great deal of what's happening right now as global warming begins to wreak havoc across the globe. The flip side to the compulsion of war is the perceived powerlessness to stop it.

If only there were some sort of international organization expressly formed to help prevent wars between peoples, to help foster peace, to help unite the nations of the globe…

Oh wait. I'm sorry. There is just such an organization, which is actually called the United Nations. Preventing war is specifically part of their charter: "All Members shall settle their international disputes by peaceful means in such a manner that international peace and security, and justice, are not endangered. All Members shall refrain in their international relations from the threat or use of force against the territorial integrity or political independence of any state, or in any other manner inconsistent with the Purposes of the United Nations."

And still, even with this, we are somehow attracted by war. (Mind you, constant anti-UN propaganda on the part of the very stupid in the world certainly doesn't help.)

This is not to discount the efforts of the millions of people throughout our history who have stood up and said "No" to war. It has been said that the only thing necessary for evil to triumph is for the good to do nothing and that has certainly not been the case with those who resist the pull to war.

In 1918, Eugene Debs spoke out against World War One – a war based on a surplus of unspent bullets and shells – with these evocative words, "They have always taught and trained you to believe it to be your patriotic duty to go to war and to have yourselves slaughtered at their command. But in all the history of the world you, the people, have never had a voice in declaring war, and strange as it certainly appears, no war by any nation in any age has ever been declared by the people."[105] Debs was put in jail for these words, thanks to legislation created to restrict speaking against violence, deceptively called *The Espionage Act*.

Those who spoke out against Hitler in Germany prior to World War Two were thrown into Concentration Camps. In the United States, on the other hand, there was an incredible opposition to the war. Too many had seen family members killed or returned home maimed in the Great War – that would be the "War To End All Wars" or World War One. This opposition fell almost utterly after Pearl Harbor, after Americans began learning of Hitler's atrocities, and after and after and after...

And after World War Two, the United States was hooked on a steady stream of military adrenaline. By 1950, the military portion of the American federal budget was $12 billion of a total budget of $40 billion. Americans weren't oblivious to this. No matter how much their government tried to tell them that the military was protecting them from that Communist boogey-man or that Fascist boogey-man, there were still groups like the War Resister's League who spoke out as best they could.[106]

Of the many military escapades the United States mucked its way into after World War Two, the one most people think of right away is Korea. This was a "war" that even American General Omar Bradley said was "The wrong war, at the wrong place, at the wrong time, and with the wrong enemy." That was in 1951 and that particular war hasn't ended, yet.

I don't need to tell you about the opposition to America's war with Vietnam. There have been movies, books, television shows, songs – popular culture has documented the moment when millions of Americans stood up against war more than any other anti-war movement probably because it is something we can take such pride in. (Just don't compare it to the worship paid to World War II...)

People from all walks of life have stood up against war, from pacifists to Generals, from teachers to professional boxers – and doctors. In 1961, a few doctors formed Physicians for Social Responsibility to educate Americans on the medical consequences of nuclear war. They did this by documenting the presence of Strontium-90, a highly radioactive waste product of atmospheric nuclear testing, in children's teeth.

Stop there for a minute.

Children's teeth.

And it didn't end there. Over more than 50 years, Physicians for Social Responsibility has shown again and again how individuals can become a force to help prevent wars.

My experience standing against war began in the mid-1980s. When it looked as though Reagan was going to start a war with Libya, a friend and I agreed jokingly to help each other move to Canada. And when the first President Bush started a war with Iraq, I saw dedicated people standing against war. I wondered how a few people standing on a corner in downtown Santa Ana thought they could exert any influence against a war-crazed government. Cynicism does that. It prevents us from seeing any hope at all and we give up. Fortunately, I've come to understand that the truth of the matter is that every voice counts and being ethical often means taking a stand for what is unpopular in the face of the popular madness of war. So, I've marched with hundreds of others through the streets of Los Angeles and I've picketed with dozens of others in a traffic circle in Orange and I've stood with just a few people at a protest that looked hopeless because upholding the idea of a fair and fulfilling relationship I have with every other person on this planet is the right thing to do.

Heroes of Dynamic Pluralism

Jack Ryan

I have a brief story to tell you about one of those who have opposed war. It's not about any protester in particular but, rather, it's about someone who stood against the forces who would oppose them.

There are all sorts of powers regularly set against those who would exercise their right to speak out against what's wrong. In the case of Eugene Debs, there was *The Espionage Act*. In the case of Martin Luther King, there was the twisted injustice of the bullet. In the case of so many in recent times who have stood up at an Occupy protest or Black Lives Matter rally or at a university or in so many towns across the country, there have been fire hydrants of pepper spray and far too many bullets.

FBI agent, Jack Ryan, was given an order to investigate anti-war groups. As a twenty-one-year veteran of the bureau, he was seen as a prime candidate to send against those who would exercise their rights as American citizens. But Jack Ryan decided not to do this. Instead, he acted ethically, in a fair and fulfilling manner towards his fellow citizens, and refused to undermine the rights guaranteed by our Constitution.

As payment for this, Jack Ryan was thrown out of his job just ten months short of retirement. He lost his pension and became homeless – all because he knew that it was more important to treat people fairly, rightly, decently.[107]

Ethics do not come cheap. When the price is paid, however, we find people we can admire and who show us what it means to be human.

There's always a reason to go to war

If there's one thing proponents of war will tell you – even as they try to convince you that the very last thing they would ever want is war, even as they remain safe and make sure others die in their war, even as they buy stock in the companies that get rich off war – it is that there is always a good reason to go to war. Absolutely. Always. Every time!

We have fallen for some of the dumbest lies warmongers have drummed up and have fought for the dumbest reasons you can imagine. Worst still, we have shouted these reasons as slogans as if to justify the stupid, wasteful sport that is war.

On the 15th of February, 1898, the battleship Maine was rocked by an explosion in Havana Harbor. The lie quickly spread that this was the doing of a Spanish mine, helping launch the United States into war against Spain with the rallying cry, "Remember the Maine! To hell with Spain!" Of course, none of the five inquiries into her wreckage – not in 1898, or again in 1898, or in 1911, or in 1974, or in 1998 – could conclude that a mine brought down the Maine and, as it turned out, most concluded the explosion came from inside the ship. And still, we went to war.

There were plenty of slogans in World War One – they needed all they could get. Was the entire world caught in bloody turmoil over the assassination of an Archduke in Sarajevo? No, they just had a lot of guns and bullets and shells and somebody needed to use them and, hell, no one had better plans for the Somme anyway. One of the least known slogans for the war probably summed it up the best. Penned by Randolph Bourne, it idealizes "War is the health of the state." What better way to sum up complete insanity but with an insane statement?

In 1964, we believed that one US aircraft carrier and one US destroyer and four US fighter bombers were somehow endangered by three small Vietnamese torpedo boats. We wiped out the Vietnamese, found we liked the taste of it, and called it the Gulf of Tonkin Incident. Lyndon Johnson used this story – you know, that we were so threatened by the folks we massacred – to get us into the Vietnamese War.

War drums were always being battered during the 20th century. When I was just a boy, in the 1970s, our class was shown a Cold War surplus film made in the early 1960s called *Red Nightmare*. The plot was as simple as it was stupid. "Jerry" wakes up one morning to find that "the Reds" had taken over – evil and speedy those Reds were. All of his rights are taken away and the world he knew has become a nightmare. My balls might not have dropped yet but my bullshit detector was on full alert. With lies like that, it's no wonder so many of us grew up to become cynics.

And yet, somehow, we still fell for the dumbest lies of all time.

After the tragic events of September 11, 2001, it was shocking how many of us fell into lockstep behind the second President Bush's call for war against a nation that had no involvement in the tragedy. "Weapons of Mass Destruction," the administration shouted long and hard and – surprisingly – so many of us fell for it. I remember watching Secretary of State Colin Powell presenting the most obvious lies before the United Nations. "You see these buildings that look like trailers? Well, they're bombs! Bombs, I tells you! You can see they're bombs because they're Iraqi! That's all you need to know!" He might as well have been that obvious the way people bought it. Of course, they were all proven to be lies by and by – but by that time thousands upon thousands of Iraqis were dead. By the "end" of the war (a nebulous term if there ever was one), hundreds of thousands of Iraqis were counted dead with millions more maimed, scarred, and wounded.[108]

And for what? Turns out, it doesn't even matter. The Unites States has sent its fighting men into harm's way for any reason they can think of. As an example, I'm going to list just a few of the times in the 20th century the United States sent its armed forces to another country. This is just an example and not even a complete list:

Colombia/Panama (1901)	China (1926)	Zaire (1979)
Colombia (1902)	China (1927)	Iran (1980)
Honduras (1903)	China (1930)	El Salvador (1980)
Dominican Republic (1903)	United States[109] (1932)	Sinai (1980)
Syria (1903)	Cuba (1933)	El Salvador (1981)
Ethiopia (1903)	China (1934)	Libya (1981)
Panama (1903)	Newfoundland (1940)	Sinai (1982)
Dominican Republic (1904)	Bermuda (1940)	Lebanon (1982-1983)
Morocco (1904)	St. Lucia (1940)	Egypt (1983)
Panama (1904)	Bahamas (1940)	Grenada (1983)
Korea (1904-1905)	Jamaica (1940)	Honduras (1983-1989)
Cuba (1906 – 1909)	Antigua (1940)	Chad (1983)
Honduras (1907)	Trinidad (1940)	Persian Gulf (1984)
Nicaragua (1910)	British Guiana (1940)	Italy (1985)
Honduras (1911)	Greenland (1941)	Libya (1986)
China (1911)	Netherlands (1941)	Haiti (1986)
Honduras (1912)	Iceland (1941)	Bolivia (1986)
Panama (1912)	World War Two (1941-1945)	Persian Gulf (1987-1988)
Cuba (1912)	China (1945)	Honduras (1988)
China (1912-1941)	Germany (1945-1949)	Panama (1988)
Turkey (1912)	Austria (1945-1955)	Libya (1989)
Nicaragua (1912-1925)	Italy (1945-1946)	Panama (1989-1990)
Mexico (1913)	Japan (1945-1952)	Columbia (1989)
Haiti (1914)	Philippines (1944-1946)	Philippines (1989)
Dominican Republic (1914)	China (1945-1947)	Liberia (1990)
Mexico (1914-1917)	Korea (1945-1947)	Saudi Arabia (1990)
Haiti (1915-1934)	Italy (1946)	Kuwait (1991)
China (1916)	Greece (1947)	Iraq (1991-2012)
Dominican Republic	Palestine (1948)	Zaire (1991)

(1916-1924)		
China (1917)	Germany (1948)	Sierra Leone (1992)
World War One (1917-1918)	China (1948-1949)	Bosnia (1992-1996)
Cuba (1917-1922)	Korean War (1950-1953)	Herzegovina (1992-1996)
Mexico (1918-1919)	Taiwan (1950-1955)	Kuwait (1992)
Panama (1918-1920)	China (1954-1955)	Somolia (1992-1995)
Soviet Union (1918-1920)	Vietnam (1955-1975)	Bosnia (1993-1995)
Croatia (1919)	Egypt (1956)	Macedonia (1993)
Turkey (1919)	Lebanon (1958)	Haiti (1994-1995)
Honduras (1919)	Haiti (1959)	Macedonia (1994)
China (1920)	Thailand (1962)	Liberia (1996)
Guatemala (1920)	Cuba (1962)	Central African Republic (1996)
Soviet Union (1920-1922)	Laos (1962-1975)	Bosnia (1996)
Panama (1921)	Zaire (1964)	Albania (1997)
Costa Rica (1921)	Dominican Republic (1965)	Sierra Leone (1997)
Turkey (1922)	Israel (1967)	Cambodia (1997)
China (1922-1923)	Zaire (1967)	Guinea-Bissau (1998)
Honduras (1924)	Cambodia (1968)	Kenya (1998-1999)
China (1924)	Cambodia (1970)	Tanzania (1998-1999)
China (1925)	Cyprus (1974)	Afghanistan (1998)
Honduras (1925)	Cambodia (1975)	Sudan (1998)
Panama (1925)	Lebanon (1976)	Liberia (1998)
Nicaragua (1926-1933)	Korea (1976)	East Timor (1999-2001)
		Serbia (1999)

As I say, this is only a partial list.[110] A complete list would fill a whole other book – one that I highly recommend someone write! This list includes more than 150 wars, raids, assaults, battles, and the like, more than one for every year of the century! Even if you scoffed at such a number and claimed it could be only half that you still end up with more than 70.

We all know there are too many wars and yet we keep on starting them. Even in the 21st century, sitting comfortably in 2016, I can tell you about more than 20 instances of US military action in such places as

131

Sierra Leone, Yemen, East Timor, Afghanistan, Philippines, Côte d'Ivoire, Iraq (of course), Liberia, Georgia, Djibouti, Haiti, Pakistan, Lebanon, Somalia, Libya, Nigeria, Jordan, Turkey, Chad, Mali, Cameroon, Syria and Uganda. In just about every instance, I'm sure you can find someone to provide you an excuse or lie to make you feel better about why we were there – but I can promise you it has nothing to do with ethics.

War is what happens when you have excised any attempt at being fair and fulfilling. War is what happens when you throw away ethics.

What are the lessons of war?

Any discussion of the ethics of war wouldn't be complete without including some of the lessons humanity has learned after millennia of war. After all, we wouldn't senselessly kill each other century after century unless we were taking away some valuable lessons, would we (he intoned sarcastically)? Let's take a look at some of the lessons of war...

Sam Colt's automatic pistol was one of the most valued weapons of the oxymoronical Civil War. It's said that Colt stole the concept from the English while visiting Calcutta in 1830. When he returned to the states without any money to finance production, he went into medicine as a bogus "Dr. Coult," preaching the value of nitrous oxide.[111] (This display of doing something completely unethical for the least ethical ends is a great example of the opposite of the Santa Claus Effect.)

World War One gave birth to the propaganda techniques of Ivy Lee and George Creel, previously mentioned. Freshly equipped film crews were capturing all the lies Americans could gobble up. In one case, the war footage of Donald Thompson actually came with German help. He asked and they happily destroyed a windmill for him. Sometimes faked pictures worked better than the real thing. Captain F. E. Kleinschmidt, who travelled with the Austrian army, explained: "In real life a man who has been hit by a bullet does not throw up his hands and rifle and then fall in a theatrical fashion and roll a few times over. When he lies in the trenches and is hit he barely lurches a few inches forward and quietly turns on his side. The real picture is not as dramatic as the fake picture."[112] On a more practical level, World War One gave us the tank and the machine gun, which proved to be very useful in every other war since.

If nothing else, World War Two taught us that we could have an "honorable" war. Just think of all the people we saved and people we put in concentration camps.

… wait. Back up.

This book wouldn't sell very well if I made it sound as though the United States illegally rounded up thousands of people of Asian descent, disenfranchised them, and put them into our own grossly unethical mass prisons. Even if it was what we did, the truth never sells well.[113]

Just think of all the people we saved from German concentration camps and then think of all those folk we locked away as being in resorts with barbed wire and guard towers. There. That sounds better.

Never forget, World War Two also gave us napalm, invented by Harvard professor, Louis Fieser in 1942. Originally meant as a rubber substitute, it was instead used as an incendiary to kill Asian peoples for thirty years. (Hell, who needs a rubber substitute, anyway!) It was proudly produced and refined and improved upon by Dow Chemicals until 1969. Napalm's effectiveness was so horrific that the United Nations passed a resolution deploring its use in 1972.[114]

The Korean War taught us a lesson we should have learned long before, which is: You can say anything and people will believe you. In 1950, Harry Truman said about some anger half a world away, "A return to the rule of force in international affairs would have far-reaching effects. The United States will continue to uphold the rule of law." In the conflict that followed to oppose "the rule of force", about two million Koreans (north and south) were killed. Apparently, there was some confusion over the meaning of words like "oppose" and "force."

The lesson from the war in Vietnam could easily have been "how better to drop bombs." After all, the United States dropped more bombs on Vietnam than in all the theaters of World War Two – three times more![115] Go take a look, on your globe or Internet map, at the dozens of nations involved in World War Two and then look at Vietnam and consider what that many bombs does to one small nation.

Sadly, however, that doesn't appear to be the only lesson from Vietnam. The next lesson was how to brutalize people worse than we'd ever done before and then get away with it. Future Senator and Presidential candidate, John Kerry spoke of US atrocities as "not isolated incidents but crimes committed on a day-to-day basis with the full awareness of officers at all levels of command." Appearing before the Senate Foreign Relations Committee in April 1971, Kerry said, "Over 150 honorably discharged and many very high decorated veterans testified to war crimes committed in Southeast Asia." He went on to retell how American troops, "had personally raped, cut off ears, cut off heads, taped wires from portable telephones to human genitals and turned up the power, cut off limbs, blown up bodies, randomly shot at civilians, razed villages in fashion reminiscent of Genghis Khan, shot cattle and dogs for fun, poisoned food stocks, and generally ravaged the countryside of South Vietnam." All this was "in addition to the normal ravage of war."[116]

During the Cold War, when all mankind was threatened with annihilation, we took away from it more weaponry than we could ever imagine as "defense" budgets grew and grew, defending us against a threat we ourselves created. We built weapons instead of peace.

It seems we Americans may have run out of lessons to learn from war. After all, in the wars of the 21st century thus far all we've seemed to learn is how to torture and gain the nickname "Death from Above," lessons that might have some value but surely don't require us to learn by doing.

Perhaps the real lesson is that there is no lesson. War is as barbaric and wasteful as it ever was. Certainly, there's nothing the ethics of Dynamic Pluralism, with its tilt towards treating others in a "fair and fulfilling" manner, can hope to gain.

The Spoils of War

If there are no good reasons for war and no good lessons to be had by this time, surely there must be some reason why we keep shoving any sense of ethics aside in our continual pursuit of war. Perhaps these lay in the final victory, the spoils of war.

If you include military influence around the world, which holds sway over international policies such as monetary and social policy, the United States has done very well for itself. Estimates put the number of US military bases located outside of the US at between 700 and 1000.[117] Even multiple time Republican presidential candidate Ron Paul put the number at 900.[118] That many military bases equates to that much influence. Consider for a moment how we might feel if Somalia had a military installation in Idaho and you get some idea how that influence is spread.

Of course, in recent times, wars have been driven less by nations and more by the influence of multinational corporations. War allows them to exploit the conquered and oppressed and keep their shareholders happy. Places with abundant natural resources have simply become the victims of nations like America. When was the last time we had a war where there *wasn't* oil? American corporations have depended on the poorer countries for 100 percent of their diamonds, coffee, platinum, mercury, natural rubber, and cobalt. They got 98 percent of their manganese from abroad, 90 percent of their chrome and aluminum. And 20 to 40 percent of certain imports (platinum, mercury, cobalt, chrome, manganese) from Africa.[119] The cheapest way for corporations to get at these raw materials is far too often the costliest way for us: through armed conflict.

When imperialism results from corporations and not countries, the profits are funneled not to a country but to investors. This may explain why so many Americans were curiously disappointed when oil prices didn't go down after we took over Iraq. Corporations are seen as people in the United States and when they practice Imperialist tactics the recriminations fall back on the nation whose army does the fighting and not on the faceless corporate slugs who reap the reward.

Whatever spoils are found benefit the wealthiest few – as they always have, after all. For all the blather Americans spout about "supporting the troops" who return home from these outings, they certainly don't benefit. No matter the rhetoric, "supporting the troops" has never been of importance to the US government. Even back in the 1930s, when 17,000 World War One veterans, their families, and affiliated supporters marched on Washington, DC, demanding the US government remember the promises it made, President Herbert Hoover found it easier to call in Douglas MacArthur (yes, that Douglas MacArthur) and George Patton (yes, that George Patton) with their troops and their bullets and their complete lack of irony to move in with the police (because when all you have is the entire US Army at your back it's good to bring some cops) and treat the veterans as we always do... like shit.

Next time you want to see how much we honor our veterans and how much we honor peace, just take a look at the budget for the Veterans Administration and put it next to the budget for all of our militaries. At the very least, you'll know what an ant looks like beside a mountain.

Perhaps the only spoil of war then, beyond those reserved to multinationals and those who would sway the world with might, comes down to what Ambrose Bierce famously said about war being god's way of teaching Americans geography. And he said that over a century ago.

People throughout history have spoken about the morality of war. Now that we know the difference between morals and ethics, we can clearly agree that in the light of Dynamic Pluralism there is nothing ethical about war. No matter how they advertise it, those who side with war are not on the side of ethics. Anyone interested in pursuing an ethical path of creating a fair and fulfilling relationship does not resort to war.

Remember that when someone tries to convince you that another person is the enemy, their interests are not your own. Consider the greatest enemies of the 20th century. It wasn't the Russian people who hated the American people or the American people who hated the Russian people. It was the leaders of each country who convinced their people that it was right to hate, that it was ethical to hate.

And, of course, they were wrong.

Chapter 8
Ethics and Equal Rights

This is what ethics and rights look like

This is a story about Bob Bing, a man who has no apples. Of course, the apples are a metaphor and could refer to money or jobs… or even apples. This short passage explains the disaster that happens when we forget the simple rules of life with regards to ethics and basic human rights.

…and is in no way meant to disparage The Apple Company or any of its fine products…

One day, Bob decided to join the American Peel n' Pit Lovers Emblem (which was, oddly enough, referred to as Amp-n-Ple).

BOB
I'd like to become a member of the Ameri -

Amp-n-Ple Prez
We don't allow your kind in here.

BOB
Why? Is it my race?

Amp-n-Ple Prez
Race? No, that's not it – although we do restrict Swedish memberships… they're so snooty…

BOB
Could it be because of my sexual preference?

Amp-n-Ple Prez
We don't care if you're a man or a woman or if you're married to a man or a woman… although we don't allow people in with cats, just because…

BOB

Is it my level of education? I know all about apples of all –

Amp-n-Ple Prez

No. You pass all the educational requirements and you've already paid your fee. We keep anyone who can't out because we don't allow any poor or stupid Amp-n-Ple-ites... unless they're white, of course.

BOB

Of course. So, then, what is it? What's keeping me out?

Amp-n-Ple Prez

We saw you eating an orange. You're a sick, sick man.

Equal Rights... for All?

If ethics can be found in the fair and fulfilling relationships one individual has with another, nothing speaks more about our understanding of ethics than the rights we afford others. Make no mistake, the rights afforded to others here in America and in most of the world have improved remarkably in the last hundred years. Woman and men of all races and colors were finally recognized by the United States as individuals who should have the right to vote. The federal government recognized the injustice of segregating African Americans and persons of color. Homosexuals were even allowed to serve their country openly in the military.

And yet, there is still so far to go. As a society, we still have not come to a fundamental understanding. We need to recognize that when it comes to rights there are no "minority groups." There are only individuals with the inalienable right to be free.

No one loses when a group of people are afforded the rights ethically due to them. Indeed, we are all minimized by the fact that women do not have the same rights as men, that the government still has the power to discriminate against a certain race or people, or that certain people are not allowed to marry for no more reason than because some old, white guys think it's gross. Seen in this light, we should all be shamed.

There are always threats to our rights and always will be so long as people do not understand their ethical duties of creating fair and fulfilling relationships with every individual. In the United States, we've had more than our share of laws and rulings restricting rights. We've had *The Espionage Act*, *The Alien and Sedition Acts*, *Plessy v Ferguson*, *The Patriot Act*, and the humorously titled *Defense of Marriage Act*. If those don't go far enough, operatives of the government have been known to arrest people for standing peaceably on the street.[120]

In this chapter, I'll look at some of the ways we still don't understand the ethics of equal rights and what it would mean to understand some of these issues ethically. People are bound to disagree on moral (that is religious) grounds but I will show how important equal rights for all are under the ethics of Dynamic Pluralism.

The Issue of Race

Any discussion about the rights we afford others in our society should probably begin with our concept of "race." "Race," is horribly misconceived as a subdivision of humankind based on physical characteristics but this is a subdivision that does not exist in biology.[121] We create that distinction to excuse our treatment of others based on something we don't like about them.

Take Black Americans, for instance. Their subjugators, torturers, humiliators, murderers, and owners – you know, our Founding Fathers – needed to think of them as different because of the horrific way they treated them. Indeed, in the Dred Scott decision of 1857, Chief Justice Roger B. Taney ruled "A Negro had no rights a white man was bound to respect."[122]

Even after they were no longer slaves, Black Americans were still thought of as different by whites and even a threat. When Black Americans dared stand up for their rights during the Woodrow Wilson administration, J. Edgar Hoover explained the resulting riots (beatdowns on those with the impunity to ask for equality) as due to "the numerous assaults committed by Negroes upon white women."[123] In 1963, George Wallace used his inaugural address to decry rights for Black Americans with the lines "segregation today . . . segregation tomorrow . . .

segregation forever."[124] Segregation was just one way the white males in American government kept Black Americans separated and deprived of rights.

Another way was in restricting the rights Black Americans fought so hard to win. This is still done to this day. The Voting Rights Act of 1965 was purely a temporary measure and the "Right to Vote" for all Americans is still not a right. It had to be renewed in 1970, 1975, 1982, and 2006. And even in 2006, there were lawsuits to challenge the constitutionality of the Act. Then, in 2013, much of the Act was struck down by the Supreme Court. In addition, so-called "Voter Fraud" cases requiring government ID spring up more and more, the results of which would favor white, affluent Americans over everyone else. It's not hard to imagine that this scene from the early 1960s, when a black teenager named James Crawford brought a woman into a polling place to vote, might one day be repeated:

Registrar: What do you want?

Crawford: I brought this lady down to register.

R: (after giving the woman a card to fill out and sending her outside in the hall) Why did you bring this lady down here?

C: Because she wants to be a first class citizen like y'all.

R: Who are you to bring people down to register?

C: It's my job.

R: Suppose you get two bullets in your head right now?

C: I got to die anyhow.

R: If I don't do it, I can get somebody else to do it. (No reply.) Are you scared?

C: No.

R: Suppose somebody came in that door and shoot you in the back of the head right now. What would you do?

C: I couldn't do nothing. If they shoot me in the back of the head there are people coming from all over the world.

R: What people?

C: The people I work for.[125]

The people he worked for were people with ethics. Though they might not have considered it this way, they were at the forefront of a dynamically pluralistic ideal of fairness and fulfillment.

And yet, equal rights still do not exist for all Americans any more than they exist for all Black Americans. Consider the "Papers, Please" anti-Hispanic laws that began in Arizona, which permit racial profiling against people with brown skin.[126] This is a strange mirror image of the "walking while black" phenomenon.[127] Both groups are discriminated against with laws that disproportionately favor whites and manifest a prison population absurdly tilted against them.

Not to be forgotten, there is also the American Native. Displaced from their homelands, wiped out by folks of the ever-encroaching United States, and left in an impoverished state, the American Indian is regarded as even less than a separate race. Native Americans have been treated as subhuman by the United States for centuries. In 1862, when the American government refused to honor their treaties, leaving the Dakota Sioux Indians desperate for the resources they had been promised, the local U.S. government agent said, "If they are hungry, let them eat grass or their own dung."[128]

And it has ever been so. Let me give you an example. Let's say a government agent came to your door and said, "Sorry. We can't fund your children's schools. Guess you'll just have to suffer." Now, let's say you met with your neighbors and decided to help fund the schools by opening a casino but the government wouldn't let you do that without someone else's approval. That's just what happened to many Native Americans.

They continue to persevere despite the disregard of the rest of America, with creativity and ingenuity that should be praised but so often is ignored. That is how all those who are discriminated by their "race" get by. Those who succeed should be applauded but, more often than not, we use such differences as a way to perpetuate the idea that they are a "different race."

Ethics does not simply mean accepting those of different races. It means understanding that no such distinction exists. We are all equal and equally deserving of fair and fulfilling relationships.

In closing, I should mention that none of this covers how we treat those outside of our country. As shown in separate chapters, the issue of our differences – be they of culture or nationality or any other man-made distinction – is one that can only be surmounted with ethics.

The Issue of Women

The idea of restricting a person's rights based solely on which organs they have is as obviously ludicrous as it is unethical. After all, had women possessed more physical strength at one time things would be very different. And yet, this is exactly how things have been throughout history.

When the Mother Goddess image, so important throughout early history for understanding humanity's relationship to the Earth, was replaced with the male god images it happened through domination and strength. Temples of the Goddess were destroyed and her image nearly obliterated. Since that time, the search for equality for women with men has been long and difficult.

This search continues today. In 2016, women still made at best only 80% of the pay a man made for the exact same job with the exact same performance.[129] Women are still not guaranteed equal rights with men in the U.S. Constitution. The last time women tried with an amendment as unthreatening as "Equality of rights under the law shall not be denied or abridged by the United States or by any state on account of sex," it was shot down. Women have had to ask men for the right to vote, the right to serve in the military, and the right to have a surgical procedure on their own bodies (which will be addressed shortly).

Any fair and fulfilling relationship is an equal one. As in the other cases listed here, Dynamic Pluralism requires the rights of all individuals to be equal.

The Issue of Poverty

If you find yourself wondering about the justice in our capitalist system, consider how it treats those with the least capital. This is not to say that all would be perfect under a socialist system but, rather, that when you have a system based on greed it becomes difficult to fulfill a sense of fairness towards those impacted by the greed of others.

Not only does our lack of ethics make it difficult (if not impossible) to prevent poverty but it also blinds us to causes and effects and how we fit in relation to others. Quite simply, when it comes to poverty, there are those with the ability to help others and those who need help. Each entity has an ethical relationship with the other. Helen Keller explained this phenomenon very well. "I had once believed that we were all masters of our fate – that we could mold our lives into any form we pleased... I had overcome deafness and blindness sufficiently to be happy, and I supposed that anyone could come out victorious if he threw himself valiantly into life's struggle. But as I went more and more about the country I learned that I had spoken with assurance on a subject I knew little about. I forgot that I owed my success partly to the advantages of my birth and environment...Now, however, I learned that the power to rise in the world is not within the reach of everyone."[130]

A brother of mine had another way of looking at this. As we were driving through Seattle, Washington one day in his new car, he told me a story about a homeless man he had seen begging on a corner. "All I want is money to buy booze," he insisted the homeless man told him. He used this as an excuse not to help others because, as he said, none of them have the nerve or honesty or what have you to admit that all they want is booze or drugs. He simply could not accept that people are hungry or without shelter often through no fault of their own.

This deception becomes even more strange in a society as wealthy as ours, one that could easily afford to exercise ethics. We throw countless billions of dollars into war, sports, reality TV, fast food, blockbuster movies, video games, and sex but somehow cannot put aside a few bucks to feed a hungry child.

Instead, we create excuses why people aren't helped.

Recently, when discussing the unemployment benefits so many in our society rely on when faced with the loss of a job, Georgia Republican John Linder painted the picture of lush benefits to lazy freeloaders, claiming that unemployment benefits present too much of an allure.[131] According to this person, unemployment benefits are better than actually working, causing people to jump out of their jobs and live the good life of the unemployed. This, of course, is crazy and senseless. But his goal wasn't to make sense. His goal was to turn the helpless into the enemy, to blame the victim for the crime.

The same thing recently happened when so many politicians and pundits called for drug testing for those struggling to make ends meet on welfare.[132] The argument goes something like this: "Those lazy welfare recipients – you know, the poorest of the poor – are so rich and entitled that they sit around and take drugs all day!" Of course, nothing could be less true. In fact, when such drug tests were mandated in Florida, only about 2% of the recipients tested positive.[133] The total amount saved by the state by catching those 2% was about $260 each month while the cost of those tests ran into the millions. This example was repeated in state after state where such testing was mandated.[134]

Of course, no one really expected to catch millions of dopey, drugged out welfare manipulators, any more than they believed the "Welfare Mom in a Caddie" story back when I was a kid. But when you don't care about ethics or people, it's easier to demonize than to help.

Sometimes, it's easier to kill. Just before Martin Luther King, Jr. was assassinated in April of 1968, he had turned his focus from race to war to poverty. As he said, "… the evils of racism, economic exploitation, and militarism are all tied together…"[135]

Martin Luther King, Jr. was launching what he called The Poor People's Campaign, to address the issue of economic injustice for all Americans. He spoke of "the evils of capitalism" and asked for "a radical redistribution of economic and political power." Shortly after that, he was assassinated.

The hunger of one child may result in the death of millions if that hunger prevents the child from saving those millions. This means the hunger of one child is the same as the death of millions. And the triumph of one individual is the triumph of millions. We are each connected. Martin Luther King, Jr. understood this and because his message carried to millions of others, his assassin failed.

Ethics defeat assassins and feed children. That may sound a bit extreme but ethics are meaningless otherwise.

The Issue of Immigrants

Rarely is there a group of people more reviled in American society than the immigrant. Politicians use hatred of immigrants to win elections. Bigots use hatred of immigrants to explain what's wrong with a world that long ago left them behind. And, let's face it; people just hate eating their vegetables… which are mostly picked by migrant labor.

Hatred of immigrants is a U.S. tradition. In the 19th century, we hated the Jews and the Irish. In the early 20th century, we hated the Eastern Europeans. In the late 20th century, we hated anyone who came up from the south. And so far in the 21st century, well, we hate anyone who looks in any way like they came from the middle east… or from the south… or pretty much anywhere. We're not picky.

Ronald Reagan's Secretary of Education, William Bennett – a white man, though you'll surely find that bigotry is an equal-opportunity menace – once called Western Civilization "our common culture… its highest ideas and aspirations."[136] He was speaking out against "Political Correctness," which is what some people call what the rest of us refer to as "decency." Others use the term "Multiculturalism" to refer to what the rest of us call "we all come from somewhere, dumbass." The Ayn Rand Institute equates "Multiculturalism" and "Political Correctness", treating those of other cultures with decency, with the practices of Nazi Germany.[137] To them, decency equals death camps. Considering what we know of Rand's Objectivism, this should come as no surprise.

Spreading hate about people different from ourselves may be easy but it's not ethical. Immigrants fight a lot of battles many of us already in this country would never consider fighting: Bureaucracy, Hate, Discrimination, Acclimation, and the Unknown. All they are trying to do is find a decent life for themselves and maybe their families as well. All they want is what we want.

And treating them ethically, creating fair and fulfilling relationships, recognizes them as what they truly are: Equals. Brothers and Sisters. Friends in a world where we have too few.

The Issue of Sexuality

This is the part of the book where I talk about the rights of gays, lesbians, transgender brothers and sisters, and those who have not traditionally been recognized in the sexual norm, so brace yourself. I, myself, am too painfully in the norm and certainly do not claim to be an expert otherwise. But if the point of ethics is to create fair and fulfilling relationships, as Dynamic Pluralism instructs us to do, I can't help but think this would apply to folks with differing sexual agendas than my own. After all, you have relationships with them, too, even if your political or religious leader would rather you didn't – and shame on them if they do.

I wrote several encapsulations of the history of gay rights for this section but inevitably threw them away because none of that really has any meaning for the matter at hand. Gays, lesbians, and transgender folk could have been giant lizards roaming the earth and devouring Tokyo for all you know – the point is any relationship that restricts their rights as equal individuals is unethical. And who are you to talk, anyway?

One recent Pope actually claimed that gay marriage poses "a threat to the future of humanity."[138] There's a certain unavoidable logic here. If there was nothing to stop gays from marrying, it is possible (however absurdly remote) that everyone would turn gay. This could lead to the reduced production of babies and then – blammo – no more humanity. Where that logic goes astray is that it's not like gay people are going to say "Okay, you got me. If I can't marry the person I love, I guess I'll go make a baby with someone I'd rather not engage in sex with." The fear that Pope was displaying, that too many people still display, is simply the fear of the unknown. And just because something is beyond your comprehension, shut away in a walled city with a funny hat, doesn't make it terrifying. I had that problem with dogs once. Then, I found out they're cute and they give kisses.

Are homosexuals or transgender people different from so-called "straight" folk? Sure. Of course. But then, they'd have to be – and good for them for trying something different at the buffet. This does not make them somehow exempt from ethical treatment, even if you don't "get them."

On a personal level, I had a best friend once who was gay. He's still gay but we're no longer friends. The friendship ending had nothing to do with his sexuality or mine or any misunderstanding. We simply grew apart. But I miss him every day of my life and I wish him well. And I will defend his right to love who he loves because I still have a relationship with him. His love enriched my life – and that is what ethics do.

When it comes to the matter of education, let's defer to one of the wisest of our founding fathers, Thomas Jefferson. Democracy itself and thus the health of our nation would be threatened, Jefferson taught, without an educated populace. An educated citizenry is the best protection from the powerful, wealthy, and unscrupulous who would seek to undermine the ideal of a government run by and for ordinary citizens. The antidote, therefore, is a vigorous support for the expression of unpopular views, widespread literacy, substantive debate, a common familiarity with critical thinking, and the mandate to question authority (i.e. the "experts").[139]

This ideal could not be farther from the educational system that presently exists. In our system, children from poorer neighborhoods attend underfunded schools where they are prepared for low-paying jobs. There is no emphasis on critical thinking but, instead, they are prepped for one meaningless test after another meant to secure funding that might otherwise be further stripped from them by politicians looking to score political points. Wealthier families put their children into private schools (recently re-branded as "charter schools" to somehow remove the stench of money and privilege) where they are taught to blindly follow a system that ignores the rest.

Unpopular views such as science (evolution), history (any wrong America has done), and cultural empathy are removed as often as possible. Critical thinking remains outside of the United States' standard curriculum. And what about questioning authority, which Jefferson specifically encouraged? When was the last time you saw anyone encourage children to question authority?

Education funding is a complicated mix of local and federal monies. Most comes from local property taxes, meaning that wealthier neighborhoods end up with better schools. If you look at the actual federal budget for 2015, you see that education amounts to not 20% of the budget – not 10% of the budget. Our federal commitment to education that year was a measly 4% of the federal budget. National "Defense", the manufacture of weapons and the killing of people, gets 22% of that pie.[140]

Schools should be revered places that create our future leaders. Teachers should be paid like NBA stars. The tools of teaching should be the most cutting edge and innovative in the world. Politicians say you can't throw money at a problem, but they have no problem throwing money at the goal of killing people. The end result is that we value killing people more than 5-to-1 against educating our children. Schools are dilapidated hovels. Teachers have to take second jobs. School books are out of date embarrassments of ignorance.

The ethics of Dynamic Pluralism encourage us to create fair and fulfilling relationships and nothing is more fair to a child or more fulfilling than a good education. As it stands today, our educational system is the hallmark of a citizenry bereft of ethics.

The Issue of Health Care

We Americans live in a society where health is not a civil right. Society does not owe you health. And while this is obviously not fair or fulfilling, the stupidity of it is equally obvious. Consider the cost that goes into the treatment of disease that could be saved were the most common diseases prevented, both here and around the world. And yet, while most of the wealthier countries consider health care a right, we Americans remain short sighted.

None of this is new. It's not like we can't do simple math. (One sick person plus another sick person equals more sick people.) Throughout our history, we have moved towards the prevention of diseases with improved sewage and waste treatment, better health care facilities, the fortification of foods, water fluoridation – these were all done by governments looking to improve the health of their citizens in the face of small-minded tyrants fed only by their greed.

We've seen those very same people in our own time. When President Bill Clinton attempted health care reform, we saw groups like the Coalition for Health Insurance Choices and the Health Insurance Association of America tell us why a healthier society would spell ruin for us all. Thomas Scarlett's "Killing Health Care Reform," which appeared in *Campaigns & Elections* magazine, stated: "Through a combination of skillfully targeted media and grassroots lobbying, these groups were able to change more minds than the President could, despite the White House 'bully pulpit'… Never before have private interests spent so much money so publicly to defeat an initiative launched by a President."[141] And this wasn't just to defeat an initiative. This was the unethical use of power to keep people sick.

The Coalition for Health Insurance Choices even sponsored a now-legendary TV spot, called "Harry and Louise," which featured a middle-class married couple lamenting the complexity of Clinton's plan and the menace of a new "billion-dollar bureaucracy."[142] The message was "doing the right thing is hard and it's better to be lazy and apathetic," and people listened.

Later, when President Obama attempted health care reform, he was beaten by more lies and deceit. Americans were told that "health care," when not run by enormous private corporations who determine if you can get care or not, meant "death panels."[143] Somehow, "death panels" would be legalized and you should be terrified of them. And people were. People were so afraid that a sensible approach to reforming a health care industry that insures fewer and fewer, pays out less and less, and rakes in more and more would mean some spooky, Boogeyman kind of "death panels" that the reform we ended up with simply meant more money to the insurance companies.

It may not be a crime but it should be. What is less ethical than telling lies simply to scare people out of defending themselves? Or denying people health simply because of their economic fortunes? And if you're going to allow one person or corporation the right to make the call as to who gets health care and who doesn't, how can you be sure you'll be one of the privileged few?

Those who would defend our broken system often claim we have the best health care in the world, which is true just so long as you only look at the richest of Americans. Those without do without. They suffer and die because we lack the ethical will to stand up for them. Others engage is what is delicately referred to as "medical tourism." This means they travel to third-world nations where treatment is cheaper, both in cost and quality, for what should be provided here.[144]

One of those treatments offered for fewer and fewer Americans is abortion. This procedure is performed on a woman's body, inside a woman's body, and yet has been prevented mostly by men. It seems equally fair that any government run by women should vote mandatory castration for all men, doesn't it?

Those who would prevent women the legal right of abortion – let alone the ethical right to their own bodies – claim it is a moral issue. Based on our earlier findings, that morality is a relationship between an individual and that individual's higher power, they are both right and wrong. An individual would be right to not have an abortion based on their religious beliefs. That same individual would be wrong and therefore immoral to prevent another person from having an abortion because they are not involved in the moral decision. It is between the person and their higher power – NOT YOURS.

Another way of looking at this "moral" argument, which is also known as the "right to life" argument, was revealed by the late Carl Sagan:

> There is no right to life in any society on Earth today, nor has there been at any former time (with a few rare exceptions, such as among the Jains of India): We raise farm animals for slaughter; destroy forests; pollute rivers and lakes until no fish can live there; kill deer and elk for sport, leopards for pelts, and whales for fertilizer; entrap dolphins, gasping and writhing, in great tuna nets; club seal pups to death; and render a species extinct every day. All these beasts and vegetables are as alive as we. What is (allegedly) protected is not life, but human life.[145]

Those who would deny a woman her right to health care via abortion have a history of not honoring their so-called "respect for life." Many support the death penalty, some with the claim that they can judge the worthy from those unworthy.[146] Others seek to pass laws to define "life" so narrowly, such as with so-called "Personhood" laws, that a woman's monthly cycle makes her a murderer in their eyes.[147] Some commit murder, killing doctors in their zeal for saving lives.[148]

Finally, too many of those who oppose abortion or wish to refuse people the right to health care, simply do it out of selfishness, ignorance, or hate. None of these are ethical traits. There's no argument to be made as to the ethics of what they do.

We Americans live in a society obsessed with violence. Most television news broadcasts focus on one kind of violence or another. Politicians find issues of violence "sexy" because they bring in more donations than when a politician addresses real issues. Our highest grossing movies are violent. Our biggest TV shows are violent.

And, yet, our hunger is not slaked. Some young people involved in gun violence think of it as little more than a video game. We see our elected representatives gunned down in the street without stopping for a moment to suggest that there may be too many guns out there.[149] Still, we love our guns. In fact, according to a 2009 survey, the idea that certain people should not have guns and that we as a society should not encourage gun violence was at an all-time low![150]

There's an incredible irony about our love of guns that is uniquely American. Back in October of 1980, history tells us that John Hinkley tried to assassinate President Reagan by shooting him with a .22 caliber revolver. Reagan's press secretary, James Brady, caught one of those bullets instead. So, to recap: a Republican President was the victim of an assassination attempt that wounded his Republican press secretary. James Brady used this experience to push for tighter gun control legislation. You'd think Republicans would have supported this but it ended up passing under a Democratic President. The Brady Handgun Violence Prevention Act was opposed by Republicans (many of whom claimed to be Reagan's friend) and the National Rifle Association. It has since been rendered so toothless that we see the shootings of elected officials on the news… and few people recognize the irony.

That said, the ethics of Dynamic Pluralism is absolutely opposed to violence of all kinds. You cannot create a fair and fulfilling relationship that involves violence. It doesn't matter if you're shooting a person or a target, stabbing your finger or a knife, or even raising your voice. Violence of any kind is unethical. (We'll discuss the difference between what is ethical and what is necessary in the closing chapters.)

Not only is violence not seen as unethical in this country, we fail to see the lack of ethics in the way we resolve violence. The answer most people give when dealing with a person found guilty of violence has been for a long time: prison. Lock them away. Throw away the key. That's what they'll say. Some more extreme people will also include the death penalty. *Kill 'em*, they'll say. *Kill 'em all.*

Those people are usually missing any sense of irony.

Is the death penalty ethical? Absolutely not. Even the question is absurd.

"Can I kill someone and call it ethical?"

No.

"What if I have permission?"

There's no way you can create a fair and fulfilling relationship with a person after you have killed them. Absolutely no way. And, no, their ghosts don't count. The death penalty has been abolished by sensible nations and encouraged by the crazy ones. Which side are you on?

The option, then, is incarceration. Our prison system has been built on centuries of reform. These reforms were necessary because, prior to them prisons were little more than asylums, hell holes where those found guilty faced a life of suffering. Reformation rather than retribution was the key.

And, if you think about it, that's an ethical way of looking at it. Retribution, favored by those good folk who want to see the guilty suffer, does nothing to create any sense of fairness or fulfillment. All it does is destroy relationships.

Now, there may be some readers reacting negatively to this idea. You may think Dynamic Pluralism is too "pie in the sky." But look down the long road and tell me where the solution lays. Retribution only fosters resentment and builds a class of citizens resentful of the other. Rather than encouraging the guilty to become active members of society, you encourage them to get retribution for your retribution. Or, as Ghandi said, "An eye for an eye only makes the world blind." It may be difficult to turn against the impulse for retribution but consider the characteristics that reform promotes: compassion, empathy, understanding. These are the characteristics of ethics. That's what we're looking to achieve.

These are not theoretical issues, either. The only prison reform of late has been the privatization of prisons. Run by corporations looking only at their bottom line, private prisons run on leaner budgets that mean more deprivation, less living space, fewer rights, and less humanity. Even if a private prison embraces the idea of reform, the way they are run is retributive, taking more and more from those marginalized from society. And you cannot expect ethics in an atmosphere that is unethical. If you do, I'll refer you to Einstein's definition of insanity.[151]

The violence in our system of law enforcement does not end with the prisons, either. Nor does its lack of ethics. One such ethical violation is false arrest. Every week it seems there's a new story of a person who spent years in prison, his pleas of innocence unheard, to find he is released because he was arrested falsely. Then, far too often, the person is still treated like a criminal by society – despite their innocence. So often, violations of ethics – of our right to humanity – end up this way. Victims of malicious prosecution or excessive force are often dismissed with the comment, "The police wouldn't have done that if they weren't guilty. They must have done something to bring it on themselves." So, too, people dismiss "Stop and Frisk" practices or arrests attributed to DWB (Driving While Black). To make such a claim, however, is to abdicate your responsibility to behave ethically and is therefore unethical.

This applies equally to the issue of preventative detention, a practice increasingly on the rise that deprives the victim of due process and the acknowledgement of the simple fact that they did nothing wrong. And yet, it increases in state law enforcement as well as federal.[152] In 2011, the U.S. government took such violations of simple rights a step further with indefinite detention.[153] With the National Defense Authorization Act, signed into law by President Obama, you don't have to be guilty, you don't have to be given a trial, you don't have to do anything wrong – and they can throw you in a hole for life.[154] They don't even need to tell anyone.[155]

Simply put, the more violence you allow, the more you say, "That's not as bad," the worse things will get. You have to draw an ethical line long before more people are arrested for no reason or the wrong reason. You have to speak up before elected officials have to fear the bullet of someone who didn't like the way they voted. The line is simple. It's easy to see. Violence is unethical.

And so, this chapter closes as it began. Because there can be no rights, according to Dynamic Pluralism, if every individual does not share in those rights. You cannot create a fair and fulfilling relationship, otherwise.

Those rights go beyond race, sexuality, education, and the like. They are tied more strongly to such concepts as dignity, humanity, and equality. Those basic rights take on less validity as we deny them to others and inspire the world when we share them with the ethical goal of creating fair and fulfilling relationships.

Chapter 9
Ethics and Food

This is what ethics and food looks like

This is a story about Bob Bing, a man who has no apples. Of course, the apples are a metaphor and could refer to money or jobs… or even apples. This short passage explains the disaster that happens when we forget the simple rules of life with regards to ethics and food.

…and is in no way meant to disparage The Apple Company or any of its fine products…

One day, Bob wasn't feeling so good. He'd eaten a bunch of lovely apples and realized he was growing a large tumor out of the side of his head. The tumor was the size and shape of an apple! So, naturally, he went to see his doctor.

BOB
Doctor! Doctor! You've got to help me. I've got a tumor like an apple growing out of my head!

Doctor
On the upside, you can buy some crust, some sugar, and some cinnamon and make some pie.

BOB
That's not funny at all.

Doctor
What can I say? I'm a doctor, not a comic.

BOB
I could have told you that. But what should I do?

Doctor

Let me take a look at that thing. Wow! That's some big apple you've got on your melon!

BOB

Doc!

Doctor

Sorry. No more jokes. Let me ask you, have you been eating a lot of apples lately?

BOB

Quit joking around. This is serious!

Doctor

I'm not joking. I ask because a recently developed, genetically modified apple has entered the market and could be playing pinkus with your genes.[156] That could be causing your tumor.

BOB

Seriously?! But I eat apples to prevent just this sort of thing – to "keep the doctor away!"

Doctor

Fortunately for us doctors, "health" always falls far below "profit."

We used to call it food

Once upon a time, long before your parents were born, in a time when elves and dwarves and dragons roamed the earth... food meant food. It meant something edible made out of edible things. It meant things you ate to help you grow big and strong and live a long and happy life.

Then... things changed.

We found we didn't like having an unreliable food supply, such as when a potato blight moved from the Atlantic coast of America to European shores. By autumn of 1845, the disease had wiped out the Irish potato crop. By November, corpses lined the Irish roads. The living ate

the dead. A million people died and a million more fled the country.[157]
So it should probably come as no surprise that we shifted towards a more reliable food supply.

With a reliable food supply came the convenience of eating what we liked when we liked. We could shop at local grocery stores, supermarkets, mini-marts, and even over the Internet. We could select from a hundred brands of breakfast cereal. We could buy a week's worth of food that had been frozen for years. We didn't have to buy any food that had been touched by human hands if we didn't want to or we could buy food with dirt still on it.[158] We were catered to, placated, patronized, propositioned, pasteurized and…

… eventually, things got out of hand.

The crossroads of ethics and food come somewhere between the Great Potato Famine and Instant Mashed Potatoes that have no recognizable "potato" in the ingredients. At their core, ethics are about relationships and we each have an intimate relationship with our food. So, let's take a look at it and see if we can find something ethical.

It's What's For Dinner

Meat. Since pre-history, humankind has eaten meat. Meat was essential in the discovery of fire. Why, if it wasn't for the hunting of meat, there'd be nothing to separate early men from early women.

Now, we don't really hunt meat. We actually gather it at the market. So much for that distinction.

As of 2015, the beef industry alone was valued at 105 billion dollars and the United States ate nearly 25 billion pounds of the stuff each year.[159] I'm the last person to judge anyone for eating meat. While I was once a vegetarian, my back-slide began with a single steak each year. My one vice… well, my one steak, at least. Then, my wife tempted me with some really good barbeque and all bets were off. My job, then, has been to educate her on what goes into the beef and steer her (no pun intended) towards the highest quality, lowest-hormoned, best grass fed beef we could find.

And that's important because a lot passes for food that you would never eat, especially when it comes to meat. The USDA grade of meat supplied to schools for our children's school lunches is rated in quality beneath anything you'd buy in the supermarket. It's not good enough for processed foods. Hell, even fast food doesn't want it.[160]

Most of this comes from industries – beef, pork, poultry, and whatever else meets your idea of meat – that have been let off the hook when it comes to regulation. In 2000, the group Public Citizen released an updated look at Upton Sinclair's seminal novel, *The Jungle*, with their own look at America's meat inspection.[161] It opens with the quote, "Plant managers say the rule is - there are no rules! We (plant managers) write our own regulations." It demonstrates a history of poor regulation, de-regulation, and so-called self-regulation in America's meat, turning the USDA sticker into little more than branding by the meat industries.

And we've seen where that leaves us, right? Or have you forgotten the chicken shit in your steak? The meat industry's answer has been irradiation, which is also known as "cold pasteurization." The problem with this, however, is that it encourages shortcuts and misses the problem entirely.[162] Stop trying to sell sick meat and you won't need to "cold pasteurize" it!

And chicken shit is only a small part of the problem. If you want to talk about really sick meat, let's go to the heaviest hitter: Mad Cow. Mad Cow, also known by the catchy Bovine Spongiform Encephalopathy (BSE), is not just the last word in "Hey, you've got a sick cow there," but also a perfect example in what happens when ethics and food have nothing to do with each other.

Americans have an expectation that their government will protect them from brain-eating diseases, which is what the human form of Mad Cow known as Variant Creutzfeldt-Jakob disease (vCJD) does. When the relationship between the American people and its government breaks down, due to industry lobbyists influencing our elected officials to look the other way when it comes to brain-eating diseases, you can hardly call that fair or fulfilling.

Sadly, this is exactly what happened. The multinational giant Monsanto developed a bovine growth hormone, ironically called recombinant bovine growth hormone (rBGH), to fatten cows faster. The goal was obviously cheaper meat. But cows treated with growth hormones (rBGH) require more energy-dense food.[163] In this case "energy-dense food" means meat, and what's cheaper to feed to cows than other cows too sick to survive? As it so happens, Mad Cow occurs precisely when you do this.

There was nothing illegal in this and it is certainly not the intention of this book to cast such an accusation. The proper approvals were provided by the government. All the correct forms were completed. Politicians were paid off in just the right and properly legal manner.[164]

And people died. The first American death by Mad Cow was Charlene Singh, of Fort Lauderdale, Florida in 2004.[165] As of 2006, the number of people who died from Mad Cow hit 160.[166] And, of course, mad cow has since been found in US cows, something the laissez-faire regulators told us wouldn't happen.[167] The number of other deaths and the number of deaths to come vary wildly based on who signs your paycheck.

The producers of the meat, the producers of the hormones, the government inspectors, the government officials, and all the people in between – all of them – were plainly unethical. They didn't care about what would happen to those who ate the meat no more than the folks who feed their meat chicken shit care if you get sick or not. If ethics means anything at all, it should mean you don't feed people tainted meat, diseased meat… poison.

Not to ignore the other side of the ethical equation, what ethical considerations are there even when you do eat healthy meat? (I believe I have just created an oxymoron.) What is the result of a diet with meat? After all, there are about 1.5 billion cows in the world – yes, that's billion – each releasing a conservatively estimated 200 liters of methane into the atmosphere each day.[168] As a greenhouse gas, methane is 23 times more powerful than carbon dioxide so how much better would the world be – how much better off would we be – without all those cows, which would happen if we didn't eat all that meat? Vast lagoons of pig shit cover huge areas of the United States because of our love of pork chops.[169] And the consequence of the chicken in our diet is unbelievable. According to Environmental Defense, if every American skipped one meal of chicken per week and substituted vegetarian foods instead, the carbon dioxide savings would be the same as taking more than half a million cars off U.S. roads.

According to the Center for Science in the Public Interest, it takes roughly seven pounds of corn to grow one pound of beef; five times as much water to grow feed grains for cattle as to grow fruits and vegetables for humans; and roughly ten times the acreage to raise cattle for food as to raise comparable plant food calories for direct human consumption.[170] The bottom line is: eating meat is unethical. If you eat meat, you are doing harm to other people. Those people could be your children or your neighbor or your neighbor's children.

One way or the other, in a post-mad-cow world, in a world of climate change, in a world with more than seven billion people, eating meat has ethical consequences. I have to face this fact just as much as you. Maybe I won't enjoy barbeque the same way or maybe not quite so much but that is a choice we have to make.

What the "cool kids" are eating

Even if you don't look far into the future – the 50 or so years we have left before every climate change nightmare runs rampant – you should at least acknowledge that you have an ethical duty to the way your children eat. There may be no relationship so profoundly shared as the one you have with your kids so, you would think, that should be the one that counts. And, if it's not your kids you're specifically looking after, if you are like me and have no children of your own, it may be your nieces, nephews, neighbors, heck even the kid up the street. Shouldn't you care about them?

And yet, the evidence shows we don't. And it's not the kid's fault. They don't make most of their dietary decisions; many of those choices are made on their behalf.

If you look at the National School Lunch Program (NSLP) alone, you'll find many dietary decisions made on behalf of our nation's children. According to the USDA's own numbers, over 31 million meals were served as part of this program in November of 2012 alone.[171] That's a lot of food. And I mention this because I myself was in the NSLP as a young person and ate many of those meals. I remember the bad jokes about the bad food – but, sadly, they're not all jokes. Most of the food is fatty and unhealthy, not just indigestible as so many of my fellow NSLP'ers could attest.

School lunch programs – you know, food to keep our nation's next generation from starving – are horribly underfunded and rely on handouts up to 20% of the time. Handouts are not always the most nutritious thing around. David Ludwig, director of the obesity program at Children's Hospital in Boston put it this way, "School districts are under intense budgetary pressure, and often-times nutrition is at the bottom of the priority list."[172] In other words, we would rather not spend our money on feeding our kids. You can imagine the ethical implications in that.

This means we give our children the cheapest food imaginable. The meat is not only the most likely to be contaminated with pathogens, but also the most likely to contain pieces of spinal cord, bone, and gristle left behind by Automated Meat Recovery Systems (contractions that squeeze the last shreds of meat off bones).[173] As we've seen, this can be countered by irradiation (and blindly hoping for the best). Another method of making school lunch meat less likely to poison kids is by treating the meat with ammonia, a method usually reserved for dog food.[174] Anyone who has eaten an NSLP meal knows what I'm talking about.

Some of you may be wondering, "What about the rest of the food? The fresh fruits and vegetables? The healthy grains and hearty dishes that help our children grow big and strong?"

Okay, enough jokes.

Some of you may remember when the Reagan Administration declared ketchup a vegetable to help demonstrate the "nutritional" value of school lunches.[175] Well, don't get too nostalgic because it didn't end there. People would still rather make excuses than do right by their kids. Just recently, Congress determined pizza was a vegetable because it sometimes comes with a little tomato sauce.[176] (This is school lunch pizza so who are we kidding?)

In the face of all this, I wonder where the outrage is. So many groups shout "What about the children?" and their concern for children when it comes to their own pet peeve.[177] Yet, there's so little outrage about our national lack of ethics when it comes to providing nutrition to our own children. You might say, "That's not my kid," but it could be your kid or her friends, or neighbors, or peers. It is an entire generation for whom we have an incredible responsibility. Here, at the very least, we should witness ethics.

And, yet, this is just the tip of the iceberg. I haven't mentioned what they eat on their own time…

Happy Meals

I feel I should mention up front that this section of the book is going to annoy parents who try their best to feed their children nutritious food but feel like they might not know what they're doing. On the other hand, it will be enjoyed by grandparents who watch their own children try to feed their grandkids nutritious food but know they don't know what they're doing. I don't think either can be reduced to an ethical level. Trying your best to create a fair and fulfilling relationship is all ethics can ask. Trying and failing just happens sometimes.

The big relationship that hasn't been mentioned is between kids and the companies that market food at them. And I mean right at them! The ethics of advertising have already been covered but this seems like a good time to talk about some of the specifics on how food is sold to children – not to their parents, but to children. A study in 2006 found that children were exposed to 40,000 ads each year directed straight at them on television alone![178] And this only goes up as children spend more hours of their day on the Internet, where advertising makes up so much of social networking. Most major ad agencies, if they are not focused directly on children, have entire divisions devoted to children. Children's advertising often takes on sweet, benign sounding names like Small Talk, Kid Connection, Kid2Kid, and Just Kids, Inc. with a number of industry publications such as *Youth Market Alert, Selling to Kids*, and *Marketing to Kids Report.*[179] The relationship advertisers have with your kids is not meant to be fair or fulfilling; the question of ethics is never asked. With millions of dollars devoted to manipulating children, parents hardly stand a chance.

Just take a look at soda. You don't need a battery of studies to tell you it's bad for you. It's full of sugar! It's called "Liquid Candy". And yet, we're surrounded by it in our stores, in our restaurants, in our schools. It's ubiquitous everywhere you look. According to one Harvard

School of Public Health report, Americans drank over 10 billion gallons of the stuff in 2008.[180] The big soda companies like to push press releases touting the decline in soda consumption but neglect to share how much more money they make in energy drinks, sweetened waters, and so forth. All of these drinks make you fat, rot your teeth, weaken your bones, and make you sick. In short, they're poison.

So, why do so many parents let their kids drink the stuff? Is it fair to poison your kids? Does soda give them a sense of fulfillment? No. On the contrary, it's addicting.[181] But the soda makers don't care about any of this. Their business is not ethics; their business is to wear down the busy, overwhelmed parent who just wants his child screaming for that next sugar fix to quiet down for a moment. And I hate to break it to you, but giving them more sugar probably won't work.

Food manufacturers prey on the busy parent as well, ignoring any ethical obligation they have. Very often, they'll disguise their opportunism in a cloak of convenience. Just look at Lunchables, and the many Lunchable ripoffs, handy and convenient mini-meals all packaged up for the busy parent to give to their child. Mind you, nobody is telling the parent that those "meals" are full of fat and salt and chemicals and all sorts of things that aren't exactly good for their child. And it is interesting how such products are rarely advertised as healthy, just convenient. It's a trade-off, obviously; you're trading the ethical nature of your relationship with your child for whatever you get out of convenience.

And that brings me to the most blatant violator of food ethics: The Happy Meal. No matter what branding it is sold under, turns out there's very little happiness to be found there. In them, you'll usually find:

1)   A main course made of a burger or chicken nuggets,
2)   A side dish made of processed potatoes deep fried and smothered in salt, and
3)   A soda. A nice, big, sugar-filled, gonna send your child through the roof and running right towards adult-onset diabetes soda.

What the hell is so happy about that? You've seen what goes into the burger (chicken pellets). The chicken nuggets are often made the same way the National School Lunch Program gets its meat. (Riddled with bacteria and soaked with ammonia, they call it "pink slime".)[182] The French fries are about as nutritious as... well, what do you expect? They're French fries![183] And then, of course, there's the soda.

Now, I know that some of you – probably those representing fast food restaurants – would argue that many restaurants now offer "healthy" alternatives. Sure they do. And we've seen how much they advertise those. When was the last time you saw McDonald's advertise an apple? To ignore the power advertising has over your kids and to ignore the way they are manipulated is to ignore your ethical responsibility to them – or to anyone for that matter.

What does the Happy Meal say about our society? What does our addiction to convenience, sugar, and fat tell us? It says that we are impoverishedly rich, that we possess a ghetto wealth. We've fallen for the easy ploy that deprives us of health and happiness, of ethics.

There was once a McDonalds at Dachau. Where once thousands upon thousands of people were slaughtered in the name of anything in the whole damned world BUT ethics, once stood a restaurant that served some of the foods I've mentioned here. It may still be there. I think that provides a pretty apt symbol so let's move on.

Fat... So?

Where does this all lead? What does it mean to replace concern with convenience when it comes to our kids? What happens when we decide we'd rather be selfish than caring and we're fine allowing our children to be fed like dogs? When we trade in a healthy skepticism and begin believing the lies of those who do not care about our well-being, what happens?

I don't need to tell you what happens. You can see it all around you. We live in a nation of paradoxically obese and undernourished people. It's not difficult to understand: cheap, empty calories from cheap, empty eating that never satisfies us and leads us to more cheap, empty eating makes us fat without providing the nutrition our bodies require.[184] So, we get fatter and sicker because being fat, despite what you might think, is not just a sign of having too much food. It's an indicator signifying a lack of ethics with those we should care about and an existential crisis within ourselves.

The rise in obesity in America from the 1960s to today is staggering, rising from 13% of the population to easily one third of all Americans. In 2010, two-thirds of American adults and a third of American children were overweight or obese.[185] The number of overweight adolescents has tripled since 1980.

This doesn't come from too much healthy food. It comes from too much crappy food, too many Happy Meals, too much soda, too much "just shut up and I'll give you whatever you want," and too little caring.

Beyond that, though, there is also an existential dimension to this story of fatness. Despite America's expanding waists, we somehow convince ourselves that we're still not fat. We have become masters at deceiving ourselves. We see a picture of a guy we would think of as just a bit overweight by modern standards without realizing that he was considered a circus freak only 100 years ago.[186]

In the end, our lack of honesty with ourselves and others is the single most damning indicator of our lack of ethics towards others and existential dishonesty with ourselves. Dynamic Pluralism demands honesty. We need to realize that we're only hurting ourselves. We are not passively allowing this to happen. We are actively turning away from ethics with every bite.

Now, we call it "FOOD"

I opened this chapter by discussing how food has changed in the last few hundred years and how it's going to continue to change. Make no mistake about it. As our society changes, as humanity's impact on the world changes the world itself, the way we look at food has to change as well. But that certainly doesn't mean we should abdicate any ethical imperative for fair and fulfilling relationships with others when it comes to what we eat. Ethics insist that we still treat each other, through our relationship with foods just as much as anything else, with care and compassion.

And that isn't easy to do these days, let me tell you. My wife and I had supper with some friends at their home the other night. Did we know if the food was prepared in a clean kitchen? Were we certain the food wasn't spoiled? Could we know if the chicken was organic and humanely raised or that the cheese wasn't filled with hormones, steroids, antibiotics, and other tasty additives? No. Of course, not. We had to trust that everything was good and good for us, which is just how many of us approach eating and just why ethics are so important.

We live in a time when food is no longer really food. It's "FOOD," disingenuously branded with a caveat in the small print. Sometimes, juices labeled as "grape" or with the name of some other fruit are mostly made of apple juice. Other times, juices have added arsenic as well.[187] Genetically modified foods, which are just about the ultimate in "FOOD," range from dairy products to produce to meat to sweeteners.[188] If you're eating it, someone has probably genetically modified it. As if that wasn't enough, our "FOOD" doesn't even taste like food. There's an entire flavor industry to change the way your food tastes which, according to a 2010 Dun and Bradstreet industry report, consisted of 569 firms employing 21,433 people and generating $33.4 billion in annual revenues.[189]

"FOOD" doesn't even need soil to grow. Now, it is raised in a toxic sludge of polybrominated diphenyl ether (PBDE) flame retardants, triclosan, nonylphenol detergent breakdown components, heavy metals, dangerous viruses, dioxins, PCBs, pesticides and hundreds of other toxic chemicals known affectionately as "biosolids".[190] Biosolids are not new; they've been around since the 1970s. Entire books have been written about them, including 1995's terrific *Toxic Sludge is Good for You!* by John Stauber and Sheldon Rampton. But we've learned since then, haven't we? Not necessarily. In San Francisco, in fact, toxic sludge was handed out as "organic biosolids compost".[191] Companies still market the toxins as a soil additive for farming.[192]

At this point, you're probably thinking there have to be government watchdogs to watch after us, like the FDA or the USDA or the EPA. And you'd be right. The only problem is that those watchdogs are not necessarily watching over you. They are openly lobbied by the companies looking to poison you to help their bottom line and earn their shareholders money.[193] They are underfunded by greedy politicians and selfish voters who would rather keep their money than protect their neighbors or themselves. And, sometimes, the people you hire to protect you are just as devoid of a working system of ethics as you are and end up stabbing you in the back.[194]

What happens as a result? We see genetically modified corn turned into fuel for cars or high fructose corn syrup, which was rebranded once people found out just how bad it was as "corn sugar,[195] " a name that fortunately did not stick. A compound used in the making of plastics, Bisphenol A (BPA), becomes linked to obesity, diabetes, cancer and heart disease.[196] But the worst thing? The absolutely worst thing is all the other things you don't know about and you're not going to be told about because someone would rather make a buck.

That's the connection between food and ethics.

If knowledge is power, knowing what you're eating and being aware of what you're putting in your body removes some of that power from those who would do you ethical and bodily harm. You should be able to trust people and it is through the use of the ethics of Dynamic Pluralism that you will create that trust once again.

Killing Ourselves With Food

While this book does not include a lot of anecdotal references to ethics and how far they have slipped from our grasp, or how a working system might change how we see things, I feel compelled to include one note of personal experience. I would strongly suggest that the next time you go out, you dedicate yourself for just an hour or so (anymore and you might get sick) to the amount of food we in the United States surround ourselves with. You'll find food in clothing stores, food in toy stores, and food in book stores (providing any remain).

Some time ago, my wife and I were at an office supply store and it was chock-full of food. Why is that? Why must we have food in our office supply stores? Would a store that sold paper and staplers create a less fair or fulfilling shopping experience if it did not also try to ply you with chocolate, salt, and fat?

But I haven't told you about the most shocking display. There, beside the chips and crackers and cookies and snack cakes and candy bars and mints and gum and other munchables stood a tall display of bottled water. Now, I am going to allow the rebuttal that people get thirsty. We can dispose of that right away. Yes, people get thirsty.

But look at this picture and tell me if you see what I saw. This tall display was entirely disposable, as is so much else in our society. It would soon be thrown out as garbage. In addition, those bottles of water, once drunk, would be thrown out as well.

In the off chance someone might be thirsty and the possibility of making a buck might present itself, people had created a great deal of garbage. In the off chance that someone would walk into an office supply store and say, "I'd rather fancy a snack and a drink," people had created a great deal of garbage. In the name of convenience with no consideration of what all that garbage (and you know where there is that much, there is an entire chain of stores filled with more) would do to future generations, people had created just an awful mess of garbage.

And here's the reason I bring this up, here's why I found this so astonishing: All of that garbage could have been eliminated, all of it could have been avoided, with a water fountain. Are you concerned that your customers might be thirsty? Then, put in a water fountain. But these folk weren't concerned with anyone's well-being: not the consumer, not you, not their kids. Nobody's.

They just wanted to make a buck and hadn't a shred of ethics to guide them.

Chapter 10
Ethics and Overpopulation

This is what ethics and overpopulation looks like

This is a story about Bob Bing, a man who has no apples. Of course, the apples are a metaphor and could refer to money or jobs… or even apples. This short passage explains the disaster that happens when we forget the simple rules of life with regards to ethics and overpopulation.

…and is in no way meant to disparage The Apple Company or any of its fine products…

One day, Bob wanted an apple but couldn't find any. He went to the apple stand and asked about the apples.

BOB
Where are all the apples?

Apple Stand Owner
We don't have any more. There are so many people in town, we sold our entire supply. You might want to check the supermarket. They get apples from all around the country.

So, Bob went to the supermarket but they, too, were out of apples.

BOB
Hey, where are all the apples?

Supermarket Owner
We don't have any more. There are so many people in the country, we sold our entire supply. You might want to check with an apple conglomerate. They get apples from all over the world.

So, Bob went to see an apple conglomerate but they, too, were out of apples.

> BOB
> Wait! Where are all the apples?

> Conglomerate PR Rep
> We don't have any more. There are so many people in the world, we sold our entire supply. You might want to check at the fuel pump. They get apples from everywhere!

So, Bob went to the –

> BOB
> Hold on a second! Fuel pump?!

And, Bob went back to the Conglomerate PR Rep.

> Conglomerate PR Rep
> Sure, we make far more money converting apples into biofuel than we ever made selling them for food.[197]

Where'd All These People Come From?

I'd like to close Part 2 with three chapters that address the broader issues of what humanity, with its lack of ethics, is doing to itself. If we can agree that our individual actions have consequences – and here's hoping we can do that – then it's no stretch to agree that the actions of humanity as a whole have even more powerful consequences. Some refer to such issues as overpopulation, energy consumption, and climate change in relation to what effect they're having on the earth. For the purposes of Dynamic Pluralism, however, I would like to simply discuss the effect such things have on us, on our ethical responsibility.

Long ago, when there were fewer people living on the planet, common sense told us that burning fires or clearing brush made little difference. Our impact on the planet and on each other was minimal, if measurable at all. But it's like crowds at Christmas: If you walk into an empty shopping mall, things are great. Salespeople fawn all over you. The selection is endless. Stores are clean and bathrooms are shiny. Now, fill that same mall with people on December 24th (or, worse, Black Friday). Suddenly, salespeople can no longer even talk to you, let alone help you. Your choices are minimized as items are torn off the shelves. Navigation through the packed stores becomes nearly impossible and the bathrooms… well, let's not talk about what happens to the bathrooms.

What might have been common sense once upon a time is nothing more than pig ignorance today (with no offense to the pigs). While there are still plenty of people who will lie to you and tell you nothing is wrong (and, statistically, things just get worse as the population increases), the facts refuse to listen. Our race has long passed the point where we need to worry about there being too few of us and has entered the phase where we are putting an unhealthy burden on the planet and reducing our chances of surviving on it. Simply put the more people we have, the worse off we are.

This is not a new idea. We can turn once again to Thomas Malthus and his warning of the strain too many people put on resources to remind us how long we've known this to be true. Since then, the warnings have only been exceeded by our ability to ignore them.

And it's not like our planet has not done its level best to help keep us in check. The human race has survived the black death, smallpox, cholera, malaria, influenza, AIDS, and high cholesterol. We've been beaten by wars and hurricanes, earthquakes and tornados, pestilence, famine, and daytime talk shows. It would seem that even nuclear holocaust won't wipe us out (if you believe popular fiction, Mad Max films, and the Nuclear Regulatory Commission).

You might say this all began with the first towns or cities: Çatal Hüyük in Turkey and Jericho in Israel formed in 6,000BCE.[198] From that point on, humanity was more than just another pest on the planet's skin.[199] Animals had already been domesticated by this time and farming was common. In fact, our love of grains predates our love of city life. On the other side of the world, by the middle of the third millennia BCE, corn had become a staple and it wouldn't reach European shores until the last years of the 15th century CE when Columbus' men brought the oddity back from Cuba.[200] This was a Europe that had already survived the worst nightmare the Earth could throw at it, the black plague.

Crop rotation came in the 18th century in response to a need for greater crop yields. With new machines like Jethro Tull's seed drill and better types of ploughs to aide in the revolutionary idea of crop rotation, Malthus was made to look like an idiot.[201] That wasn't all. The introduction from Holland of clover, which nitrogenized the soil and revitalized the land, increased crop yields even further. (It should be noted that the need for still greater yields as populations increased led to the use of chemical nitrogen fertilizer that led to nitrogen pollution and environmental devastation. The direct byproduct of overpopulation is unavoidable carelessness.)

More people in the 19th century meant more markets and more markets meant more production and more environmental impact. British textile mills witnessed sulphuric acid pollution and Scottish bleachers died from chlorine gas poisoning.[202] In America's Pacific Northwest, rampant deforestation followed railroad expansion.[203] And in large cities around the world, the effects of water and air pollution were more and more apparent throughout the 1800s.[204]

When, in the mid-19th century, Earth's human population crossed the billion people mark, the voices of reason for population control began to be heard.

Robert Dale Owen, in his pamphlet titled *Moral Physiology*, spoke simply to the burden too many children put on one family: "Is it not notorious, that the families of the married often increase beyond what a regard for the young beings coming into the world, or the happiness of those who give them birth, would dictate? In how many instances does the hard-working father, and more especially the mother of a poor family, remain slaves throughout their lives, tugging at the oar of incessant labour, toiling to live, and living only to die; when, if their offspring had been limited to two or three only, they might have enjoyed."[205]

When later, he spoke on what he called morality, the parallels with Dynamic Pluralism are astonishing: "If we were taught to consult, in every thing, rather the welfare of those we love than our own, how strongly would these arguments be felt! No man ought even to desire that

172

a woman should become the mother of his children, unless it was her express wish, and unless he knew it to be for her welfare, that she should. Her feelings, her interests, should be for him in this matter an imperative law."[206]

Much of Owen's material was later used in Charles Knowlton's *The Fruits of Philosophy*, a book republished by Annie Besant in England. Besant was put on trial for obscenity in 1877, a trial that was thrown out of court on a technicality.[207] Besant, and her co-defendant Charles Bradlaugh, spoke eloquently about the new threat of overpopulation that would result from slowly improving living conditions and sanitation; on the overcrowded conditions in slums, rife with immorality and incest; on the effects of pauperism that led to a death rate of one in three infants; and on the need for freedom from prosecution for those publicizing the facts about contraception.[208] However correct, even tame by today's standards, such ideas were, they would take much more time to catch hold.

This, of course, brings us to the question, "When will such ideas catch hold?" When will we say "enough is enough" and decide we have enough people? On a personal level, restricting reproductive rights is clearly the opposite of Dynamic Pluralism's mandate for "fair and fulfilling" treatment. On a societal level, the repercussions of overpopulation restrict the possibility of such "fair and fulfilling" relationships. I'll address those shortly.

From a global population of one billion people in the 19th century, humanity grew to two billion by the mid-1920s, to three billion by 1960, to four billion by 1990, and has added an additional billion people every decade since then. The math couldn't be simpler: the more people there are, the more there are to make more people.

As hard as this has been to acknowledge, those in power were aware of this all the way back in 1974. The U.S. National Security Council under the direction of Henry Kissinger released *National Security Study Memorandum 200*, which addressed this very issue. Its complete title was *National Security Study Memorandum 200: Implications of Worldwide Population Growth for U.S. Security and Overseas Interests* and it addressed the expanding world population – not in terms of our ethical responsibility but in a much cruder outlook. *NSSM*

173

200 addressed the threat of national security in the face of an out of control population. Quite simply, more people mean fewer resources and hungry people are scary people. It advised President Gerald Ford to encourage population control in India, Bangladesh, Pakistan, Indonesia, Thailand, the Philippines, Turkey, Nigeria, Egypt, Ethiopia, Mexico, Colombia, and Brazil, advocating contraception and other population reduction measures.[209] The report advised, "In these sensitive relations, however, it is important in style as well as substance to avoid the appearance of coercion." Well... that was nice of them.

Why the warning? Because geometric population growth, as discussed in the Introduction, leads to an equally increased rate of resource depletion, pollution, and poverty, while diminishing available arable land, potable water, and clean air at the same rate.

We are breeding ourselves at such a rate that, should it not lead to extinction, will certainly reduce our ability to be ethical people. Let's take a look at just where our growing population has taken us.

What Are All These People Doing Here?

Let's say you were trying to make your relationship with another individual as fair and fulfilling as you possibly could. What resources might you need? When it comes to matters affected by overpopulation, those resources might include:

- Clean water,
- Wholesome food,
- Good soil,
- Clean air,
- Forests to help clean that air and water,
- Energy resources to help get you that food,
- Biodiversity to help maintain the ecosystems we depend upon for all of the above,
- Healthy oceans and wild lands to help maintain that biodiversity,
- And so on.

When it comes to maintaining fair and fulfilling relationships, it turns out you need much more than just good manners. Actually, this may be what good manners are all about. I doubt Miss Manners would advocate depriving anyone of air.

And yet, as there are more and more people we find there are fewer and fewer of these resources. Here's an experiment you can try at home. Stock the largest room in your home with all of the food and water and air and soil and forests and fuel and oceans and wild life you think you might need to survive. Next, add seven billion people. Gets a little crowded, doesn't it?

And yet, we've been trying to pack all that into a finite space. And, yes, the Earth is a finite space with finite resources. We've been trying to grow more food and raise more livestock while not polluting the land or water with the many chemical fertilizers and animal waste (cow poop) that come from it while also looking for a place to put all this waste, which includes human waste, while not polluting the oceans or destroying the… it's just not possible. The juggler can only handle a finite number of balls.

The World Bank estimates that the amount of arable land per person – that is, the amount of land available to grow the food you eat – has been cut in half since 1960 while the amount of use we get from that land has increased. And yet, the population density per square meter and carbon dioxide emissions per person have nearly doubled in that time.[210]

According to one recent estimate, the ecological pressure of a US resident measured by the amount of resources each one uses is 13 times that of a resident of India and 52 times that of a resident of Somalia. When considering ethics, we have to consider how fair and fulfilling our relationships are with these people. Fulfilling for us? Maybe so, but hardly fair. And certainly not fulfilling for them. The answer does not lie in having everyone consume as much as Americans, not unless the question is "How do we all kill ourselves?" And that's where it is leading. Since those first towns I mentioned a while back, more than 80% of the world's forests have been destroyed.[211] Considering the traditional metaphor of the forests as the earth's lungs, how well would you do with 20% of your lungs?

Not so sure about your lungs? How about your stomach?

As I've already mentioned, the need for profits and the strain of production for so many people have led to the manufacture of food many of us would no longer identify as food. "Pink Slime" is called meat. We have genetically modified crops even bugs won't eat.[212] Some "food" is so unidentifiable; it has gained the epithet "Frankenfood." Many crops are grown in "monocultures," vast plantations with only one single plant made incredibly unhealthy due to the lack of biodiversity so that tons of harmful chemicals are used to shut out such diversity while tons of other chemicals are used to keep the crops alive – hardly a plan for healthy living.

And all these efforts to feed more and more people have consequences. Each year, more wild lands are appropriated for agricultural purposes. More agriculture requires more water. Of all the water on the earth, only about 1% is fit for human use in industry, agriculture, or even drinking.[213] That single percentile becomes less and less usable the more we dirty it with, in the case of agriculture, chemical fertilizers, biosludge, waste, and so on.

Some have indicated that the solution to our water problem, and ultimately our food problem, lies in desalination. Unfortunately, even without the incredible costs involved in processing and transporting the water from areas where there is water to areas where there is not, there is still one inescapable draw back. It is referred to as saline brine, a toxic by-product of desalination that is very hot due to how desalination is completed. This is dumped back into the water, polluting it for humans, fish, and the entire planet.

Doesn't sound like a solution to me.

The problem is that food and water production becomes prohibitively expensive in terms of waste and destruction of other resources when there are so many people who need food and water.

And this only gets worse when you consider that quite a bit of that food doesn't go towards feeding hungry people. Instead, it gets turned into biofuel. As mentioned in the beginning of this chapter, more and more crops that once fed people are being turned into fuel to feed machinery. Wealthy nations like to drive and that means poorer peoples have to starve. In recent years, food riots have become almost common in many countries as wealthier nations (including the United States) have taken food from their mouths just so they wouldn't have to walk somewhere.[214]

This all sounds a bit dour and I wouldn't want to leave you with the impression that nothing is being done about it. More and more, people are beginning to recognize that unlimited growth – which is a bit of a misnomer since population growth often means the diminishment of so many other things – is simply not going to work.

Groups such as the World Population Foundation and Population Connection have been at the forefront of a movement that encourages people to take the long view of history, to look beyond our immediate (and some might say outdated) impulse of unlimited procreation and consider such factors as stewardship, leaving a world in which future generations can thrive, which could also refer to ethics.[215]

Such appeals for ethical behavior, however, are more often than not fought over tooth and nail. Without a sound understanding of what ethics are, it seems that anyone can pick up a road apple and call it ethics. This is precisely what some politicians in the United States did in the 2012 election cycle when they moved to restrict a woman's right to contraception, safe and legal abortions, and other rights to her own body.

The United States is not alone in this. In many countries, church-owned hospitals and clinics are exempt from having to allow women any rights over their own bodies, including what surgical procedures are performed. And, where hospitals and clinics allow women any rights, there are always doctors, nurses, and even pharmacists who are happy to ignore any ethical obligation they may have toward their patient in favor of some dogmatic belief.

Dogma, it would seem, is a key word here for it is dogma that insists that, somehow, god wants us to kill ourselves through reproduction. And this is ironic because so many of the same religious nuts are dead-set against sex. It's not uncommon for religious nuts to push their beliefs on others and deep into a woman's uterus – there are far too many examples to state here. But one does ring out with equal parts of irony and gall. In 2007, Mexico's largest anti-abortion group vowed to stop pregnant women from accessing safe and legal abortions, literally forcing women to bear children.[216] The gall is apparent and the irony is that so much of the underdeveloped world sits in Latin America and Africa.

Of course, Mexico is not alone in this. In 2007, a Muslim organization in India protested the idea that sex education should be taught in schools.[217] One protester gave voice to the lunacy of such protests, "How will we digest the fact that a 10-year-old boy or girl will be taught how to use a condom?" I am tempted to respond with the sarcasm fitting such a disconnection with reality but will simply observe such a disconnect as an equal disconnect with ethics.

Such disconnections are not so unusual. The same kinds of questions are given voice every day in the United States in protests, on right-wing "talk radio," and in the homes of people too ignorant to realize how simple facts add up. What these folk refuse to see is that when people are given the resources to plan their family, they often have fewer children. Smaller families slow population growth and the pressures on our resources. In other words, it makes life more fair and fulfilling for everyone.

Fortunately, the idea of slowing population growth has begun to catch on – if slowly. According to the World Bank, the world population growth rate has dropped just a mere .2% from 1960-2010. That doesn't mean that the growth rate is in the negative numbers, just that it is growing just a bit slower than before. Much more still needs to be done and the watchword that has come out in the past couple of decades has been: sustainability.

Sustainability is based on the idea that we can't grow our way out of the problem of overpopulation and we can't drop the population back to a manageable level right away. It is the incrementalist middle road also known as "slow growth." It begins by recognizing a few human behaviors that are making things worse, such as:

- having too many children
- agricultural burning
- overconsumption of resources
- failure to recycle
- production/disposal of toxic waste
- improper disposal of human waste
- improper disposal of garbage
- misuse of pesticides
- overcrowding
- economic dependence on growth

- depletion of soils by overfarming
- erosion from removal of vegetation
- urban sprawl
- over-fishing
- removal of carbon sinks (often called "forests")
- inefficient use of fuel
- urbanizing farmland
- urban growth where water is scarce
- eating meat

There are a few more facts that are helpful to keep in mind as well. These facts were not produced by some flower-children hippie organization, either, but by a Danish businessman named Eivind Drachmann Kolding who put forth his manifesto in the belief that such realizations were necessary from a business viewpoint, which is about as "conservative" as you can get. The manifesto is as follows.[218]

We consider the following to be self-evident facts:

- Planet Earth has limited dimensions, implying that there is a limit to what it can sustain.
- Man is a biological, cultural and social being, implying that there is a limit to what he can be made to suffer.
- Man has the right to search for happiness, but no right to destroy planet Earth.
- Man is part of the biosphere, and the biosphere is prerequisite for human life. We merely have the power to destroy it - which does not entitle us to do so.
- Improving nature is beyond the reach of mankind. We need to satisfy ourselves with living in, off and with it - the latter being a must.
- The number one reason why Planet Earth is increasingly endangered is the ongoing expansion of production and productivity in countries already overconsuming.
- If today the poor parts of the world were to have a standard of material wealth comparable to the present rich world, this would require seven more Planets Earth - which we do not consider realistic.
- All over the planet considerations and rights associated with nature and human life are giving way to a statutory, global boundlessness for money and its managers.

- The social and cultural poverty of the rich world is closely intertwined with productivity increases, global economy, money's fundamental rights of freedom and the democratic deficit.
- Only a consistently democratic organisation can handle such overall conditions, and above all the discrepancy between economic power and common sense.
- Gradually, our production of knowledge has grown so fragmented as to produce massive ignorance, non-knowledge and downright stupidity.
- Our respect for common sense has to be reinstated, experience-based knowledge rehabilitated, and expert knowledge reduced to what it actually is, mere technicalities.
- State-of-the-art technologies have grown so complex and immense that no human systems, let alone humans, can control the emerging risks.
- It does make a difference whether a dairy or a nuclear plant goes down. We need to develop technologies that will take us back to manageable types of risks.
- Technologies have to be developed that allow and call for democratic administration practices.
- Such basics are not confined to the latitude of the ordinary political framework. With some caution they should be seen as absolutes for which only the means are debatable.

These are all important things to remember. Here's the problem: they don't mean anything. They are only facts, facts we should all recognize but simply facts. As a result, "sustainability" has come to mean many things to many people. In the United States, it means maybe not buying that second home or second car. In Somalia, it means maybe having a glass of clean drinking water.

We have the tools to tell us where we've gone wrong, such as the (Un)Happy Planet Index (HPI).[219] We know that we are dependent on fossil fuels just to make food grow, which should give us pause. Even with humanity's incredible resistance to change, we should already know these things. We should see them.

"Look at fishery production. We built bigger ships, larger nets, and now the fish populations of the oceans lakes and rivers are lower than they've been since 1970," observed David Pimentel, PhD professor of entomology and agricultural sciences, Cornell University. "Look at the Colorado River. As it flows south, California, Arizona, and Colorado take a big piece out of it to support their populations. By the time that river reaches Mexico, it's dry. What technology do we have available, short of manipulating the climate, that can double the flow of the Colorado River?"

Sustainability has become nothing more than lip service paid to a devastating dilemma. Even President Bill Clinton's Council on Sustainable Development found, "From an economic point of view, a reduction in the rate of population growth would bring important benefits." It also added, "In short, we find no convincing economic argument for continued national population growth."[220] We knew this stuff nearly 20 years ago. So why no national agenda to slow growth? Why no call from the Earth's greatest superpower to save the planet from its primary residences?

The reason is simple. Our systems of understanding our own behavior have not developed to the point where such a thing is possible. I'll give you an example. The United States is often referred to as an "Ownership Society," as if that's a good thing. But is ownership good? Not in the least. Ownership reduces value. We know this because the minute we drive our newly purchased car off the lot, it immediately loses value. We know this because of the age-old saying, "The grass is greener on the other side." We value more the things we do not own.

Another example of how we have not developed enough to comprehend the situation is in our belief that life is sacred when it clearly is not. As Carl Sagan explained in Chapter 8, "There is no right to life in any society on Earth today…"

We don't see human life as sacred either. We enforce a death penalty. We allow the poor and hungry and sick to die before their time. We wage wars that kill millions. And our greed takes care of the rest. If life was sacred, overpopulation would be seen as blasphemy and, yet, there are many who protect it as if it were divine.

The problem with Sustainability or any measure to curb population growth or greed or selfishness is that without a system in place for understanding value, it is doomed to fail. Ethics is that system for understanding value. The key to understanding that relationships only work when they are fair and fulfilling is also the key to understanding the value of those relationships.

You cannot legislate decency. A fundamental shift in the way humanity sees its relationship with itself and others has to occur. We have to begin understanding that our actions have consequences and the only way we can do this is by seeing each relationship we have as a matter of ethics. Otherwise, the consequences will be dire.

Where Are They Going?

So, here you are, a citizen of the Earth. You are sailing through space on a rock 8,000 miles wide with more than seven billion other people. As you look around day after day and puzzle at all the crowds and the limited resources, you wonder, "Where are all these people going?"

The answer? They're not going anywhere.

And you'll have more joining you very soon.

Even the United Nation's most conservative estimates project a global population of nine billion by 2050 – but, hey, what's a couple billion people between friends?

The answer? That's two billion more people between you and your friend, a rather crowded dinner party. And the dinner party will get more and more crowded as the effects of overpopulation increase global warming and desertification and reduce the amount of habitable land available to you and your now nine billion other fellow citizens of the world.

And there's much more than that to worry about. More people also bring with them:

- Even less adequate supplies of fresh drinking water as well as a greater demand for sewage treatment and effluent discharge.
- An increased depletion of natural resources, especially fossil fuels.
- Increased levels of air pollution, water pollution, soil contamination and noise pollution.
- More rapid deforestation and loss of ecosystems that sustain global atmospheric oxygen and carbon dioxide

- balance; with more than eight million hectares of forest lost each year.
- More species extinctions from reduced habitat in tropical forests due to slash-and-burn techniques that sometimes are practiced by shifting cultivators, especially in countries with rapidly expanding rural populations.
- Increased incidences of hemorrhagic fevers and other infectious diseases from crowding, lack of adequate sanitation and clean potable water, and scarcity of available medical resources.
- Far more starvation, malnutrition or poor diet with ill health and diet-deficiency diseases (e.g. rickets).
- Wide spread unhygienic living conditions for many based upon water resource depletion, discharge of raw sewage and solid waste disposal.
- Over-utilization of infrastructure, such as mass transit, highways, and public health systems.
- And, let's not forget, housing prices like you wouldn't believe.

Keep in mind, this is a conservative estimate. World population growth rates have slacked off .2%, after all. But we are reminded by Carl Sagan about the evils of an exponential growth rate. As he put it, "Never underestimate an exponential."[221]

The sad truth, of course, is that it does not have to be this way. We don't know how much human life the planet can support but we have let our ignorance and selfishness guide us all the same.

We need a new tool with which to guide us and that tool is ethics. When we see that our relationships only work when they are fair and fulfilling, we will understand that overpopulation harms each relationship we have: with each other, with animals, with the world. It is my hope that this will lead to an understanding that humanity will probably survive with a mere five billion people. Heck, it did in 1990.

Chapter 11
Ethics and Energy Dependence

This is what ethics and energy dependence looks like

This is a story about Bob Bing, a man who has no apples. Of course, the apples are a metaphor and could refer to money or jobs… or even apples. This short passage explains the disaster that happens when we forget the simple rules of life with regards to ethics and energy dependence.

…and is in no way meant to disparage The Apple Company or any of its fine products…

One day, Bob wanted an apple but couldn't find any.

BOB
That's because the apples grown on this side of the ocean are shipped over to the other side of the ocean, and the apples grown on the other side of the ocean are shipped over to this side of the ocean.

And shipping apples or oranges or any produce takes oil. And despite its present ubiquity, oil reserves are running low.

BOB
Sure, but can't we use something else to ship the apples?

Something else?

BOB
Yes! I mean, not oil because that just makes climate change worse.

That's the next chapter.

BOB

And not nuclear power because that'll turn the apples into radioactive fruit. But, there has to be something!

We should look into that...

Hungry For Fuel

Bob makes a good point. Our dependence on energy has gone to an absurd level. Look around you at all the things within reach that consume energy: cars, lights, phones – you may be reading this book on something that consumes energy. Energy consumption has become so necessary for everyday life that we seem to have forgotten that the energy has to come from somewhere.

And where does that energy come from? It either comes out of the ground as fossil fuel or is obtained through the dangerous process of nuclear power. Much of the world benefits from so-called "renewable" resources: wind, solar, hydro-electric, etc. And others get their power through experiments with biomass.

While there are some ethical concerns to each of these, most of our concerns do not stem from the power sources themselves but instead come from the oblivious idiots gobbling up the fuel as fast as they can. In a way, fuel has become food just as we turn food into fuel. We gobble up more fuel every day and it is our insatiable appetite that creates the most pressing ethical dilemma.

How do we create ethical relationships that are fair and fulfilling while selfishly consuming? In an effort to answer this question, let's look at each of the main power sources, each type of fuel, beginning with the one we can't get enough of: oil!

A Taste for Oil

Fossil fuels. Petroleum, coal, and natural gas.

Humanity has been utilizing fossil fuels since before the days of Alexander the Great and, yet, it wasn't until the 19th century that we really began to catch on to their many uses. In 1855, Benjamin Silliman

Jr. was asked to research and report on some mineral samples from the Pennsylvania Rock Oil Company. He found that 50% of the black tar could be distilled into a first-rate burning oil, while an additional 40% could be distilled for still more purposes.[222] Now, in the 21st century, we utilize fossil fuels in fertilizers, lubricants, asphalt, roofing, wax, weed killer, paint solvents, cosmetics, dry cleaning, disposable shopping bags, rubbing alcohol, Styrofoam, detergents, and of course toothpaste.

Why did we put fossil fuels in our toothpaste? Because once upon a time it was cheap, and never underestimate the ability of unethical people to capitalize on anything in cheap supply. Later, once we had petroleum in everything from the food we ate to the oceans we fished in, oil wasn't as cheap as we tried to pretend it was – and we pretended really hard.

Between 1950 and 1975, world fuel consumption doubled, oil and gas consumption tripled, and the use of electricity grew almost sevenfold.[223] This electricity figure is important because before the days of any alternative, electrical generators of every kind were powered by – you guessed it – fossil fuels. Even today, some studies have fossil fuels generating at least 65% of the world's electrical power.[224] That mostly refers to petroleum but don't count out coal.

With a finite supply of fossil fuels – and, yes, that is finite, as in "used up one day" – we kept burning it, and eating it, and spilling it, and wasting it as if we'd have it forever. There was no way we could still believe fossil fuels were cheap – that went out the window the minute we starting going to war over it.[225] But we did continue to waste it.

One way we wasted fuel was with inefficient, gas-guzzling cars. We Americans have been really good at that, from our fish-finned Fords in the 1950s all the way up to our personal tanks: some referred to simply as SUVs and others more mockingly called Hummers. With so much petroleum wasted on something as silly as driving your own personal tank, ethics clearly have not been understood.

But waste was not the only thing we did with oil. We spilled it, too. Lots of it. Here is a list of just a few of the larger oil spills since I was born.[226] We can only assume the amount of oil was rounded down by oil company PR men...

- 38 million gallons when the Torrey Canyon ran aground on March 18, 1967 off the Isles of Scilly, England. In 2010, Britain was still feeling the effects of this environmental tragedy.[227]
- 35.3 million gallons when the Sea Star supertanker collided with the Brazillian tanker Horta Barbosa on December 19, 1972 in the Gulf of Oman.
- 88,000 tons of crude oil when the Jakob Maersk tried to enter the port of Leixões, near Porto, Portugal on January 29, 1975.
- 7.7 million gallons when the Agro Merchant ran aground and broke apart near Buzzards Bay, southeast of Nantucket Island, Massachusetts on December 15, 1976.
- 81 million gallons when a well blowout occurred in April 1977 at the Ekofisk oil field in the North Sea. (Score extra points if you realize this gave us at least 30 years to realize the dangers of off-shore drilling before the BP Gulf of Mexico disaster.)
- 68 million gallons when the Amoco Cadiz ran aground on Portsall Rocks, off the coast of Brittany, France, on March 16, 1978.
- 140 million gallons when the oil well Ixtoc 1 blew out on June 3, 1979 in the Gulf of Mexico. (Yep, another warning.)
- 87 million gallons by the Atlantic Empress and Aegean Captain off the coast of Trinidad and Tobago in July and August 1979.
- 80 million gallons by the Nowruz Field in the Persian Gulf on February 4, 1983.
- 78 million gallons by the Castillo de Bellver on August 6, 1983 off Cape Town, South Africa.
- 43 million gallons by the Odyssey on November 10, 1988 off Saint John's, Newfoundland.
- At least 10 million gallons by the Exxon Valdez in Prince William Sound, Alaska on March 24, 1989.
- 19 million gallons by the Kharg 5 off the Canary Islands on December 19, 1989.
- 240-460 million gallons intentionally dumped to the Persian Gulf by Iraq in January 1991.
- 42 million gallons by the Haven off Genoa, Italy on April 11, 1991.

- 70 million gallons by the ABT Summer off the coast of Angola on May 28, 1991.
- 88 million gallons from an oil well in Fergana Valley, Uzbekistan on March 2, 1992.
- 84 million gallons from a pipeline near the Kolva River in Russia on September 8, 1994.
- 20 million gallons by the Prestige off of Spain on November 13, 2002.
- 10 million gallons from the Israeli bombing on the Jieh power station in Beirut on July 15, 2006.
- 206 million gallons (a very conservative estimate) from the Deepwater Horizon into the Gulf of Mexico.

And these were just some of the bigger spills on record, which are just a fraction of all the oil spilled in the time I've been alive. A conservative total from these spills is over 1.6 billion gallons of oil.

Here's an experiment you can try at home. Go to your local beach and dump 1.6 billion gallons of oil in it. Odds are you won't like what you find.

To give you some idea of just how oil hungry we are in the United States, I'd like you to guess just how long 1.6 billion gallons would last one oil-obsessed nation.

One year?

Five years?

Nope. Two days.

Two.

With the United States' average daily oil consumption in 2009 of 840 million gallons each day, all the biggest oil spills in the last 50 years would only slake our thirst over one, short weekend.

And if you think 1.6 billion gallons of crude spills were a travesty, that's just the start of it. In Russia's northern oil fields, more than five million gallons are spilled every year, year after year.[228] Hundreds of oil spills in the Niger River Delta have amounted to over 2,300 cubic meters of toxic pollution every year, year after year.[229] A crack in the ocean floor off the coast of Brazil, created by Chevron in 2011 in its search for oil has now spilled so much oil we still don't have an accurate number.[230]

None of this happened by accident. This all resulted from our greed for "cheap oil." Sadly, many of us still think of it as cheap, too –

or, when we do realize it comes at a price, we only see the price to us, the cost per gallon at the pump. But the price goes far deeper than that.

Drilling by Texaco in Ecuador in the 1960s and 1970s led to an ecological disaster unimaginable to most people. Thousands have died. Tens of thousands have been poisoned by toxic waste pools and devastated land, poisoned water supplies and a landscape raped in the name of "cheap oil."

The campaign for justice for the people of Ecuador says this on their website: "Texaco's oil extraction system in Ecuador was designed, built, and operated on the cheap using substandard technology from the outset. This led to extreme, systematic pollution and exposure to toxins from multiple sources on a daily basis for almost three decades.

"In a rainforest area roughly three times the size of Manhattan, Texaco carved out 350 oil wells, and upon leaving the country in 1992, left behind some 1,000 open toxic waste pits. Many of these pits leak into the water table or overflow in heavy rains, polluting rivers and streams that 30,000 people depend on for drinking, cooking, bathing and fishing. Texaco also dumped more than 18 billion gallons of toxic and highly saline 'formation waters,' a byproduct of the drilling process, into the rivers of the Oriente. At the height of Texaco's operations, the company was dumping an estimated 4 million gallons of formation waters per day, a practice outlawed in major US oil producing states like Louisiana, Texas, and California decades before the company began operations in Ecuador in 1967. By handling its toxic waste in Ecuador in ways that were illegal in its home country, Texaco saved an estimated $3 per barrel of oil produced." [231]

As usual, we fail to realize that what we do to others we do to ourselves. For instance, we're not just killing a few thousand Ecuadorians for so-called cheap oil. That poison gets back to us in many ways: through the food chain, through legal repercussions, and through our culpability to a crime. More immediately, each thing we poison means one more thing we've poisoned. How high does that number have to reach before we recognize our ethical responsibility?

For a clear example of ethical culpability, just look at the Gulf of Mexico. After the decimation of the Gulf by British Petroleum's Deepwater Horizon, there were plenty of oil-industry-endorsed politicians calling for more drilling, as if unable to add one and one. Empty of ethics, they just wanted their own greed satisfied right away without a care for their families or their children or their communities – their world. Now, as a result of Deepwater Horizon, much of the Gulf of Mexico is dead.[232] An immense "dead zone" has resulted and spreads.[233] This was the same Gulf that so many relied on for their livelihood, for their homes, and for food. Simply put, we've poisoned ourselves.

And oil isn't getting any cheaper. In fact, it's running out. When something is finite, wishing just doesn't help. We're now entering the age of "peak oil" and it should come as no surprise. In 2009, the world consumed more than 3.5 billion gallons of oil each day. Even if you ignore what so much consumption does to global warming (addressed in the next chapter), you don't need an advanced math degree to realize that's a lot of oil. And with finite resources, those 3.5 billion gallons are getting harder and harder to find.

This has turned our energy craving to other fossil fuels, specifically coal and natural gas. Americans tend to like both of these because we are told we have lots of them. Coal is the resource most people are familiar with. In the U.S., we've been mining coal since the 1740s.[234] Coal is something you can hold in your hand, you can burn, and you can threaten to put into someone's stocking at Christmas.

Coal is also incredibly dirty. It's a major producer of carbon pollution, leading not only to increased climate change but also immediately impacting the health of animals (including human beings). Burning coal releases large amounts of mercury that enters the food chain through fish and goes right on up to children… that would include your children. In addition, coal pollution causes 12,000 emergency room visits and wracks up $100 billion in health care costs every year.[235]

Mining coal is incredibly risky, either through traditional mining techniques or through strip mining. Traditional mining techniques include bribing lawmakers so they don't enforce mining regulations and paying lip service to local media when a few dozen miners get killed in sub-standard mines. Strip mining can lay bare up to 10 square miles and pour hundreds of millions of tons of waste material into as many as a dozen "valley fills" - some of which are 1,000 feet wide and a mile long. By 2011, the EPA announced that this covered as much as 48,000 kilometers/12 million acres in West Virginia, Kentucky, Virginia, and Tennessee, which used to be forests and habitats, streams and rivers. And it was all destroyed by an unquenchable greed for cheap coal.[236]

But, of course, none of it comes cheap. Recently, politicians and public figures paid off by the coal lobby attempted to spread the myth of "clean coal," but there's a reason it's called a myth. The amount of energy it presently takes to create actual clean coal is more than the clean coal itself creates. It's a losing proposition.

And that leaves us with natural gas. While it may be clean-burning, our greed for more and more energy has led energy companies to extract it (along with more petroleum and coal seam gas) through the dangerous method of "fracking." Short for "hydraulic fracturing," fracking forces the natural gas out of the earth, releasing a stream of chemicals and by-products into local water tables and air, soil and rivers – basically, you end up with a toxic mess everywhere, including:[237]

- 2,2',2"-Nitrilotriethanol
- 2-Ethylhexanol
- 5-Chloro-2-methyl-4-isothiazolin-3-one
- Acetic acid
- Acrolein
- Acrylamide (2-propenamide)
- Acrylic acid
- Ammonia
- Ammonium chloride
- Ammonium nitrate
- Aniline
- Benzyl chloride
- Boric acid
- Cadmium
- Calcium hypochlorite
- Chlorine
- Chlorine dioxide
- Dibromoacetonitrile 1
- Diesel 2
- Diethanolamine
- Diethylenetriamine
- Dimethyl formamide
- Epidian
- Ethanol (acetylenic alcohol)
- Ethyl mercaptan
- Ethylbenzene
- Ethylene glycol
- Ethylene glycol monobutyl ether (2-BE)
- Ethylene oxide
- Ferrous sulfate
- Formaldehyde
- Formic acid
- Fuel oil #2
- Glutaraldehyde
- Glyoxal
- Hydrodesulfurized kerosene
- Hydrogen sulfide
- Iron
- Isobutyl alcohol (2-methyl-1-propanol)
- Isopropanol
- Kerosene
- Light naphthenic distillates, hydrotreated
- Mercaptoacidic acid

- Methanol
- Methylene bis(thiocyanate)
- Monoethanolamine
- NaHCO3
- Naphtha, petroleum medium aliphatic
- Naphthalene
- Natural gas condensates
- Nickel sulfate
- Paraformaldehyde
- Petroleum distillate naptha
- Phosphonium, tetrakis(hydroxymethyl) -sulfate
- Propane-1,2-diol
- Sodium bromate
- Sodium chlorite (chlorous acid, sodium salt)
- Sodium hypochlorite
- Sodium nitrate
- Sodium nitrite
- Sodium sulfite
- Styrene
- Sulfur dioxide
- Sulfuric acid
- Tetrahydro-3,5-dimethyl-2H-1,3,5-thiadiazine-2-thione (Dazomet)
- Titanium dioxide
- Tributyl phosphate
- Triethylene glycol
- Urea
- Xylene

Once again, greed for energy leads to destruction of land, poisoning of people, and other assorted devastation. And since the energy companies can afford to bribe elected officials, fracking is nearly done with impunity.

That isn't the end of where our greed will lead us for sources of fossil fuel, either. There are also tar sands, plentiful in Canada and filled with heavy metals such as vanadium, nickel, lead, cobalt, mercury, chromium, cadmium, arsenic, selenium, copper, manganese, iron and zinc. It is certainly not environmentally friendly and, you guessed it, is just as certain to run out.

Fossil fuels kill in the short term. They kill in the long term. And we excuse ourselves by ignoring our ethical responsibility to others. When you fill up your car's gas tank or when you use electricity (which I am doing right now as I write this) or when you eat, because agriculture is dependent upon fossil fuels, you become responsible. Dynamic Pluralism says that ethics come from relationships that are fair and fulfilling. You cannot have a fair and fulfilling relationship when you are killing others to feed your greed for energy.

And I refuse to allow anyone to employ a false equivalency, which have become so popular of late. A false equivalency is when you justify your actions by showing someone else who does it, without taking their circumstances in mind, as in the *Live Earth* concert mentioned previously. Therefore, if anyone says to me that I am not allowed to suggest that the use of fossil fuels (by billions of people all over the globe) is unethical because I use them as well, I will remind them that I am at least trying to make things better for us both (in an act that is both fair and fulfilling) instead of just trying to make excuses.

The Nuclear Option

Here's an experiment you can do at home: Go to a family member or a friend and propose a new kind of power plant. It's not very efficient and requires lots of subsidies, paid by your family member or friend. It's incredibly dangerous with hundreds of thousands already dead, diseased, or displaced in its wake. The waste it generates will be around to poison everyone for thousands of years – one type, Plutonium-239, will be toxic for at least 24,000 years and probably as long as 100,000 years – and the fact that anyone can make nuclear weapons out of the waste makes it even more dangerous.

Now, ask your family member or friend for the money to build it.

You've now entered the nuclear energy field.

Somehow, power companies have convinced us and have, more importantly, convinced our government that nuclear energy will save us from the dire consequences of fossil fuel related climate change. They say, "Look at the situation your greed for energy has put you in! Here's a more dangerous energy source to save you!"

We should be able to see through a lie that obvious.

In 1954, the Chairman of the United States Atomic Energy Commission, Lewis Strauss, spoke to the National Association of Science Writers about the future of nuclear energy. He said, "Our children will enjoy in their homes electrical energy too cheap to meter... It is not too much to expect that our children will know of great periodic regional famines in the world only as matters of history, will travel effortlessly over the seas and under them and through the air with a minimum of danger and at great speeds, and will experience a lifespan far longer than ours, as disease yields and man comes to understand what causes him to age." He was telling them a fairy tale. Their children, and their children's children, have seen global climate change as a consequence of energy addiction, nuclear tragedies that have terrified the world, and a constant refusal to face the truth he might have been proud of.

Take the price of nuclear power to begin with. What are you going to charge your customers? Will you charge them $1 per kilowatt hour (kWh is the standard unit of measure used in billing electricity)? How about $10/kWh? In December 2011, the World Nuclear Association pegged the price at no more than 1.42 cents/kWh.[238] That's just over a penny an hour.

What would that penny an hour cover?

According to the World Nuclear Association once again, that would bring you over $65 billion in U.S. subsidies from 1950-2006.[239] That's right. You get to charge and they give you money on top of it, just so long as you keep making outrageous promises. You'll need those subsidies, too, because each of your reactors could cost you as much as $5 billion just to construct – less if you avoid pesky safety regulations.[240]

And you'll be asked to build plenty of those reactors, too. The world is running out of dirty fossil fuels and climate change gets worse by the day. You may be asked to build hundreds of plants, even thousands! But, don't worry, you won't be able to build a fraction of those in time to make any change. Just make your promises and take the subsidies and you'll be fine. (I can't say the same for your children but, heck, you've already shown that you don't care about them.)

You'll want to pick up some uranium for any reactors you build and my advice would be to do it quickly. According to the U.S. Department of Energy Office of Environmental Management, the price of uranium increased tenfold from 2003 to 2007. In just four years, it increased to the low, low price of just $100/pound.[241] The price increase was so dramatic that some retirement advisers actually suggested investing in uranium, an act so ironic I cannot begin to wrap my mind around it.[242]

And that's it. All your bases are covered. Just hire a few people too uneducated to know about the dangers of…

Ah, but I haven't covered the dangers, have I?

I won't kid you. Nuclear energy has a rich and storied history of unfortunate... non-beneficial... oopsies. Let's just say there have been enough accidents for the International Atomic Energy Authority to create a handy, quick-reference scale of devastation: Their scale ranges from level 1 (Anomaly) to level 7 (Major Accident). I don't know if I should be happy or not that there's no level 8; I can't help but wonder if level 8 is when we realize these aren't just accidents.

Here's a sample of some of those accidents with some idea of what each level on the scale means.[243]

Level 2 (an "incident")

Year	Location	Official Description	What That Means
1981	Tsuraga, Japan	More than 100 workers were exposed to doses of up to 155 millirem per day of radiation.	16 tons of waste spilled into Wakasa Bay. Seaweed in the area was found to have radioactive levels 10 times greater than normal. Cobalt-60 levels were 5,000 times higher than previous highs recorded in the area.[244]
1999	Ishikawa, Japan	Control rod malfunction.	A chain reaction went unchecked for 20 hours, killing two workers.[245]
2006	Forsmark, Sweden	"Degraded safety functions for common cause failure in the emergency power supply system."	According to Swedish nuclear expert Lars-Olov Högland, "It was pure luck that there was not a meltdown. It was the worst incident since Chernobyl and Harrisburg."[246]

Level 3 (a "serious incident")

Year	Location	Official Description	What That Means
1989	Vandellos, Spain	Loss of highly radioactive Cobalt-60 source.	When one of the turbines caught fire, the wisdom of not having any fire-fighting equipment was put into question. The fire raged for four hours but authorities insisted no radiation leaked.[247]
2003	Paks, Hungary	Partially spent fuel rods undergoing cleaning in a tank of heavy water ruptured and spilled fuel pellets.	For 14 days, the reactor leaked radioactive gas, which according to spokespersons was just fine for the environment.[248]
2005	Sellafield, UK	Release of large quantity of radioactive material, contained within the installation.	Quoting The Guardian, "The highly dangerous mixture, containing about 20 tonnes of uranium and plutonium fuel, has leaked through a fractured pipe into a huge stainless steel chamber which is so radioactive that it is impossible to enter." Barry Snelson, managing director of British Nuclear Group, Sellafield, later stated, "Let me reassure people that the plant is in a safe and stable state."[249]

Level 4 (an "accident with local consequences")

Year	Location	Official Description	What That Means
1977	Jaslovske Bohunice, Czechoslavakia	Damaged fuel integrity, extensive corrosion damage of fuel cladding and release of radioactivity.	Two men died in the cleanup after a 4.5 ton radioactive rod shattered to pieces.[250]

1993	Tomsk, Russia	Pressure buildup led to an explosive mechanical failure.	A cloud of radioactive gas, 14 miles square was released.[251]
1999	Tokaimura, Japan	Fatal overexposure of workers following a critical event at a nuclear facility.	Radiation levels rose as high as 15,000 times higher than normal and a third of the workers reported serious health conditions. Police had to cordon off a 6km wide "forbidden zone" around the plant.[252]

Level 5 (an "accident with wider consequences")

Year	Location	Official Description	What That Means
1952	Chalk River, Canada	A reactor shutoff rod failure, combined with several operator errors, led to a major power excursion of more than double the reactor's rated output.	Millions of liters of water, some 10,000 times their normal radiation level, was pumped 1,600 miles away from the reactor after a meltdown caused the reactor's four ton lid to be literally blown off.[253]
1979	Three Mile Island, US	Severe damage to the reactor core.	The United States' worst nuclear meltdown (to date) was fortunately contained. The U.S. Nuclear Regulatory Commission released no data about the accident and claimed that the radiation was contained and any release was "negligible."[254] And yet, studies have shown increased cancer rates in the area.[255] So much for "negligible."

Year	Location	Official Description	What That Means
2011	Fukushima, Japan	Reactor shutdown after the 2011 Sendai earthquake and tsunami; failure of emergency cooling caused an explosion.	It's difficult to estimate casualties with a disaster that was trebled by earthquake, tsunami, and radiation. It is clear, however, that thousands will die of cancer with maybe a million additional cases resulting.[256] More than 80,000 people lost their homes.[257] A vital fishing industry has been decimated. And 8,000 square miles of precious land – the size of New Jersey – has been lost to radiation.[258]

Level 6 (a "serious accident")

Year	Location	Official Description	What That Means
1957	Kyshtym (Mayak), Russia	Significant increase of radioactive material to the environment from explosion to a high activity waste tank	Not much information was released by the then Soviet Union about the only level 6 "accident" on record but we do know that it released a radioactive cloud that spread for hundreds of miles. Over 10,000 people were displaced with reports of some with their skin literally falling off.[259] The death toll reported by the Soviet Union was 200 due to cancer but you can be sure it totaled more. Kyshtym left a dead zone reaching 800 kilometers from the reactor, which is still uninhabitable today.[260]

Level 7 (a "major accident")

Year	Location	Official Description	What That Means
1986	Chernobyl, Ukraine	Widespread health and environmental effects. External release of a significant fraction of reactor core inventory.	The world's worst nuclear disaster – and I certainly do not have the space in this book to do it justice. Here, then, are just a few damning statistics:[261] • The Chernobyl accident equaled 500 nuclear bombs used in Hiroshima in 1945. • Around 17 million people were contaminated with radiation to some degree. • Displaced persons from contaminated areas of the Ukraine totaled 143,000. • Of the 600,000 people who took part in liquidating the effects of the disaster, 100,000 died or are handicapped. • Cases of leucosis and thyroid cancer exceeded the average by as much as five times among the Chernobyl victims. • During the 14 years after the disaster, 300,000 died in the Ukraine alone from radiation sickness. • After the horrible disaster, 95% of the power plant's fuel (about 180 tons) remained within a hastily constructed, temporary sarcophagus along with thousands of tons of radioactive debris. A new sarcophagus for the remains was completed in 2016 but there are doubts as to how effectively it will contain the still deadly site.[262]

The radioactive remains of Chernobyl, Kyshtym, Fukushima, and the many others not even mentioned here will remain with us for spans of time we can hardly imagine. And we must face the fact that we're handing this poison down to our children – and theirs – and theirs – on and on.

Those whose job it is to sell us nuclear energy, a job well described in Chapter 6, would like us to forget as much of this as possible. They would like us to forget that the price of nuclear energy is far greater than we can imagine. They would like us to forget that any energy source this dangerous just isn't worth it. And they'd like us to forget about what happens after we're gone even in the best of circumstances.

That's right. I still haven't mentioned the waste.

That's the best part.

You've probably figured out by now that all the radioactive clouds and irradiated water and horrible, radioactive junk for all those disasters doesn't just go away. No, it disperses enough for PR men to breathe a bit easier (far, far away, of course). But it doesn't go away.

And neither does the waste.

Nuclear fusion is an incredibly wasteful process that generates all sorts of goodies for us to hand down to those who are sure to curse our graves. If you were thinking that nuclear power was fine if not for the disasters, I should remind you that nuclear power is generated (at present) through boiling vast amounts of water. You might say a radioactive rose by any other name would have just as many radioactive thorns.

And then, there's also the spent fuel rods, the solid waste from nuclear generators, to take into consideration. A large nuclear reactor produces about 30 tons of spent fuel each year and there are currently about 400 plants around the globe. Welcome to 1,200 tons of waste annually.

Spent fuel rods must be stored in shielded basins of water (spent fuel pools). The water provides both cooling for the still-decaying uranium, and shielding from the continuing radioactivity. After a few decades some on-site storage involves moving the now cooler, less radioactive fuel to a dry-storage facility or dry cask storage, where the fuel is stored in steel and concrete containers until its radioactivity decreases naturally ("decays") to levels safe enough for other processing. This interim stage spans years or decades, depending on the type of fuel. Most U.S. waste is currently stored in temporary storage sites requiring oversight, while suitable permanent disposal methods are still being discussed.

As of 2011, the United States had accumulated about 72,000 metric tons of spent nuclear fuel from nuclear reactors.[263] After 10,000 years of radioactive decay, according to United States Environmental Protection Agency standards, the spent nuclear fuel will no longer pose a threat to public health and safety.

There you go. Just 10,000 years. Nobody has really figured out how much 10,000 years of radioactive storage costs, so it's difficult to figure into the price. It's also difficult to figure out how we're going to keep all that radioactive waste safe, since spent fuel rods can be used in making nuclear weapons. Will the United States even be around in 10,000 years? Because no other empire has even come close.

Our answer to nuclear power has been, as with so much else, to let someone else come up with the answer. This should come as little surprise. After all, we used to dump nuclear waste in the sea and then blast holes in the sealed barrels that held it to help the barrels fill with water, the better they should sink.[264] And for decades, we pointed phallic figures of war at the Soviet Union and the rest of the world and dared someone to blink. Many of these missiles are still with us. Somehow, we just can't seem to take our consequences seriously.

If you haven't stopped to consider where ethics comes in, let me bring that up right here. Because ethics provides perspective and puts consequences front and center. When your focus is on creating fair and fulfilling relationships, it is difficult to avoid the poison you're creating to feed your greed for more energy.

No energy supply that kills is an ethical one. The answer lies somewhere else.

We've had biofuel for a long time.

You might say that oil is a type of biofuel, since it takes biological organisms to create oil. Well, that and millions of years of compression beneath tons of earth. We call them fossil fuels and not fast fuels for a reason.

One type of biofuel we're all probably familiar with is alcohol. It can be made from corn, barley, potato, sugar or Billy Bob's secret still; one way or the other, it packs quite a kick! It can fuel your car, too!

At present, most Americans know about biofuel through ethanol, which is a blend of gasoline and corn-derived alcohol. We'll hear how important its use is in the media and there's a general feeling of (dare I say) arrogance about it. After all, ethanol has helped revitalize American farms, has cut our dependence on foreign oil (a tad), and burns cleaner than gas alone.

I hate to be the one to burst the bubble of those who believe this but… no. True, ethanol does burn cleaner than gasoline but that reasoning is similar to a murderer pleading before a judge that he has killed fewer people this year. As we'll discuss in the next chapter, global climate change remains out of control and a little corn won't stop that. Maybe if we took the gasoline out of the equation, it might help but… where would you get all that corn?

The fact is we didn't need ethanol to help American farms. There are plenty of people hungry for corn in the U.S. and outside of the U.S.[265] Feeding people is what farming is supposed to be about. Turning food into fuel just doesn't make sense.

I know this sounds like a contradiction. We need the fuel we've been getting from corn but we also need the food that, let's face it, corn is. The answer? Get the fuel without using food. Since biofuel is generated based on the content of starch/cellulose in the plant (starch/cellulose = sugar = alcohol), it would seem that we should be looking for a plant that can generate more starch.

The problem with corn is that, while it might taste great barbequed or popped, it's just not that good for making ethanol. A single hectare of corn can generally only produce about 172 liters of vegetable oil, or biofuel.[266] You also have to take into consideration the nutrients it takes out of the land and the pesticides and fertilizer it takes to grow. As a fuel source, ultimately, you want to look towards a source that is easier on the land, easier to grow, and let's not forget: not food. Because taking food out of a starving child's mouth so you can joyride in your SUV is the definition of unethical.

Generating 273 liters of vegetable oil per hectare, far out-producing corn, our attention thereby turns to kenaf. Grown for thousands of years in Africa where its leaves have been consumed by humans and animals alike, its fiber has been used for cordage, and its woody core is perfect for fuel. Kenaf is considered a hardy plant that requires a minimum of fertilizers, pesticides and water in comparison to conventional row crops. There. In one short paragraph, you've increased your yield by over 100 liters.

But there must be more. In fueling an energy hungry world, we must still do better.

And we can, with hemp. Debates over the use of hemp always tend to break down over questions about whether marijuana (which is actually not the same as hemp) should be legalized. I'm going to avoid those questions by stating here and now that marijuana should be legalized. Any argument against legalization relies so much on superstition, childishness, and outright lies that it does not belong in any adult discussion from the get go.

Producing 363 liters of oil per hectare, the use of hemp would double the ethanol yield. Hemp can be grown for food or fiber or fuel. Hemp can be used to make paper, plastics, shirts, and lunch. It produces twice as much fiber per acre as cotton and four times as much as a tree plantation. It can grow in any climate and, as it is unpalatable to insects, does not require pesticides. And, yet, its use is illegal in most of the United States and do you know why?

… neither do I.

But, okay. Let's say you have been brainwashed to believe that hemp will, as George Carlin put it, "infect your soul, curve your spine, and keep the country from winning the war." Could there be some other alternative to putting someone's breakfast in your gas tank?

There is and it is called jatropha. Jatropha grows around the world in any number of climates and soil types and can produce 1,892 liters of oil from a single hectare. And best of all, nobody has yet found a way to call it a devil plant.

So, why aren't we using jatropha? Or hemp?

Why aren't we using algae, which some studies have shown to produce 5,000 gallons of oil per acre per year?[267] (By comparison, jatropha yields 202 gallons per acre per year and corn yields a pitiable 18 gallons per acre per year.)

Why? Because our present system of ethics – which is no system at all – makes it perfectly acceptable to take food out of a child's mouth and put it in our car so we don't have to walk an extra few feet. The ethics of Dynamic Pluralism show what a travesty this is. When you realize that you have a relationship with the people you are starving just so you can drive your car, you understand the consequences of your actions. It is just possible that this realization will help us move away from using corn as a fuel and let us enjoy how it tastes once again.

Is the answer renewable?

Renewable energy sources can generally be broken down into the following categories: wind, solar, hydroelectric, geothermal, and tidal. It is the hippy idea of energy: cheap and generally harmless. It is also the energy of the geek: difficult to explain and hard to fit into a Ferrari. As a result, it's often mocked by those too stupid to understand or too selfish to care.

The fact is, renewable energy sources take us out of the old paradigm of "burn this and make it go" and into the future. Solar energy is clean and easy to generate and gets cheaper and more effective all the time. Tidal energy has an incredible potential using the earth's own rhythms. Geothermal energy taps into power beneath our feet. And, as there are those who laugh at wind power while endorsing an energy policy that left so much of the Gulf of Mexico dead, allow me to quote Bill Maher with regards to the safety of wind power: "You know what happens when a windmill malfunctions in the ocean? It makes a splash."

Truly, it would appear the answer to all of our energy problems may lie with renewable energy.

While that will very likely prove to be true, let me provide a few words of caution. Too often, our greed turns even good things into bad. The example of how this happens lies in another renewable energy source: hydroelectric.

During the 20th century, many nations found hydroelectric to be a great contributor to their need for more and more energy. In less than 200 years, the United States constructed 80,000 dams and in the golden age of dam building that was the 1960s five dams were completed every day. In the wake of this, our rivers became little more than waterways for generating electricity. Across the country, habitats were destroyed and countryside ruined in our greed for energy. Now, in the 21st century, we are learning that we needed those rivers for more important things than just energy. We needed them to keep us alive!

And so, my word of caution with regards to renewable energy sources is to remember hydroelectric. If we dot the map with a million windmills or cover the southwest with photovoltaic cells, what is that energy worth? If we destroy our shores with tidal plants, how are we better off?

Renewable energy is terrific in that it can bring power to those who need it without killing the environment like fossil fuels or just plain nuking the crap out of us like nuclear power plants. In this way, it helps facilitate ethics. But going overboard throws ethics away once again.

There must be a way to live with ethics while providing energy.

Ethics and the Energy Economy

Sometimes, you happen on to things by chance. When petroleum was discovered in Pennsylvania in 1857 and thereafter distilled for lamp oil, I'm sure a great many sperm whales breathed a sigh of relief because up until that time, whales were being slaughtered for oil to read by.[268] But the time for hoping we happen on an answer to our energy addiction by chance has long passed.

The options currently on the table are inexcusable. Proponents of fossil fuels tell us to ignore the mess as they tear open the earth in a desperate search for more fuel. Those who support nuclear energy insist it is safe while hiding one disaster after another. Biofuel proponents sell a bill of goods based on starving those who cannot afford artificially skyrocketing food prices. And renewable energy advocates know that as good as their choice may be, it still might not be enough.

What is enough?

Is a car of our own enough? Is constant entertainment in the form of a thousand television channels, radio, and endless amusement on the Internet enough? Are amusement parks throughout the country enough? Is the Las Vegas Strip, a glorious red flag of energy waste, enough? How about floating all-you-can-eat cruise ships? All of these consume energy, some in vast amounts. How much is enough?

The problem with not having a working system of ethics is that we are not equipped to make difficult decisions such as when we've had enough. Our current laissez-faire system of capitalism, which is far less lazy that many think, tells us to consume, consume, consume, and that "the market" will adjust. In the end, though, the market just keeps consuming until it is we who must adjust either to global climate change or nuclear "accidents" of several stripes or children starving for want of fuel… I mean food.

A working system of ethics provides the bearings we need to decide right and wrong. In the case of Dynamic Pluralism, we know it is wrong to keep consuming because that kind of behavior only creates unfair and unfulfilling relationships with others. Greed does not create happiness; it just creates more greed.

We cannot grow our way out of our current energy consumption dilemma any more than we can grow our way out of our rampant population growth. We must stop and reprioritize. Yes, this means consuming less energy. Maybe we shut down Las Vegas once a week. Maybe we turn our vast media machine towards encouraging less selfishness. Or, more importantly, maybe we each see how our energy consumption might possibly be unethical and maybe we choose as individuals to change things.

In the end, that might just be enough.

Chapter 12
Ethics and Climate Change

This is what ethics and climate change looks like

This is a story about Bob Bing, a man who has no apples. Of course, the apples are a metaphor and could refer to money or jobs... or even apples. This short passage explains the disaster that happens when we forget the simple rules of life with regards to ethics and global climate change.

...and is in no way meant to disparage The Apple Company or any of its fine products...

One day, Bob wanted an apple but couldn't find any. There were no apples and no apple trees. The soil had become so toxic that they couldn't grow and the availability of water so scarce that he couldn't water the trees if he tried.

BOB
This isn't exactly a happy ending, you know?

I know. We need to work on that.

Environmentalism: A Long History

I've already mentioned at length how connected we all are and nothing connects us quite like the damage we are doing to our planet. And, make no mistake, any "damage" to our planet is actually damage to ourselves and our children. Due to interconnectivity, we are only hurting ourselves. And yet, one of the things that divides us the most has told us for many lifetimes just how true this is.

I'm referring, of course, to religion. Even if you chose not to believe in any of the many (and similar) messages the world's religions hand down to us, there's no denying their antiquity. Religions hold old truths realized by those far less developed than we like to believe ourselves to be. And yet, they tell us things we prefer to ignore.

Chapter 5, Verse 32 of the Koran reminds us about how we're all connected: "[I]f anyone slew a person—unless it be for murder or spreading mischief in the land—it would be as if he slew the whole people. And if anyone saved a life, it would be as if he saved the life of the whole people."

Environmentalism appears built into the Torah's DNA, from green design (Numbers 35:4) to cautions against pollution (Deuteronomy 23:12).[269]

In the Christian Bible, god tells the first humans to "Be fruitful and multiply." It would seem through this simple message that being fruitful is the goal here, as it is mentioned first.[270] Therefore, it would seem to be good, Christian reasoning that if multiplying made being fruitful impossible, you'd cut back on the multiplying. Sadly, though, this is the situation that so many people on the planet contributing to global climate change is putting us in.

None of the eastern traditions of Hindus or Buddhists provide the authority over nature that western religions seem to provide. In fact, these traditions puzzle many in the west as nature religions, since nature is held in such reverence.

It would seem that if we simply listened to the gods so many of us profess to believe in, we would be fine. And yet, we don't.

We don't even listen to ourselves, to the rich and insistent voice of centuries of environmentalists throughout history. The idea of taking care of our home, of being responsible citizens of the world, did not originate with the hippies.

The Sumerian epic of Gilgamesh dates back to the 3rd millennia BCE and, already, environmental concerns were clear. Areas of what is now southern Iraq are described as covered in vast tracts of cedar forest. Gilgamesh defies the gods to cut down the forest and, in return, the gods curse Sumer. In that same millennia, another Sumerian wrote about the earth turning white, indicative of soil erosion and salt buildup.[271] The Sumerians would later be the first people to pass laws protecting their remaining forests.

The Hindu practice of "simple living" dates as far back as the 2nd millennia BCE, extolling the sacredness of all life and reminding us that true happiness does not come from without.[272] This practice continued in various Abrahamic and Buddhist movements throughout the world inspiring such practitioners as Abraham, Moses, Gautama Buddha, John the Baptist, Jesus, Muhammad, Francis of Assisi, Ammon Hennacy, Rabindranath Tagore and Mahatma Gandhi.

Around 200 BCE, the first nature reserves in the world were established in Sri Lanka. Early environmentalism did not come to the west until the 7th century, when Cuthbert of Lindisfarne (later canonized as Saint Cuthbert) instituted special laws to protect the Eider ducks and other seabirds nesting on the Farne Islands, off the British shore.

It wasn't until the 14th century that there were enough people for human beings to really get a sense of the mess they were making. The middle of that century saw the first attempts at public health laws after the decimation of the bubonic plague. A few years later, in 1366, Paris mandated the disposal of animal wastes from the city's butchers outside the city. Similar laws in New York and Philadelphia would still be disputed nearly 400 years later. By the end of that century, Cambridge had passed the first urban sanitary laws in England and Parliament made illegal the dumping of garbage into rivers, streams, and other waterways.

It would seem that as far back as those hundreds of years ago, we began to understand our place in this world and how we needed to preserve it lest in destroying our planet we destroyed ourselves.

... or so it would seem. There are always those who would ignore the obvious. In 1420, with the colonization of the Madeira Islands, Portuguese settlers decided to clear the island of its natural forests to make room for farms and help fertilize the soil. The laurisilva forest burned for seven years.[273]

In the late 16th century, deforestation became a problem throughout England as industry's desire for coal led to what was seen as a cheap coal substitute: England's lumber. By 1700, rapid industrialization stripped England of much of its forests.

On the topic of saving forests and hippy environmentalist philosophies, allow me to introduce the first "tree huggers." These would be the Bishnois Hindus of Khejadali, many of whom died to protect their trees. In 1730, the Raja Abhay Singh needed fire wood to burn lime to construct his palace in Jodhpur. His advisors told him the only place to find wood would be the Bishnoi villages. When he came for the trees, the Bishnois put themselves between the trees and the axes and many died for this act. The Bishnois were compelled by their beliefs to "be compassionate towards all living things".[274] For this, they were killed.

By the 19th century, many people understood a clear connection between what was done to the environment and the climate. This was displayed with the eruption of Mount Tambora (in what is now Indonesia) in 1815. The eruption was so huge and threw so much smoke into the air that the following year was known as "The year without a summer," due to the ash in the atmosphere blocking the sunlight.[275]

In America, George Perkins Marsh spoke in favor of conservation throughout the 19th century. He argued that deforestation could lead to desertification and that "the operation of causes set in action by man has brought the face of the earth to a desolation almost as complete as that of the moon." The term "ecology" was coined around that time by Ernst Heinrich Philipp August Haeckel. We knew about acid rain as far back as 1872, the same year America set aside its first national park and created Arbor Day, a holiday devoted to the earth.

The fact is, we know these things to be true: that our existence has an effect on the planet, that if we do not preserve our world, we waste it, and that to behave as if we do not know this is to shame ourselves with our perfidy. It's not the world we destroy, but ourselves, and that makes ethics especially difficult.

What We've Done to Our Home

While it can be said that humanity has known the need to take care of our world and the impact we can have upon it for hundreds of years, it cannot be said that we acted in that manner. If anything, our attitude has been to use things up even quicker and care less, almost as if we're afraid we'll get caught. It reminds me of a recent Internet posting: "Climate change is real so there's nothing we can do about it."

Ethics tells us that being responsible for something means more than saying you're sorry or simply acknowledging guilt. That's only the first step. Ethics are not passive. In order to create fair and fulfilling relationships, you have to ensure that it's possible for such relationships to exist. Accepting guilt is a start – but it's taken hundreds of years to get that far.

You can go back hundreds of years further still and come up with clear examples of how we've destroyed our environment. Consider the infamous damage to the ecosystem on Easter Island (or Rapa Nui). Some said it was wiped out when the island's inhabitants destroyed the trees so they could roll their huge stone figures into place. This was the accepted view for a long time. Then, some claimed the island was decimated by Portuguese sailors and the rats they left behind.[276] Those who dodge the issue of responsibility by saying, "See, it wasn't the natives who had an effect on their environment! It was the Portuguese!" miss the point entirely. It was still humans who did that.

And they – we – would continue to do that. This is not to say that the damage done to our environment has been the result of malicious intent, either. On the contrary, it is the position of this book that just as there is no way to move in a new direction without understanding ethics it is equally difficult to see the direction we are headed without understanding ethics.

Take oil, for example, one of the primary ingredients for the mess we're in. In many ways, it was oil that kept us from causing irreversible harm to the planet. When whaling was such a huge industry, during the 17th, 18th, and 19th centuries, one of the most lucrative products extracted from whales was whale oil. Whale oil made a terrific illuminant because it glowed brightly and cleanly. It also wiped out a staggering number of whales until they were nearly gone from the oceans. In the 1860s, however, kerosene hit the market, a cleaner-burning and cheaper alternative.[277]

Around that same time, ivory was in great demand and hunters were out shooting elephants at an alarming rate. Elephant ivory made everything from jewelry to figurines to billiard balls and more. The search for ivory was so great that by 1864 England alone imported a million pounds every year. To get that ivory, for just that one country, over 8,333 elephants had to be butchered. The slaughter became so bad that the New York Times ran an article about the Great Disappearing

African Elephant Scare in 1867.[278] Enter oil, and an ivory substitute called celluloid. Fewer elephants were killed and folks could still play billiards.

Fossil fuels have even helped save the trees, if you can believe that. Back in the 16th century, the devastation of the Spanish Armada had cost Spain in ships but it also cost them in trees. The construction of just one gigantic, two-thousand ton ship used over one thousand oak trees. Soon, there were laws aimed at preserving the dwindling forests, such as not being allowed to cut down a tree without planting two in its place.[279]

But simple conservation wouldn't save the forests in 19th century United States. With the growth of the railroads, lumber was at a premium. Wood was used to build bridges, wagons, carriages, crew accommodations, locomotive fuel (three thousand cords a month), telegraph poles and, above all, the ties that held the rails in place. In 1850 America had 9,000 miles of track, and that grew by 1890 to 164,000 miles of track. Worse still, this was all temporary. The timber used in railroad ties and telegraph poles lasted no more than seven years before rotting and needing to be replaced. Growth could not be maintained if every mile had to be replaced perhaps as much as a couple of times each decade.

Again, the answer was found in fossil fuel, specifically a thick black by-product of distilled coal tar we call creosote. This coated the timber and preserved it for as much as thirty-five years, saving the railroads and some of the forests.[280] Another product we get from the distillation of coal tar is aspirin, in case the thought of thousands of miles of oily lumber leeching into ground water gives you a headache.

We often find that the seeds of our downfall lie in our ingenuity. Take plastic… please.

The Polyethylene polymer was created in 1935. Water resistant and an excellent electrical insulator, plastic was cheap, durable, and had a thousand and – well, many more thousand – different uses. Now that we've filled the earth's landfills, parks, gutters, oceans, and forests with millions of tons of the stuff, we find out plastic takes about a hundred years to decompose.[281] And once it does decompose, it releases toxins in a display of bad karma you don't want to hear about.

The same goes for CFCs. Created as a refrigerant, they also happened to be a long-term science experiment about how much damage we cause our environment without looking. Released into the atmosphere since the 1920s, each CFC molecule can stick around for over a century, taking out ozone as it goes. We're still using it – oh, maybe not so much in the United States but in plenty of other places around the world – and we're still wiping out our ozone layer (if only a bit slower than before).

And while you're asking yourself why, I'll remind you that it's because we don't have a working system of ethics. Without the ethics of Dynamic Pluralism, it's perfectly normal to say, "But I need to work for the company that makes toxic chemicals to feed my family," and ignore the fact that you're poisoning them.

That's why environmental legislation hasn't worked. You can't mandate caring for the earth. And believe me, it's been tried plenty of times. How about a brief chart?

1903	The first US National Bird Reserve on Pelican Island, Florida	1909	The first North American Conservation Conference
1948	The World Conservation Union founded	1956	Fish and Wildlife Act
1963	The Convention on International Trade in Endangered Species of Wild Fauna and Flora	1964	Wilderness Act
1966	National Wildlife Refuge System Act	1966	Endangered Species Preservation Act
1968	National Trails System Act	1968	Wild and Scenic Rivers Act
1969	National Environmental Policy Act	1970	Earth Day
1970	Environmental Protection Agency (EPA) founded	1970	Clean Air Act
1970	Resource Recovery Act	1971	Greenpeace founded
1972	The first Conference on the Human Environment	1972	The United Nations Environment Programme founded
1974	The Convention for the Protection of the Marine Environment of the North-East Atlantic	1974	Marine Mammal Protection Act
1974	Marine Protection, Research, and Sanctuaries Act	1974	Noise Control Act
1974	Clean Water Act	1974	Ocean Dumping Act
1975	Coastal Zone Management Act	1975	Energy Policy and Conservation Act
1976	National Forest Management Act	1977	Surface Mining Control and Reclamation Act

1977	Soil and Water Resources Conservation Act	1979	The Convention on Long-Range Transboundary Air Pollution established
1982	Coastal Barrier Resources Act	1982	Emergency Wetlands Resources Act
1988	Ocean Dumping Ban Act	1988	Intergovernmental Panel on Climate Change (IPCC) established
1988	Montreal Protocol on substances that deplete the ozone layer	1990	National Environment Education Act
1991	The Protocol on Environmental Protection to the Antarctic Treaty	1992	The Earth Summit in Rio de Janeiro
1992	The United Nations Framework Convention on Climate Change	1993	The International Convention on Biological Diversity
1993	World Ocean Day	1997	The Kyoto Protocol
2002	The Earth Summit in Johannesburg	2016	Paris Climate Treaty

With all of these laws and conventions, reminders and summits, how is it we are still making the earth uninhabitable for human life? Because they're just not enough. When President George Bush signed amendments expanding the Clean Air Act in 1990, he called himself the "environmental president." But in less than two years those amendments were seriously weakened by a new rule from the EPA, allowing manufacturers to increase their hazardous pollutants into the atmosphere by 245 tons a year.[282]

The tragedy of the EPA is that it is only as good at protecting the environment (which is in its name, after all) as the current administration and those bribes it takes from big business wants it to be. In recent years, the EPA has backpedalled from doing anything about climate change or even protecting the environmental laws already on the books. And when British Petroleum devastated the Gulf of Mexico, the EPA looked on... and did nothing.

When the United States did cooperate with global efforts, such as when President Bill Clinton committed to the protocols of the Rio de Janeiro Earth Summit, we actually helped make the world a better place. From 1993, when President Clinton committed to the protocols, to the year 2000, US carbon emissions actually dropped. And considering that the United States creates about 25% of the world's carbon emissions, that's saying something. We can be adults and do our part.

Or we can follow the example set by the second President George Bush and insist we're protecting trees by allowing industry to cut more of them down.[283] Even when we do elect a presidential administration friendly towards actions to save our planet, such as when President Obama signed the Paris Climate Treaty in 2016, we Americans still need to worry if opposition members of Congress (and even members of the President's own party or the next administration) will work against such measures for political points or simply due to a well-placed bribe.[284]

The fact of the matter is the textbooks we read in school are wrong. It won't be politicians signing legislation who will help us out of this problem because it is those same politicians taking bribes from unscrupulous business interests who got us into it. This is why you hear politicians tell you that protecting the environment is "bad for business." "Bad for business" is a euphemism for "unprofitable to the guy bribing me."

What we need are ethics, providing an understanding of our place in the world, the significance of our actions, and an incentive towards building fair and fulfilling relationships. Otherwise, we travel down the same road that has brought us here. And where is "here?"

Let's take a look at that.

What We're Still Doing To Our Home

We live in a world where 90 million tons of greenhouse gases are pumped into the atmosphere by human beings every day and we seem to think that it will have no effect, perhaps float out into a magical "no pollution" zone inhabited by unicorns, angels, and teenagers who respect their parents.[285] We know greenhouse gases in the atmosphere have increased astronomically because we've been monitoring them from the Mauna Loa Observatory since 1958, along with many other places. A 2010 study found that 97-98% of the climate researchers most actively publishing in their field support the tenets of ACC (Anthropogenic Climate Change) outlined by the IPCC (Intergovernmental Panel on

Climate Change) – and yet, we chose to believe politicians bribed by oil companies instead.[286]

We listen as these politicians tell us that saving the forests and not covering the land with concrete is the same as Communism. We drive our gasoline-gobbling cars even as huge chunks of ice melt away in Antarctica, Iceland – everywhere! The glaciers of the earth are disappearing before our eyes. In 2010, we experienced the hottest summer ever recorded in modern history, the 34th exceedingly hot year in a row, and listened to politicians tell us not to fear because it snowed somewhere last winter.[287] And we continued to listen to such people, as each year grew hotter than the one before.[288]

Sadly, a little snow in the winter isn't going to help us. The ice caps have helped protect us from an increasingly warming planet for a long time, acting as massive mirrors to reflect solar radiation away from the planet. Less ice equals less protection and less solar radiation that gets reflected away. In other words, the hotter it gets – the hotter it gets.

And all this melting ice is playing havoc where there once was permafrost. Melted permafrost means, at the very least, instability for roads, pipelines, other infrastructure, and worse still.[289] It also destroys the ecosystems that rely on the permafrost. We're destroying a lot of ecosystems with our heat. A study in 2005 found up to 125 arctic lakes had simply dried up.[290] Lake Chad, formerly the sixth largest lake in the world, disappeared.[291] Even the mighty Aral Sea, diverted by thirsty humans, has essentially vanished.[292]

People are getting thirstier as more heat means less pack ice, which means less water to most people. Warmer air holds more water, thus drawing more water out of the soil, creating droughts. The United States in the first part of the 21st century experienced the worst drought conditions not just in its history, but in 500 years.[293] And drought conditions are quickly coming to the rest of the world.[294] More droughts mean more fires and more fires mean fewer trees – and things just get hotter.

Paradoxically, more heat also means bigger storms.[295] Part of why this happens is because as greenhouse gases increase, so does the temperature. Increasing temperatures allow air to hold more moisture and more moisture evaporates into the air (creating droughts). With each additional one degree of heat (Centigrade) the atmosphere's capacity to hold water vapor increases by 7%. This means that by 2011, there was 4% more water vapor over the oceans than just 30 years before. This is cumulative and creates bigger storms. Concurrently, as the land heats up, parching occurs in dry areas. These large parched spaces increase the pressure gradients that cause winds to develop. This causes more violent storms, tornadoes and higher winds.

While politicians and oil industry "scientists" don't seem to think any of this is a problem, it is common sense to understand that what we want are a larger number of milder storms and not fewer extreme storms. Extreme weather is killing us. Just ask the people whose job it is to insure folks against the ravages of extreme weather. In the thirty years leading up to 2006, insurance companies witnessed a 15-fold increase in the amount of money they paid out due to extreme weather, such as hurricanes, floods, drought, tornadoes, wildfires, and other natural disasters.[296] Weather disasters in 2011 cost $14 billion. In September 2010, Munich Re one of the world's leading reinsurers wrote "the only plausible explanation for the rise in weather-related catastrophes is climate change."[297]

And speaking of water, ever wonder how human negligence and a lack of ethics has affected the water we rely on to live? As of 2005, 40% of America's rivers and 46% of America's lakes were too polluted for fishing, swimming, or aquatic life. The Mississippi River drains an estimated 1.5 million metric tons of pollution into the Gulf of Mexico every year, resulting in a hypoxic coastal dead zone about the size of Massachusetts. The United States discharges 1.2 trillion gallons of untreated sewage, stormwater, and industrial waste into its waters annually and a quarter of its beaches are closed or under advisories due to pollution at any given time. And that's just in the United States alone.[298]

In Asia, rivers are the most polluted in the world, with three times as much bacteria from human waste as the global average and 20 times more lead than rivers in other industrialized countries. Thirty percent of Ireland's rivers are polluted with sewage or fertilizer. The Sarno is the most polluted river in Europe, featuring a nasty mix of sewage, untreated agricultural waste, industrial waste, and chemicals. Pollution of freshwater (drinking water) is a problem for about half of the world's population. Each year there are about 250 million cases of water-related diseases, with roughly 5 to 10 million deaths as a result. Each year, plastic waste in water and coastal areas kills up to 100,000 marine mammals, 1 million sea birds, and countless fish.

Our oceans are filled with plastic and waste and, quite literally, shit, even as we overfish until there's no living creature remaining. Coral, which is just as important to the ocean as forests are to the land, is being wiped out by coral bleaching and black and white band diseases – all related back to human negligence and global climate change – and how's this for ethics: Dynamite Fishing. Yes, it's just how it sounds.[299]

Our destruction of life on earth is literally working on up through the food chain. We're killing off bees, which pollinate plants so we can live. And we're doing it through colony collapse disorder, which has been linked over and over to the corporate giant, Monsanto.[300] They make the chemical that's killing the bees… and we subsidize the people doing the killing.

Around the world, we're wiping out amphibians and birds sensitive to pollution and changes in their environments. Plant species are dying off because they can't move to a more suitable climate as the world changes around them. And as we take over more and more land, we're wiping out animal life all around the world.

Yes. Us.

Who else did you expect?

And why are we doing it? I think it's because we really don't know any better. We don't have a system of ethics to tell us what's right and wrong; we don't understand our relationship to the world. We don't realize that any actions that are unfair or unfulfilling eventually work their way right back to us.

What's going to become of our home?

If things don't change – or, I should say, if things continue to change at their current rate and in their current direction – the world we live on will become a very unpleasant place. I think the technical term for it is "a shithole."

We know the glaciers and the ice caps will melt because they are melting. We know the sea levels will rise because they are rising. We know desertification will increase because it is increasing. We know oceanic acidity will increase due to carbonic acid because it's already happening. Global climate change is happening in our lifetimes.

A study from the Netherlands has already displayed that the seasons are no longer occurring at the same time every year.[301] This will disrupt millions of delicately-balanced ecological relationships and cause further harm to all life on Earth. We know mass extinctions will occur because we are already experiencing an extinction rate 1,000 times higher than what was once "normal."[302] We've even entered a new geological era, the Anthropocene Era, named after mankind because mankind is wiping out everything else.[303] At the same time, diseases are spreading because the factors that once kept them in check – cooler weather, for instance – continue to fail as global climate change increases.

In the future, this could spell disaster in ways we haven't even begun to imagine. If you think tornadoes and hurricanes are bad now, just wait. Like food shortages? You'll get plenty of it! And the ultimate absurdity global climate change could pull on us – the one deniers like to trot out as if it makes the whole thing some kind of joke – is that it could spell a big freeze coming on. The "Global Ocean Conveyor Belt", the weather system that helps keep the earth's climate regulated, could break like a dry twig. Think things are bad now? Oh, it gets worse.

But the worst thing about our future global climate change, the future we've all made possible, is not what we know will happen. It's what we don't know that's the real nightmare. The sad truth is that predictions about global climate change have never been strong enough. They've always been too conservative! We find out that the truth about climate change is always far more dire than the predictions.[304] Conversely, our response time is always far slower than we imagine it would be.[305] Even if our response took as little time as a single century, 100 years, we have little time to listen to deniers and other idiots who take a "wait and see" approach. We can already see. Look around you!

We need to act and act fast. We need to change the way we live, which means our diet, our energy consumption, our population… our ethics.[306] We need to support the people who support the environment, who are trying to save our lives. That includes Greenpeace, Friends of the Earth, the Environmental Defense Fund, The Wilderness Society, the World Wide Fund For Nature, and Earth First. The collected budgets of these six groups total less than that of a single big-budget Hollywood film. Maybe we can go without a single blockbuster?

We need to shun those who say they speak for the environment but actually act against its (meaning life's) interests, such as the Global Climate Coalition and the British Columbia Forest Alliance and others of their ilk. The Global Climate Coalition fought many efforts to help save the earth (turning a tidy profit for its supporters) until, in 2002, it could no longer pose as anyone who cared for the environment.[307] Nice name aside, the BCFA worked as a stealth bomber for those industrial interests who would destroy forests, packed with influential people and fueled with far more money than any pro-environment opposition.[308] As I've mentioned before, there are those who will do anything to lie to you and posing as someone who supports your interests with a friendly name is just one way

How are we to begin understanding basic truths – such as "When the glaciers and ice caps melt, it means the temperature has increased." How do we see through the lies of those who pose as someone looking out for our best interests while doing us terrible harm? How do we grasp that a tree farm is not a forest, any more than a pet store is a wildlife preserve? How do we rebuke the corporate lie that their "carbon sinks" make their pollution okay? (That's the same wisdom that makes a double cheeseburger and a diet coke make sense.) How do we come to understand that trees are more important than jobs, like lungs are more important than… well, jobs? Or that dominance over the earth has led to destruction?

How are you ever going to realize that you cannot claim to love your children if you are killing your children? You cannot claim to love anyone if you are killing them. You cannot lay claim to love if destruction is all you're leaving behind.

If we're going to save the planet, we're going to have to stop acting like we own it. We're going to have to understand that we have a relationship with it. Just as we have relationships in our own lives, which means we don't own the other person or the animal or any individual, we have a relationship with our home. We need to realize that relationship should be an ethical one.

That realization comes long before buying an energy-saving light bulb or driving an electric car. It comes before any other decision because it informs those decisions. Ethics is what tells us why we're making those decisions, why we're not being selfish, and most of all why it's important to think of more than ourselves.

Al Gore has said that old habits with old technology bring predictable results. In the context of this book, that means that if we continue down this road, we know where we'll end up and it's not pretty. He then went on to add that old habits with new technology can bring dramatically altered consequences.[309] Sure, we can see this as good or bad. We can try to tell ourselves that our new technology will save us from our old habits but that would be a lie. We've seen that we cannot grow our way out of our problems. We can't keep hoping for a magic bullet. That's the child's way out.

Mister Gore's point and mine as well, is that what we need are new habits. In the context of this book, that means a new system of ethics, one that works in our world. One we can understand.

While it might be difficult for some to consider climate change our fault, we cannot deny that climate change is our problem. Ethical behavior provides one avenue through which we can help resolve this problem.

Villains of Dynamic Pluralism

Climate Change Deniers. Liars in the Face of Facts.

A Villain of Dynamic Pluralism is someone who goes out of their way to infect their relationships with unfair and unfulfilling treatment, and maybe even turn a tidy profit as part of the bargain.

Enter the climate change deniers, those who tell you that it's impossible for humanity to have any lasting effect on the planet, that carbon dioxide in any quantity is a good thing, that pollution disappears the minute you stop thinking about it, and that corporate interests should always come before the interests of the people who are hurt by them. It doesn't matter to them if we know this is all nonsense; they just shout louder and louder against the mountains of proof relying on their outrage and healthy corporate sponsorships to keep them going.

They tell us we can't trust what we've been told no matter how much sense it makes.

They deny the great quote attributed to Chief Seattle: "Teach your children what we have taught ours, that the earth is our mother. Whatever befalls the earth befalls the sons of the earth. The earth does not belong to man; man belongs to the earth. Man did not weave the web of life; he is merely a strand in it. We do not inherit the earth from our ancestors; we borrow it from our children." They say you can't listen to these words because it may not be exactly what Chief Seattle said VERBATIM![310] But does that make the words and the sentiment less valid? Just because no one was there with an HD camera to film Chief Seattle, get a verified voice print and a signed (and notarized) affidavit, does that mean we should ignore his words and pollute at will?

They go on to mock the message that inspired me as a young man given by Iron Eyes Cody that we should take care of the Earth. They say that you can't trust the message because Iron Eyes Cody was an actor and not a real Native American.[311] Does that make the message invalid?

They'll tell you to ignore the lessons of history. Of Chernobyl. Of Love Canal. Of the melting ice caps and the mass extinctions.

They claim that Chief Seattle may not have said it; therefore we don't have to listen.

They try to rationalize that Iron Eyes Cody wasn't an Indian, therefore pollution is fine.

And on and on.

Meanwhile, the adults have been telling us the truth and it's time we grew up. Every National Academy of Science of Every Major Country in the World Confirms Anthropogenic Global Warming. Every Major Scientific Society in the World in Fields Related to the Study of Global Warming Confirms the Consensus. A joint statement from the National Academies of Science in 2009 stated about global climate change, "The need for urgent action to address climate change is now indisputable."[312] Of the climate researchers most actively publishing in the field in 2010, 97-98% support the tenets of ACC (Anthropogenic Climate Change) outlined by the IPCC.[313]

And the deniers are discredited around every corner. NewsCorp, a breeding ground for climate change denial in the media, has a documented record of hypocrisy. And the PR people pushing denial are also the ones who told us that tobacco was good for us and that ozone depletion was a myth.[314] They don't care about what happens. They don't care about facts. They just want to create doubt while their corporate overlords make a few trillion more.

Here's an experiment you can perform at home. Close all your doors and windows. Now, pump 90 million tons of greenhouse gases into your home every day. Makes a difference, doesn't it?

Climate change deniers can sleep just fine at night because they do not have a system of ethics that informs them about their responsibility or their place in the world. Dynamic Pluralism does this.

PART 3
How Do You Start A Revolution In Ethics?

Ethics mean so much more than simple philosophizing. They're not just a deep thought.

Now that we've talked about what the ethics of Dynamic Pluralism mean and how they can apply in a world without a working system of ethics, let's not forget where we started back in Chapter 1. Ethics can be revolutionary and change the world in unexpected, amazing ways.

But how is that done? How do you start an ethics revolution?

Chapter 13
Dynamic Pluralism as a Revolution in Ethics

Our Final Visit with Bob and just what ethics presently look like

This is a story about Bob Bing, a man who has no apples. Of course, the apples are a metaphor and could refer to money or jobs... or even apples. Let's pay Bob one last visit as he helps us understand just what is wrong with having no working system of ethics and why we need an Ethical Revolution.

...and, once again, this is in no way meant to disparage The Apple Company or any of its fine products...

One day, Bob saw someone who had an apple...

BOB
Excuse me. Can I have an apple?

1 Apple Man
As you can see, I only have one apple. If I were to give you my apple, that would leave me with no apples. And that's hardly fair, is it?

BOB
No. I guess you're right.

So, BOB went to someone with 5 apples...

BOB
Excuse me. Can I have an apple?

5 Apple Lady

I'd be happy to give you an apple, but as you can see I only have five. I really need to think about tomorrow, when I'll need another apple, and not just give away my apples without a thought. That makes sense, doesn't it?

BOB
Yes. I guess you're right.

So, BOB went to someone with 10 apples…

BOB
Excuse me. Can I have an apple?

10 Apple Citizen

I'd be happy to give you an apple, but as you can see I only have ten. I'm going to have to be wise with my apples so I have enough for my old age, and not just give away my apples without a thought. That makes sense, doesn't it?

BOB
I suppose… but what about me?

10 Apple Citizen

You should consider your retirement, as well. Maybe try someone with 100 apples…

So, BOB went to someone with 100 apples…

BOB
Excuse me. Can I have an apple?

100 Apple Honcho

An apple, eh? Well, I don't know. It's taken a lot of hard work on my part to get just these apples.

BOB

The 10 Apple Citizen said you could spare one since you have enough to eat and enough for tomorrow and enough for your retirement.

But I can't just give them away now that I finally have enough. Why don't you try someone with a thousand apples? That's so many; they're sure to give you some. That makes sense, doesn't it?

BOB
I suppose…

So, BOB went to someone with a thousand apples… and then ten thousand… and then a hundred thousand apples. But they were all far too selfish. Finally, he was sent to someone with a million apples.

BOB
Excuse me? Can I have an apple?

Apple Millionaire
Oh, look. How sad. Someone with no apples at all.

BOB
Yes, could you spare one?

Apple Millionaire
Hmmm… well, if I give one to you, I'll have to give one to everyone else without an apple, wouldn't I? Then, eventually, I'd have no apples at all. That makes sense, doesn't it?

BOB
You know what? No. It doesn't.

Apple Millionaire
Tell you what. I'll set up a Foundation to provide apples. Actually, it won't really supply that many apples. Mostly, it'll supply apple cores and old apple skin but that should shut you up. How does that sound?

BOB
Not great.

Apple Millionaire
I'll tell you what. Why don't you go to the conglomerate that holds all the rest of the apples? With all those apples, there's no way they can't spare some, right? That makes sense, doesn't it?

BOB
Sure. Okay. Fine...

So, BOB went before the Almighty Conglomerate, holder of 99% of all apple mass in the universe with 1% of cores, pits, stems, and old skin passed down in the form of taxes, wages, etc.

BOB
Excuse me?

Almighty Conglomerate
What is it you want?

BOB
I was hoping for an apple, please?

Almighty Conglomerate
Hmmm... interesting. Let me think for a minute.

BOB
Take all the time you -

Almighty Conglomerate
(DING) Very well, fill out these forms and take these tests. It's especially important that you pass the drug tests.

BOB
Drug tests? All I want is an apple.

Almighty Conglomerate
Yes, well, we can't just hand out apples to anyone, can we? After all, you are obviously inferior and therefore probably lazy or a crack addict or anything else we might think up.

BOB
I'm sorry – Did you say "Inferior"?

Almighty Conglomerate
Absolutely.

BOB
What gives you the right to say that?

Almighty Conglomerate
All our apples. And that means we can make you jump through any hoop we want if you want an apple of your own. We don't give a pit about you, one way or the other.

BOB
That's hardly fair…

Almighty Conglomerate
Look, do you want an apple or not?

BOB
It's just… I mean, if I had an apple to spare, I wouldn't make you jump through any hoops or call you inferior or –

Almighty Conglomerate
Ah, but you don't, do you? And we have made sure you'll never have as many apples as us. We've warped the system and we'll continue to warp it to our advantage with apples or promises of apples. After all, we hold all the apples. So, you are powerless as well as appleless.

One person against the power of a conglomerate that holds all the power is quite literally powerless. But a thousand persons? Or a hundred thousand? Or a million? BOB may be only one person but there are millions of BOBs out there and that's what so many who have sparked social change in the past – Ghandi, Martin Luther King, Nelson Mandella, and every movement that stems (pun intended) from the people – have realized. It's time for you to make that same realization.

So far in this book, we've discussed what Dynamic Pluralism is (in Part 1) and what a world without it looks like (in Part 2). But what about a world with Dynamic Pluralism? A world with ethics? What would that look like?

In this section, I'd like to walk you back through some of the ideas of Dynamic Pluralism and see how that would affect the world around us.

First, let's take a closer look at Dynamic Pluralism. Dynamic Pluralism tells us that ethics occur in relationships that are fair and fulfilling. We have relationships with every living creature on this planet, even with the planet itself. But what does that mean: Fair and Fulfilling? What does it mean to be "fair?" What does it mean to say a relationship is "fulfilling?"

First, let's take the cynic's view.

Fair is often defined as: "marked by impartiality and honesty, free from self-interest, prejudice, or favoritism."[315] If we're to accept that definition, it would mean that in order to be ethical you would need to be impartial and honest, free from self-interest, prejudice, and favoritism in all of your relationships. You would need to be fair in your friendships, in your marriage, in your career, in your daily interactions, and even in church. You would need to be fair to people you pass on the street. You would be required to behave fairly towards all people at all times, with all animals as well. You would need to always be fair.

For your relationships to be fulfilling, you would need to "develop the full potentialities" from them all.[316] In order to be ethical, it would seem, you would need to see that everyone everywhere was fulfilled. You would need to see that all things were fulfilled.

You would need to make it your life's work that every living thing, everywhere, throughout time, in every dimension was treated fairly and fulfilled, otherwise...

Otherwise?

That's where the cynic's view breaks down.

There is no "otherwise." I have written the past few paragraphs to intentionally lead you down what I am sure is an argument detractors of Dynamic Pluralism will make. That argument is "You can't possibly be fair towards and fulfill everyone. It's an unreasonable expectation."

There is some truth to this argument. You can't possibly make every relationship with every individual, everywhere, and at all times fair and fulfilling.

And, yet. Still. That is what Dynamic Pluralism tells us. Would it be ethical to be fair to only some? No, that's not right, either. Would it be ethical to see that only a few of our relationships were fulfilling? No. That would leave all sorts of unethical nonsense available to those who wished to be free to do whatever they desired.

So, how do we reconcile these two seemingly opposing positions?

This is the most difficult thing about Dynamic Pluralism. We can't. As human beings, we are limited. We are flawed. We are not all powerful. We are not perfect.

Ethics has never been about doing the right thing at all times. It has never been about perfection. When it has, it has failed utterly. Consider Kant's Categorical Imperative. It said that ethics involved creating one rule for everyone, which was obviously impossible. But when we're let off the hook, such as with Utilitarianism, ethics slides into the gutter.

As a human being, you can't avoid making mistakes or doing the wrong thing. You can't be absolutely fair to everyone at all times. You can't make every relationship fulfilling. It's just not possible. But you can give it your all and do your best. Ethics require you to try and make all of your relationships fair and fulfilling, with all individuals.[317] This is what Dynamic Pluralism is about. Sometimes, you're going to do something unethical; you're going to screw up now and then. But if you keep your mind focused on being ethical, you minimize those instances and create a more ethical world.

Sometimes, the bad guys are going to win. Look at the institution of slavery. Look at global climate change and the hole in the ozone layer. Look at what the United States did to the American Indians, the Vietnamese, the Iraqis, and so on. But it was ethical people doing the right thing – the heroes of Dynamic Pluralism – who set things straight where they could. They haven't made the world perfect and they may never do that but they have effected ethical change.

You may see this as disappointing because it looks like there's no winning but you must realize that there's never going to be a winner because this is not a game that can be won. Life is not about winning but about making the most of what you have. Ethics will never make things perfect but they can and will make things better.

But as long as your ethics are yours alone they are going to bump up against the ethics of someone else. The only way to prevent this is with an ethical system that builds others into the equation. It must realize that circumstances are going to change and must therefore be dynamic. It must further realize that we do not exist independently of each other and so therefore must be pluralistic.

That system is Dynamic Pluralism.

Dynamic Pluralism does not change ethics. It changes its perspective. Ethics is not "what I have in my head" as previous systems have claimed. It is your relationship with others, and thus is constructed with two people and then more.

Dynamic Pluralism does not tell you how to create fair and fulfilling relationships, as something like the Golden Rule tries to do. They are your relationships. If they are fair and fulfilling, they are ethical. How you make them so is your decision.

How Dynamic Pluralism Starts A Revolution

In previous chapters, I've talked about Labor, Advertising, War, Equal Rights, Food, Overpopulation, Energy Dependence, and Climate Change. I've talked about how not having a system of ethics has led us to precarious straits, to ledges both unforeseen and unavoidable due to our apathy, our selfishness – due to our lack of an ethical system.

We in America replace ethics will all kinds of things. We replace it with greed and with lust, with waste and with blame. We avoid responsibility and reason because we do not see our relationship to the facts.

Dynamic Pluralism is a revolution in ethics because it connects you to those facts; it reminds you of your relationship with reason and responsibility. Ethics are once again a part of the world you live in. Of course, they always have been, but now you can see it.

This does not mean that any of the topics covered in the above chapters are restricted or forbidden. In our modern world, we need to hire labor to do work. We need to advertise products and eat food and use energy. No book can hope to cover every ramification of ethics or the lack thereof, but I believe this one points the way. Living in our world is complex and nuanced and can be ethical when endeavoring to make each relationship fair and fulfilling.

With every additional person endeavoring to be ethical, we will see a revolution in ethics. They will treat others with ethics and, thus, teach others about ethics through their actions. There will be those who treat them unethically and they will speak out in their own defense, demanding ethical treatment. In this way, ethics spreads. Individual ethics cannot spread this way because they are limited to the individual. A dynamic, pluralistic system passes from person to person. This has always been the way we communicate our values and pass them along.

This is how the revolution begins.

The Revolution Has Already Begun

We have a name for unethical people. We call them "assholes."

Another clear sign that Dynamic Pluralism is something we recognize even if we don't recognize the name for it lies in the fact that we actually have a name for those who treat us unethically. We know deep down when we're marginalized or when someone treats us as if we don't have any worth or as if they're not considering us as having any value that something very wrong is going on. We just don't have a philosophical-sounding word for it.

But, as I said, we do have a word. In many parts of the United States, that word is "asshole." We use this word all the time to distinguish those people who are not creating a relationship that is fair and fulfilling. We may not think of it at the time but that's what it boils down to.

Consider a common breeding ground for unethical behavior: the automobile. Drivers are often the worst perpetrators of asshole behavior because they put the car between you and them. You have been reduced to just another obstacle for a car. So, when someone cuts you off or won't let you merge into a lane, when someone steals a parking spot or takes up multiple spots, when someone refuses to use their turn signal or runs a light, we call them assholes.

Driving a car is only one example, of course. If you look around you will see that there are many circumstances in which you could fall victim to refusing to recognize ethics yourself – neglecting the relationships you have with others who share the planet – so many ways you might be an asshole as well that this applies to everyone.

So, okay. Then, what would happen if we would stop being assholes and begin to recognize our relationships and the ethics involved in them? What would an ethical revolution mean?

Chapter 14
What Would An
Ethical Revolution Mean?

Just imagine. We've rid the world of assholes and everyone takes responsibility for their relationships, committing that each one will be as fair and fulfilling as they can make them. Humanity has become an ethical creature.

What would a world like that look like?

A lot of ideas we've held for a long time would probably change quite a bit. Some of these changes have been tried before but those attempts were external, imposed by governments and other organizations. Coming from within us, the changes would take hold like never before.

I can only guess at this point with inferences of logic as to how profound those changes might be. They could be made even more profound by people experiencing an ethical world revolution.

What happens to property?

We've discussed property a bit in this book so it should come as no surprise that ethics would probably tend to steer people away from a capitalist viewpoint of property. Without the incentive of greed, people would look at things a different way. Oh, sure. People would still want things of their own. There's nothing wrong with that. It's the impulse towards greed – to have more and more and more and take as much from others as you can – that is unethical.

Dynamic Pluralism would help regulate greed, show people when enough is enough.

Rather than watch half the world starve as the other half lives high on the hog, the people of the world would share. They would recognize their relationship with those who are starving and how their gluttony prevents hungry folk from eating and end that behavior.

If you had what you didn't need or more than you needed, you'd give it to those in need. We see that already. We call it "generosity." But that's an incorrect label for the recognition of perspective. Generosity can be better understood as ethical behavior.

How about the flip side? What do we do with the Jean Valjeans of the world who steal bread for their hungry children? Quite simply, they wouldn't exist. They wouldn't need to exist. Any potential Jean Valjean, if his children were hungry, would recognize he also had a relationship with the baker. He would talk to the baker and ask how they might work out a trade so that he might have the bread. Maybe he could work for it. Maybe he could clean. Or maybe the baker would recognize his responsibility to those who have little and work to help them as well. With everyone recognizing that their relationships must be fair and fulfilling, thievery wouldn't exist because the need to steal would be eliminated.

What happens to marriage?

Would a world of ethics mean a world in which all marriages would last forever? Hardly. In fact, marriage itself might take on a completely new meaning. Definitions could change (and we see this already) in terms of time spent together, sexual partners, roles and responsibilities. With each person working towards fair and fulfilling relationships, the puritanical inclinations towards traditional marriage would probably fade away.

Would that mean that infidelity would be tolerated? Not at all. Infidelity might not even exist. Consider that infidelity involves such unfair and unfulfilling elements as lying and cheating and you can see how that would have a problem fitting in an ethical world. Rather, marriages might flex or fade as a result. They might end but they would not break.

In most matters of relationships, human suffering would be minimized.

Human labor wouldn't end just because people realized their relationships between worker and owner or boss. But the relationship would fundamentally change. A kind of spontaneous Marxist revolution would occur, not spurred by authority but, rather, growing out of each individual.

Unions could become unnecessary, and a resulting state might mean no animosity between owner and worker. People would work together for the betterment of their company. If the corporation is unethical, people would be more inclined not to make that a part of their lives. And so on. This might extend all the way to the eradication of corporations, because competition would become more fair and fulfilling as well.

What happens to advertising?

With less competition and more cooperation – imagine that! – would there be a need for advertising? Yes, but not in the way we know it now.

Advertising would transform from an industry of lies into one of education.

Education would change as well. To make education more fair and fulfilling, facts would be taught. There'd be none of this push to teach superstition and ignorance such as "Intelligent Design" instead of evolution or global climate change denial instead of actual science. We could finally get down to the business of educating our children.

To get back to advertising, that industry would inform about real choices, real information: facts. Would this reduce the world to a drab, beige place with no imagination, Big Brother, etc. etc.? Absolutely not. As I showed with the Santa Claus Effect, if you're engaged in imagination to inspire and play, there's nothing unfair about it. But we can agree that there's a difference between lies and deceit and play and fun.

How differently would our children eat once we focused on fulfilling their needs, rather than fitting them in our schedules? The scourge of obesity helped in a hardcart by fast food might be eradicated!

Those who produce food would put people before profit and produce healthier foods. An ethical society would, as a result, be a healthier society.

As mentioned above, we would be less likely to gorge ourselves and more likely to share as well. We would no longer watch one half of the world overeat while the other half starves.

As people became healthier as a result of ethics and food, other phenomena would change their health.

To start, we would finally see universal health care. If ethics means treating people fairly and seeing that they are fulfilled, it means seeing to their health. Up until this point, universal health care has been proposed as a right, which is to say the government should give them that. With Dynamic Pluralism, we can see that it is actually an obligation on the part of the citizens – the people whose relationships express their ethics. Once again, you can see that the ethics of Dynamic Pluralism rises from the people and is not expected from a higher power.

Another health care issue that would be profoundly affected by ethics is that of abortion. Simply, if women were treated fairly, they would have the right to decide matters of reproduction for themselves. The other element of ethics, fulfillment, means it is up to the woman if giving birth would fulfill her. Dynamic Pluralism means that decisions of birth are ultimately a woman's decision and no one can say otherwise.

Does this make abortion ethical? Is it ethical to kill anything, no matter how small? No, it's not. Abortion is unethical at any stage because, according to Dynamic Pluralism, you are stopping something that is trying to live. But that does not mean it should be against the law.

Ethics do not always boil down to something you should or should not do but, rather, provides insight into our actions. Finally, the relationship is between the woman and the life form within her and must be her decision and her coming to terms with the ethics of that decision.

This is why birth control preventing conception is preferable to waiting until after conception to make that decision. It is silly and unethical to deprive birth control while making abortion illegal. In a world rife with overpopulation, matters of birth rate must be addressed without silly ideas such as "God doesn't want you to wear a condom" or, to quote the beloved Pythons, "Every sperm is sacred."

And that leaves us with overpopulation, a matter that cuts to the heart of ethics. You cannot have an ethical society if the vast membership makes such ethics impossible. An ethical society is one that is aware of the strain it puts on its environment and the limits it faces. Am I saying limitations on children would be mandated, as once done in China? No. I'm saying that a society steeped in the ideology of Dynamic Pluralism can make that decision for themselves and has no need of such mandates.

What happens to global climate change?

Having mentioned the situation our over-encumbering population has put on our planet, it seems only right that it should dovetail to the topic of global climate change. How would an ethical society change our current situation?

First, as mentioned, it would recognize the burden our astonishing numbers are putting on the planet and move towards relieving that burden.

Second, since energy consumption (in the form of fossil fuels) has helped put us into this mess, I believe that an ethical society would cut that consumption. Further, it would cut consumption of all resources. This would happen naturally as greed was eradicated and also as we reduced our numbers on this planet.

Finally, an ethical society would recognize the dilemma we have placed ourselves in with global climate change and actually do something to change the trend. Yes, that's right. They would act. They wouldn't argue in a false debate ignorant of facts. They would see the facts and act. That would, after all, be the ethical thing to do.

What happens to war?

In just about any conversation about ethics, the subject of war inevitably arises. This book has been no different. How would Dynamic Pluralism affect war?

Simply put: It would end war.

Now, I understand that's a huge statement far beyond our modern, myopic view. So, let me take this one step at a time. First, wars of conquest (fueled by greed) would end. But what if your nation is attacked by another? Obviously, Dynamic Pluralism is not acquiescence. Ethics require a fair and fulfilling relationship – but the key word there is relationship, as I'll discuss further. Where none exists, one must be built and self-defense is an important part of that when facing an aggressor. That said, as ethics spread to all peoples there would be fewer aggressors and, no matter how paranoid you might be, that means the war business would be forced to make popsicles or yo-yos or something.

In recent times, I've heard warmongers advertise with the slogan: "Support the Troops." What this usually means is "Let us wage all the war we want or else you're an enemy." At the tail end of this book, I think it's probably rather late to point out how disingenuous and plainly unethical this is. Simply, troops should be supported – with decent jobs and a happy, healthy life and NOT with more war.

One final note on war and violence goes to America's obsession with guns. Are the gun nuts right in their crazed insistence that people should be allowed to own more and more and more guns?

… Yes. They are.

And no. They are not.

While it is not unfair and unfulfilling to let a person own a gun – there is nothing wrong with possession in and of itself – there are a lot of things wrong with it in many other ways. Consider that a recent study showed that gun violence increases as much as seven times in the homes of gun owners – violence begets violence.[318] More than that, though, is the sheer waste of it. Consider what else could be made in those factories producing guns if people weren't buying so many guns. Could swords really be beaten into ploughshares? There's no way to know until people embrace ethics and look beyond their guns.

What happens to people?

Finally, what would happen to people in an ethical society? To say they'd be more ethical would be to fall into the same kind of trap bad definitions brought us at the beginning of this book, however accurate it might be. The ramifications of a working system of ethics would go far beyond such a simple declaration.

For one, an ethical people would be a more accepting people. The ingrained paranoia so utterly instinctive in so many of us these days would be replaced by the understanding that each person is in the same boat we are. We're all in this together. Ethical people would therefore be friendlier, more welcoming, and just plain nicer.[319]

Ethical people would insist on equal rights for all. That means everything the thick-headed paranoid clods of today fear it might mean: equal marriage rights, equal opportunity, equal treatment. Education for all. Health care for all. A living wage for all. Where possible, universal equality.

People would also be held to a higher standard. After all, when a society provides fairness and fulfillment – justice in every sense – these things come at a price. And it would only be right to hold people to a higher standard as they, too, are obliged by the ethics of Dynamic Pluralism to treat others with fairness and provide fulfillment.

Of course, there will be those who say, "To hell with that." There will always be unethical people. You cannot mandate ethics. All you can do is teach it and hope it takes root. But what do you do when it doesn't? What do you do when a lack of ethics is found not in the lowest of society but in those of the highest stations? You do exactly what so many have done before you, what those in the Civil Rights Movement and the Anti-War Movements have done: You protest. You raise your voice.

You make yourself heard. Because you have a right to be treated ethically. It is an existential right anchored in your DNA. You know it. You feel it whenever you are treated poorly. And just as Dynamic Pluralism tells us to treat others in a fair and fulfilling manner, so too does it insist that we should be treated the same.

Of course, there may be many other changes that I'm missing. As I stated in the first chapter, this book is not meant to be comprehensive. Surely, there will probably be ethicists in the future who see some behavior of mine that I may not even be aware of as horribly unethical. This is how we learn.

And we will learn.

Chapter 15
The Future of Ethics

You are the future of ethics. You and everyone you know, everyone else on Earth. It's a herculean responsibility spread far and wide throughout humanity.

This book has presented a picture of humanity searching for a working system of ethics but never quite finding one that worked or, at least, certainly not one that overcame our tendencies towards selfishness and greed. And yet, at the same time, we know we can be ethical because ethical people have walked among us. We admire and praise them: Jesus, the Buddha, Ghandi, Florence Nightingale, Jack Ryan and on and on. We know the tenets of Dynamic Pluralism work because they have worked before in the Civil Rights Movement, Labor Movements, Anti-War Movements and so on.

As I've written this book, a part of me has always kept in mind a quote from the Gospel of Thomas. "The kingdom of the Father is spread out upon the earth, and men do not see it." So, too, could be said about ethics.

If the same could be said for ethics, I believe that changes with this book. Now, I believe you can see it. I believe the straightforward teaching of Dynamic Pluralism, that ethics result from fair and fulfilling relationships, make ethics an achievable goal.

But, even then, are ethics easily attained? Is the goal of being an ethical person as easily achieved as 21st century philosopher Wil Wheaton posited in his famous law: "Don't be a dick!" Probably not. As a human – as a frail and fallible human – you're going to be a dick at times.

If that's the case, then how can the goal of fairness and fulfillment in your every relationship – with every living thing on earth – be possible? It's a tall order.

If you don't think you can be ethical with every living thing on earth, begin on a smaller scale. Try being ethical with only every living thing in your country. Still too hard? Try being ethical with only every living thing in your city. That should be easier. Still too much? Okay, then just be ethical with every living thing on your block. That can't be too hard, can it? How many people live on your block? How many children? How many animals?

Still too much?

Okay, start smaller. Try being ethical with every person in your family: your brothers and sisters, your parents, your cousins, your nieces and nephews. Don't even try being ethical to their pets, yet. Just those people. Can you do that?

No?

Okay, let's start even smaller still.

Start by being ethical with one person, just one person. (Keep in mind that being ethical with yourself, being fair and fulfilling, does not count. As previously stated, this is closer to existentialism than ethics.) Pick one person: your mother or father, or your brother or sister, or maybe your spouse or someone else you love. Just one person. Treat them fairly and make their well-being a priority. Make that relationship fair and fulfilling.

If you can do this, you'll realize you're not done, yet. You'll realize that once you begin treating one person ethically, you must engage in ethics with everyone else. Because you'll discover that ethics with one person and ethics with the whole world are the same thing. If you're ethical with one person then denying them a world built on ethics, meaning ethical relationships with every living thing, is to deny them ethics all together.

You'll realize your place in the world and find some perspective. Ethics, you'll understand, are both very necessary and incredibly difficult. They are worthwhile.

Now, consider how many people will try this… Simply put, the numbers are against us if we're going to bring a working system of ethics to the world.

How can this be done? Is it even possible?

Yes. Absolutely. We've done it before.

In the past 40 years or so, as our societies have become more and more computerized, we have passed on a culture so accepting of and embracing of computerization that children are far more keyed into it than any previous generation. Consider as another example the way in which our world and the way we look at the world has changed with cars. Consider how accustomed we became to the use of tobacco and then to the cessation of that use. The fact is that values passed from one generation to the next, be they values of modernization, technology, or just flat out change, become values that take hold and become ubiquitous.

This is how we've weeded out negative behavior in the past and this is how we will foster positive change in the future. This is how you create a revolution in ethics.

You take a generational approach.

Starting today, when you finish this book, you do your utmost to create relationships that are fair and fulfilling. You teach these values to your children and every child you can. As they grow up, they will then teach these values to their children. With each generation, ethics will spread.

It won't begin overnight. The first generation will have to face a populace mostly ignorant of Dynamic Pluralism. The second will still have many hurdles to overcome. But by the third or fourth generation of people behaving fairly and investing fulfillment into their relationships, these values will take hold. How can they not? When you treat another person fairly, they remember that. When you put their fulfillment first, they feel obligated to do the same. Surely there are those who feel differently but the benefits of a multi-generational approach weed those traits out.

Thus, the future of ethics is assured.

Ethical Constructions

Let me close with one final revelation that I believe to be the most profound. If at this point you find yourself saying, "Sure, ethics can change everything and make the world a better place but... I don't know," this may help change your mind.

I spent some time earlier in this book discussing the distinctions between morality and ethics, which as I mentioned is the difference between two relationships. Morality is the relationship between a person and their notion of a higher power; a moral relationship being one that is fair and fulfilling. As an atheist, I find that to be a hollow relationship because, even if you believe in a higher power, that relationship can tend to be a bit one-sided.

But what if ethics could transcend that?

Because, as it turns out, it does.

The philosopher Martin Buber (1878-1965) famously discussed an "I-Thou" relationship, which is a profound relationship with another. He considered the most profound, the "Eternal Thou", to be one with god.

As an atheist, I find it difficult to consider that an authentic relationship but, rather, a relationship more with our preconceived notions, whims, and longings for such a being. There has to be something more.

Let's look once again to Dynamic Pluralism. Dynamic Pluralism describes ethical relationships as a kind of bond between two individuals investing fairness and fulfillment. Each bond, then, becomes stronger than its individual element. Rather than one person looking only for self-fulfillment, there are now two persons moving toward the fulfillment of the relationship.

It has long been known that two heads are better than one and John Heywood once famously quoted, "Many hands make light work." Large groups of people moving in the same direction have always proven to make a difference in the world. Just look at where large groups of people, the entire human race, devoid of a working system of ethics have gotten us: war, pollution, global climate change. That's some change! It's certainly not the kind we want but it makes a great example of just how powerful that change can be. Would you like another, less disgusting one? Then cast your eyes upon the great Pyramids of the world. Huge masses of people, all working together, created structures that have lasted thousands of years.

Now, let's go back to that bond the ethics of Dynamic Pluralism creates. Then, consider what happens when each person creates a bond with two more people, then four, then eight. On and on. These bonds, or as I like to call them "ethical constructions" build on nothing more than human decency and yet there is nothing more powerful.

Consider what kind of world your children would live in if only 1% of the world was bound together in such ethical constructions. Right now, that would be a bond that included 70 million people! Their children would then go on to become CEOs, teachers, politicians – consider what it would mean to have an ethical President of the United States. Consider a leader who didn't kill. Consider a leader who looked after those in need. Consider the justice that would result when one nation bound with another out of fairness and decency.

Now consider what a human race that treated each other, that treated all living things, with fairness and fulfillment, with decency, with ethics, would mean.

"I-Thou" is the relationship Dynamic Pluralism prescribes. And the "Eternal Thou" is surely not beyond us.

Select Bibliography

This book was researched from many varied sources, from books to Internet sources and beyond. Here are just a few of the books that inspired me to write this one.

By James Burke:
> The Day The Universe Changed, London Writers Ltd., 1985
> The Knowledge Web, Simon & Schuster, 1999
> The Pinball Effect, London Writers LTD, 1996

By Al Gore:
> An Inconvenient Truth, Rodale, Inc., 2006

By James W. Loewen:
> Lies My Teacher Told Me, W. W. Norton and Co., 1995

By Sheldon Rampton and John Stauber:
> Toxic Sludge is Good for You!, Common Courage Press, 1995

By Carl Sagan:
> Billions & Billions, Random House, 1997
> Dragons of Eden, Ballantine Publishing Group, 1977

By Eric Schlosser:
> Fast Food Nation, HarperCollins Books, 2002

By Richard Shenkman:
> Legends, Lies & Cherished Myths of World History, HarperCollins Publishers, Inc., 1993

By Howard Zinn:
> A People's History of the United States, HarperCollins, 2003

Index

Endnotes

[1] Holton, Gerald James; Brush, Stephen G. (2001). Physics, the Human Adventure: From Copernicus to Einstein and Beyond (3rd paperback ed.). Piscataway, NJ: Rutgers University Press. pp. 40–41. ISBN 0-8135-2908-5

[2] Feynman, Richard (1999), The Pleasure of Finding Things Out. Perseus Books. ISBN 0-7382-0108-1

[3] The Knowledge Web, James Burke, Simon & Schuster, 1999 (p. 202). ISBN 0-684-85934-3

[4] The Day The Universe Changed, James Burke, London Writers Ltd., 1985 (p. 306-307). ISBN 0-316-11706-4

[5] A fun and educational website can be found at http://www.smm.org/catal/top.php

[6] The Dorling Kindersley History of the World, Plantagenet Somerset Fry, DK Publishing, Inc., 1994 (p. 30). ISBN 1-56458-244-2

[7] http://academic.udayton.edu/health/syllabi/tobacco/history.htm

[8] Toxic Sludge is Good for You!, John Stauber and Sheldon Rampton, Common Courage Press, 1995 (p. 25). ISBN 1-56751-060-4

[9] Richard W. Pollay, "Propaganda, Puffing and the Public Interest," *Public Relations Review*, Vol. XVI, No. 3, Fall 1990, p. 40

[10] Richard W. Pollay, "Propaganda, Puffing and the Public Interest," *Public Relations Review*, Vol. XVI, No. 3, Fall 1990, p. 40

[11] Dr Claude Teague of the tobacco company R.J. Reynolds in 1973.

[12] Prepared by Dr. Norbert Hirschhorn, this document is available on the World Health Organization's website.

[13] Toxic Sludge is Good for You!, John Stauber and Sheldon Rampton, Common Courage Press, 1995 (p. 29-31). ISBN 1-56751-060-4

[14] "Anti-America," *The National Smokers Alliance Voice*, Vol. 2, Issue 4, June/July 1994

[15] An Inconvenient Truth, Al Gore, Rodale, Inc., 2006 (p. 19). ISBN 1-59486-567-1

[16] The Knowledge Web, James Burke, Simon & Schuster, 1999 (p. 194). ISBN 0-684-85934-3

[17] The Day The Universe Changed, James Burke, London Writers Ltd., 1985 (p. 18). ISBN 0-316-11706-4

[18] http://www.worldometers.info/world-population/. In 1965, the world's population was 3.3 billion. As I wrote this book, it exceeds 7 billion.

[19] The Day The Universe Changed, James Burke, London Writers Ltd., 1985 (p. 220). ISBN 0-316-11706-4

[20] With the Royal Army Medical Corps, Evelyn Charles Vivian, Hodder and Stoughton, 1914 (p. 31), ISBN 0217908314, 9780217908313

[21] The Knowledge Web, James Burke, Simon & Schuster, 1999 (p. 153). ISBN 0-684-85934-3

[22] The Knowledge Web, James Burke, Simon & Schuster, 1999 (p. 27). ISBN 0-684-

85934-3

[23] Dragons of Eden, Carl Sagan, Ballantine Publishing Group, 1977 (p. 95). ISBN 0-345-34629-7

[24] http://www.dichotomistic.com/mind_readings_fire.html

[25] And Plato. Let's not forget Plato.

[26] http://plato.stanford.edu/entries/kant-moral/#HumFor

[27] The Knowledge Web, James Burke, Simon & Schuster, 1999 (p. 58). ISBN 0-684-85934-3

[28] http://www.philosophy.uncc.edu/mleldrid/SzCMT/prag.html

[29] And we live in a day when the legality and ethics of anything from abortion to freedom of speech often does exactly that.

[30] Online at http://www.merriam-webster.com/

[31] http://plato.stanford.edu/entries/kant-moral/

[32] http://plato.stanford.edu/entries/hume-moral/

[33] Check your thesaurus.

[34] http://www.tampabay.com/news/politics/family-values-crusader-david-caton-now-takes-on-light-rail/1070834

[35] 7,500,000,000 people divided by196,939,900 square miles = 38

[36] http://www.huffingtonpost.com/2011/12/02/europe-crisis-retirement-funds_n_1125770.html

[37] Billions & Billions, Carl Sagan, Random House, 1997 (p. 183-190). ISBN 0-679-41160-7

[38] Yiddish for "a person of integrity and honor."

[39] As this relationship usually manifests via some religious book or leader, I suppose what I'm trying to say is that this is a form of ethics in which you allow someone to stand in for a much more powerful (if absent) god figure.

[40] http://www.dailymail.co.uk/femail/article-466775/Live-Earth-promoting-green-save-planet--planet-on.html

[41] http://www.usatoday.com/news/world/iraq/2004-03-02-un-wmd_x.htm

[42] As reported in the February 17, 2008 Washington Post: http://www.washingtonpost.com/wp-dyn/content/article/2008/02/15/AR2008021502901.html

[43] http://www.huffingtonpost.com/2011/11/17/herman-cain-leader-reader_n_1099854.html

[44] http://www.economist.com/node/9832909?story_id=9832909

[45] The Pinball Effect, James Burke, London Writers LTD, 1996 (p. 253). ISBN 0-316-11602-3

[46] http://www.webmd.com/baby/features/santa-claus-naughty-nice

[47] I promised "no math" and meant it for me as well. The number is obviously not exactly half.

[48] http://well.blogs.nytimes.com/2007/12/24/talking-to-kids-about-santaand-everything-else/

[49] https://www.onfaith.co/onfaith/2010/12/08/what-we-tell-our-kids-about-

santa/2548

[50] http://thetfp.com/tfp/tilted-philosophy/79861-when-do-you-tell-your-kids-truth-about-santa.html

[51] Online at http://www.merriam-webster.com/

[52] A technical term to be explained later.

[53] A People's History of the United States, Howard Zinn, HarperCollins, 2003 (p. 564). ISBN 0-06-052837-0

[54] http://www.carsdirect.com/car-buying/why-does-a-new-car-lose-value-after-its-driven-off-the-lot

[55] A People's History of the United States, Howard Zinn, HarperCollins, 2003 (p. 244). ISBN 0-06-052837-0

[56] http://www.cdc.gov/handwashing/show-me-the-science-hand-sanitizer.html

[57] http://www.lovearth.net/gmdeliberatelydestroyed.htm

[58] http://www.counterpunch.org/2003/11/07/when-public-transit-gets-privatized/

[59] http://www.thewashcycle.com/2010/05/penn-ave-bike-lanes-aaa-is-crushing-us.html

[60]
http://money.cnn.com/2010/08/17/news/economy/private_prisons_economic_impact.fortune/index.htm

[61] http://www.nationalhomeless.org/factsheets/How_Many.html

[62] http://www.shelterlistings.org/

[63] https://www.americanimmigrationcouncil.org/research/adding-billions-tax-dollars-paid-undocumented-immigrants

[64] Lies My Teacher Told Me, James W. Loewen, W. W. Norton and Co., 1995 (p. 255) ISBN 1-56584-100-X

[65] We'll discuss hydraulic facturing, or "fracking," in Chapter 11.

[66] In all fairness, recent theories dispute the "rat hypothesis." This remains, however, the most prevalent belief.

[67] Again, I'm going with Merriam Webster.

[68] https://www.iww.org/history/library/misc/origins_of_mayday

[69] A People's History of the United States, Howard Zinn, HarperCollins, 2003 (p. 326-327). ISBN 0-06-052837-0

[70] A People's History of the United States, Howard Zinn, HarperCollins, 2003 (p. 327-328). ISBN 0-06-052837-0

[71] A People's History of the United States, Howard Zinn, HarperCollins, 2003 (p. 245). ISBN 0-06-052837-0

[72] And this demand remains unmet even as I write this book.

[73] http://www.oilcompanies.net/oil1.htm

[74] There's an oxymoron if I ever heard one.

[75] http://home.iprimus.com.au/korob/fdtcards/AlphaC.html

[76] No, I didn't forget Saddam Hussein. He was not put into power by the US, even if we were his buddies.

[77] A People's History of the United States, Howard Zinn, HarperCollins, 2003 (p. 575).

ISBN 0-06-052837-0

[78] A People's History of the United States, Howard Zinn, HarperCollins, 2003 (p. 401). ISBN 0-06-052837-0

[79] Fast Food Nation, Eric Schlosser, HarperCollins Books, 2002 (p. 36-37). ISBN 0-06-093845-5

[80] http://www.msha.gov/MSHAINFO/MSHAINF2.HTM

[81] http://abcnews.go.com/WN/mining-dangerous-job/story?id=10301377

[82] Fast Food Nation, Eric Schlosser, HarperCollins Books, 2002 (p. 178-179). ISBN 0-06-093845-5

[83] Fast Food Nation, Eric Schlosser, HarperCollins Books, 2002 (p. 202-203). ISBN 0-06-093845-5

[84] Toxic Sludge is Good for You!, John Stauber and Sheldon Rampton, Common Courage Press, 1995 (p. 15). ISBN 1-56751-060-4

[85] Toxic Sludge is Good for You!, John Stauber and Sheldon Rampton, Common Courage Press, 1995 (p. 21-22). ISBN 1-56751-060-4

[86] http://www.prb.org/Publications/Datasheets/2016/2016-world_population-data-sheet.aspx

[87] Toxic Sludge is Good for You!, John Stauber and Sheldon Rampton, Common Courage Press, 1995 (p. 17-18). ISBN 1-56751-060-4

[88] Edward J. Bernays, *Public Relations* (Norman, OK. University of Oklahoma Press, 1957), p. 38-39

[89] Edward J. Bernays, *Public Relations* (Norman, OK. University of Oklahoma Press, 1957), p. 60

[90] Some good sources to start with can be found at http://www.lung.org/stop-smoking/smoking-facts/tobacco-industry-marketing.html, http://www.no-smoke.org/getthefacts.php, http://archive.tobacco.org/resources/history/, as well as in some of the books mentioned here.

[91] Toxic Sludge is Good for You!, John Stauber and Sheldon Rampton, Common Courage Press, 1995 (p. 189-191). ISBN 1-56751-060-4

[92] According to the marketing copy on https://profnet.prnewswire.com

[93] "12 Reporters Help Shape Pesticides PR Policies," *Environment Writer*, Vol. 6, No. 11, National Safety Council, Washington, DC, Feb. 1995, pp. 1, 4-5

[94] Toxic Sludge is Good for You!, John Stauber and Sheldon Rampton, Common Courage Press, 1995 (p. 71). ISBN 1-56751-060-4

[95] Press kit from Hill & Knowlton on behalf of Partners for Sun Protection Awareness, 1994

[96] Vincent Kavaloski, "The Alchemy of Love," Forward by Chilsen and Rampton, *Friends in Deed*, p. ix

[97] http://readersupportednews.org/opinion2/276-74/5123-fox-news-lies-keep-them-out-of-canada

[98] http://mediasmarts.ca/marketing-consumerism/advertising-its-everywhere

[99] http://mediasmarts.ca/

[100] http://business-ethics.com/

[101] http://www.iwatchnews.org/

[102] As reported in the August 11, 2011 Washington Post: http://www.washingtonpost.com/politics/rick-perry-holds-the-record-on-executions/2011/08/17/gIQAMvNwYJ_story.html

[103] Many were very intentional. http://www.tahtonka.com/apology.html

[104] Lies My Teacher Told Me, James W. Loewen, W. W. Norton and Co., 1995 (p. 70-72) ISBN 1-56584-100-X

[105] http://www.prosebeforehos.com/word-of-the-day/01/20/the-anti-war-speech-that-sent-eugene-debs-to-prison/

[106] A People's History of the United States, Howard Zinn, HarperCollins, 2003 (p. 437). ISBN 0-06-052837-0

[107] http://articles.latimes.com/1987-12-02/news/mn-17461_1_fbi-agent

[108] http://www.iraqbodycount.org/

[109] Yes! The United States! This happened when President Hoover called the 3rd Cavalry and the 12 Infantry regiments against the "Bonus Army," veterans of World War One who hadn't been paid.

[110] My list was provided by the fine people at Wikipedia (http://en.wikipedia.org/wiki/Timeline_of_United_States_military_operations). You can find similar such lists provided online by Zoltan Grossman (http://academic.evergreen.edu/g/grossmaz/interventions.html) and William Blum (http://www.thirdworldtraveler.com/Blum/US_Interventions_WBlumZ.html). I'd also recommend those books suggested in the bibliography.

[111] The Pinball Effect, James Burke, London Writers LTD, 1996 (p. 114-115). ISBN 0-316-11602-3

[112] Legends, Lies & Cherished Myths of World History, Richard Shenkman, HarperCollins Publishers, Inc., 1993 (p. 271-273). ISBN 0-06-016803-X

[113] http://www.archives.gov/research/alic/reference/military/japanese-internment.html

[114] The Knowledge Web, James Burke, Simon & Schuster, 1999 (p. 217). ISBN 0-684-85934-3

[115] Lies My Teacher Told Me, James W. Loewen, W. W. Norton and Co., 1995 (p. 237) ISBN 1-56584-100-X

[116] Lies My Teacher Told Me, James W. Loewen, W. W. Norton and Co., 1995 (p. 238-240) ISBN 1-56584-100-X

[117] http://news.nationalpost.com/2011/10/28/graphic-mapping-a-superpower-sized-military/

[118] http://www.politifact.com/truth-o-meter/statements/2011/sep/14/ron-paul/ron-paul-says-us-has-military-personnel-130-nation/

[119] A People's History of the United States, Howard Zinn, HarperCollins, 2003 (p. 568-569). ISBN 0-06-052837-0

[120] http://www.guardian.co.uk/commentisfree/cifamerica/2011/oct/19/naomi-wolf-arrest-occupy-wall-street

[121] Remember "King Phillip Came Over From Great Spain" (Kingdom, Phylum, Class,

Order, Family, Genus, Species)

[122] Lies My Teacher Told Me, James W. Loewen, W. W. Norton and Co., 1995 (p. 143) ISBN 1-56584-100-X

[123] Lies My Teacher Told Me, James W. Loewen, W. W. Norton and Co., 1995 (p. 224) ISBN 1-56584-100-X

[124] http://www.archives.state.al.us/govs_list/inauguralspeech.html

[125] A People's History of the United States, Howard Zinn, HarperCollins, 2003 (p. 454-455). ISBN 0-06-052837-0

[126] http://www.factcheck.org/2010/06/arizonas-papers-please-law/

[127] http://www.huffingtonpost.com/judge-h-lee-sarokin/the-new-driving-while-bla_b_990487.html

[128] http://www.usdakotawar.org/history/andrew-myrick

[129] http://www.aauw.org/research/the-simple-truth-about-the-gender-pay-gap/

[130] My Later Life, Helen Keller, Mindstream, 1929 (p. 156) ISBN 1179301137

[131] http://www.huffingtonpost.com/2010/06/10/john-linder-unemployment_n_607589.html

[132] http://www.npr.org/templates/story/story.php?storyId=125387528

[133] http://www.rawstory.com/rs/2011/08/25/only-2-of-welfare-applicants-in-florida-failed-drug-tests/

[134] https://thinkprogress.org/what-7-states-discovered-after-spending-more-than-1-million-drug-testing-welfare-recipients-c346e0b4305d#.ofb41kcpe

[135] A People's History of the United States, Howard Zinn, HarperCollins, 2003 (p. 644). ISBN 0-06-052837-0

[136] A People's History of the United States, Howard Zinn, HarperCollins, 2003 (p. 629). ISBN 0-06-052837-0

[137] http://www.gwb.com.au/gwb/news/watch/racism.htm

[138] http://www.huffingtonpost.com/2012/01/09/pope-benedict-xvi-gay-marriage_n_1194515.html

[139] Billions & Billions, Carl Sagan, Random House, 1997 (p. 209). ISBN 0-679-41160-7

[140] http://www.usfederalbudget.us/federal_budget_actual

[141] Thomas Scarlett, "Killing Health Care Reform," Campaigns & Elections, October/Nov. 1994, p. 34

[142] Toxic Sludge is Good for You!, John Stauber and Sheldon Rampton, Common Courage Press, 1995 (p. 97). ISBN 1-56751-060-4

[143] http://www.factcheck.org/2009/08/palin-vs-obama-death-panels/

[144] http://medicaltourism.com/

[145] Billions & Billions, Carl Sagan, Random House, 1997 (p. 166). ISBN 0-679-41160-7

[146] http://www.roman-catholic.com/Roman/Articles/CapitalPunishment.htm

[147] http://www.personhoodusa.com/

[148] http://www.huffingtonpost.com/2009/05/31/george-tiller-killed-abor_n_209504.html

[149] I am, of course, referring to the brave Representative from Arizona, Gabrielle Giffords.

[150] http://www.upi.com/Top_News/2009/04/08/Poll-Gun-control-support-at-all-time-low/UPI-82781239204131/

[151] Doing the same thing over and over and expecting different results.

[152] http://www.weeklystandard.com/blogs/america-s-long-history-preventative-detention_537535.html

[153] http://usawatchdog.com/national-defense-authorization-act-indefinite-detention-bill-senate-bill-1867/

[154] http://www.veteranstoday.com/2011/12/01/the-truth-about-the-national-defense-authorization-act/

[155] http://www.forbes.com/sites/erikkain/2011/12/05/the-national-defense-authorization-act-is-the-greatest-threat-to-civil-liberties-americans-face/

[156] No kidding. http://news.discovery.com/tech/genetically-modified-apple-doesnt-brown.html

[157] The Pinball Effect, James Burke, London Writers LTD, 1996 (p. 12). ISBN 0-316-11602-3

[158] Some refer to them as "vegetables."

[159] http://www.ers.usda.gov/news/BSECoverage.htm

[160] http://www.usatoday.com/news/education/2009-12-08-school-lunch-standards_N.htm

[161] http://www.citizen.org/publications/publicationredirect.cfm?ID=7127

[162] Fast Food Nation, Eric Schlosser, HarperCollins Books, 2002 (p. 217-218). ISBN 0-06-093845-5

[163] http://www.albionmonitor.com/9612a/madcow-rbgh.html

[164] Toxic Sludge is Good for You!, John Stauber and Sheldon Rampton, Common Courage Press, 1995 (p. 55-56). ISBN 1-56751-060-4

[165] Reported by Steve Mitchell on June 21, 2004 United Press International http://www.organicconsumers.org/madcow/awful62104.cfm

[166] http://www.nytimes.com/2006/06/23/science/22cnd-brain.html

[167] http://www.cnn.com/2012/05/03/health/california-mad-cow/index.html

[168] http://science.howstuffworks.com/environmental/life/zoology/mammals/methane-cow.htm

[169] http://www.thepigsite.com/swinenews/12834/rain-puts-hog-waste-lagoons-too-high

[170] http://www.cspinet.org/EatingGreen/

[171] http://www.fns.usda.gov/nslp/national-school-lunch-program-nslp

[172] http://motherjones.com/politics/2003/01/unhappy-meals

[173] Fast Food Nation, Eric Schlosser, HarperCollins Books, 2002 (p. 218-221). ISBN 0-06-093845-5

[174] https://www.washingtonpost.com/blogs/blogpost/post/pink-slime-in-school-lunches-government-is-buying-7-million-pounds-worth/2012/03/07/gIQAKIzRxR_blog.html

[175] http://www.dailykos.com/story/2011/02/06/941664/-Ketchup-Is-a-Vegetable-

Other-Republican-Myths-Remember-Reagan

[176] http://www.huffingtonpost.com/2011/11/16/pizza-vegetable-school-lunches-lobbyists_n_1098029.html?ref=health

[177] http://www.butwhataboutthechildren.org/

[178] http://pediatrics.aappublications.org/content/118/6/2563.full

[179] Fast Food Nation, Eric Schlosser, HarperCollins Books, 2002 (p. 43). ISBN 0-06-093845-5

[180] http://www.hsph.harvard.edu/nutritionsource/healthy-drinks/sugary-vs-diet-drinks/

[181] http://www.globalhealingcenter.com/addictions/soda-addiction

[182] http://gizmodo.com/5654066/chicken-nuggets-are-made-from-this-pink-chicken-goop

[183] http://www.fitday.com/fitness-articles/nutrition/healthy-eating/the-nutrition-of-french-fries.html

[184] http://www.seattlepi.com/local/opinion/article/The-dual-burden-of-being-overweight-and-1291903.php

[185] https://www.niddk.nih.gov/health-information/health-statistics/Pages/overweight-obesity-statistics.aspx

[186] http://www.americablog.com/2010/04/100-years-ago-this-kind-of-fat-got-you.html

[187] http://thechart.blogs.cnn.com/2011/11/30/report-arsenic-in-apple-and-grape-juice/

[188] https://www.geneticliteracyproject.org/2016/03/04/dont-want-eat-gmos-foods-avoid/

[189] http://business.highbeam.com/industry-reports/food/flavoring-extracts-flavoring-syrups-not-elsewhere-classified

[190] http://gardenculturemagazine.com/garden-inputs/nutrients/biosolids-k-sewer-sludge
http://www.naturalnews.com/029504_organic_biosolids_toxic.html

[191] http://www.sourcewatch.org/index.php?title=Biosolids

[192] http://www.nviro.com/NVIRO_Soil.html

[193] http://www.reuters.com/article/2011/05/25/us-fda-lobby-letter-idUSTRE74O65Q20110525

[194] Toxic Sludge is Good for You!, John Stauber and Sheldon Rampton, Common Courage Press, 1995 (p. 99-122). ISBN 1-56751-060-4

[195] http://abcnews.go.com/GMA/OnCall/story?id=4439943&page=1
http://consumerist.com/2010/09/hfcs-rebrands-as-corn-sugar.html

[196] http://www.huffingtonpost.com/2012/02/14/bpa-chemical-hormone-obesity-diabetes_n_1276996.html

[197] And sadly, that day may not be very far away. http://www.treehugger.com/clean-technology/an-apple-a-day-keeps-the-gas-pump-away.html

[198] So much for Young Earth Creationists.

[199] The Dorling Kindersley History of the World, Plantagenet Somerset Fry, DK

Publishing, Inc., 1994 (p. 30). ISBN 1-56458-244-2

[200] Dates in this book use the notation "BCE" for Before Common Era and "CE" for Common Era.

[201] The Pinball Effect, James Burke, London Writers LTD, 1996 (p. 189-190). ISBN 0-316-11602-3

[202] The Knowledge Web, James Burke, Simon & Schuster, 1999 (p. 41). ISBN 0-684-85934-3

[203] http://www.cathedralgrove.eu/text/05-Pictures-Politics-1.htm

[204] http://www.eh-resources.org/timeline/timeline_industrial.html

[205] Moral Physiology, Robert Dale Owen, 1842 (p. 20). ISBN 0554724278, 9780554724270

[206] Moral Physiology, Robert Dale Owen, 1842 (p. 24). ISBN 0554724278, 9780554724270

[207] The Knowledge Web, James Burke, Simon & Schuster, 1999 (p. 66-67). ISBN 0-684-85934-3

[208] The Knowledge Web, James Burke, Simon & Schuster, 1999 (p. 44-45). ISBN 0-684-85934-3

[209] http://www.population-security.org/28-APP2.html

[210] http://www.google.com/publicdata/directory

[211] http://www.nationalgeographic.com/eye/deforestation/effect.html

[212] http://www.naturarx.com/health-articles/refined-food.html

[213] http://www.fcwa.org/story_of_water/html/earth.htm

[214] This article shows such riots in Tunisia and Algeria in 2011: http://www.dailymarkets.com/economy/2011/01/17/food-riots-2011-world-on-verge-of-major-food-crisis/

[215] You can find information on Population Connection at http://www.populationconnection.org and World Population Foundation at http://www.wpf.org/.

[216] http://www.chron.com/news/nation-world/article/Mexican-groups-vow-to-protest-outside-clinics-1810086.php

[217] http://www.medindia.net/news/view_news_main.asp?x=20303

[218] http://www.eco-net.dk/ENGLISH/manifesto/manifestet.htm

[219] http://www.happyplanetindex.org/

[220] President's Council on Sustainable Development, 1996 Report of Task Force on Population and Consumption
Page 16, The Implications of Slow Growth

[221] Billions & Billions, Carl Sagan, Random House, 1997 (p. 16). ISBN 0-679-41160-7

[222] The Pinball Effect, James Burke, London Writers LTD, 1996 (p. 130). ISBN 0-316-11602-3

[223] Lies My Teacher Told Me, James W. Loewen, W. W. Norton and Co., 1995 (p. 254) ISBN 1-56584-100-X

[224] http://www.mpoweruk.com/fossil_fuels.htm

[225] And we've been doing that for well over half a century.

[226] http://www.infoplease.com/ipa/A0001451.html

[227] http://www.guardian.co.uk/environment/2010/jun/24/torrey-canyon-oil-spill-deepwater-bp

[228] http://finance.yahoo.com/news/ap-enterprise-russia-oil-spills-050153139.html

[229] https://www.amnesty.org/en/latest/news/2015/03/hundreds-of-oil-spills-continue-to-blight-niger-delta/
http://www.bloomberg.com/news/articles/2016-03-03/shell-payments-don-t-bring-quick-fix-after-nigerian-oil-spills

[230] http://www.sandiegouniontribune.com/sdut-a-greenpeace-activist-holds-a-s-20160903-photo.html
http://www.reuters.com/article/chevron-brazil-idUSL1N0MW05720140404

[231] http://chevrontoxico.com/about/rainforest-chernobyl/

[232] http://www.tbo.com/news/education/6-years-later-usf-charting-long-term-effects-of-bp-oil-spill-20160418/

[233] http://www.sciencedaily.com/releases/2011/07/110718141618.htm
And here's a more "family friendly" version http://www.smm.org/deadzone/

[234] http://fossil.energy.gov/education/energylessons/coal/coal_history.html

[235] http://beyondcoal.org/dirty-truth

[236]
https://cfpub.epa.gov/ncea/risk/recordisplay.cfm?deid=225743&CFID=66364070&CFTOKEN=83472321

[237] http://www.earthworksaction.org/issues/detail/hydraulic_fracturing_101

[238] http://www.world-nuclear.org/info/inf02.html

[239] http://www.world-nuclear.org/info/inf68.html

[240] http://nuclearinfo.net/Nuclearpower/WebHomeCostOfNuclearPower

[241] http://web.ead.anl.gov/uranium/guide/facts/

[242] http://www.early-retirement-investor.com/uranium-prices.html

[243] http://www.guardian.co.uk/news/datablog/2011/mar/14/nuclear-power-plant-accidents-list-rank#data

[244] http://www.history.com/this-day-in-history/japanese-power-plant-leaks-radioactive-waste

[245] http://www.bloomberg.com/news/2011-03-17/japan-s-nuclear-disaster-caps-decades-of-faked-safety-reports-accidents.html

[246] http://www.spiegel.de/international/spiegel/0,1518,430458,00.html

[247] https://www.wiseinternational.org/nuclear-monitor/320/fire-vandellos-i

[248] https://www.wiseinternational.org/nuclear-monitor/586/serious-incident-hungarian-paks-2-reactor

[249] http://www.guardian.co.uk/society/2005/may/09/environment.nuclearindustry

[250] http://www.radio.cz/en/section/curraffrs/europes-narrow-escape-from-czechoslovak-chernobyl

[251] http://www.nuclear-risks.org/en/hibakusha-worldwide/tomsk-7seversk.html

[252] http://news.bbc.co.uk/2/hi/asia-pacific/461446.stm

[253] http://www.agreenroadjournal.com/2014/04/1952-nrx-reactor-melted-down-in-

ontario.html

254 http://www.nrc.gov/reading-rm/doc-collections/fact-sheets/3mile-isle.html

255 http://www.washingtonpost.com/wp-srv/national/longterm/tmi/stories/study022497.htm

256 http://alexanderhiggins.com/nuclear-expert-fukushima-10-times-worse-than-chernobyl-1-million-cancers/

257 http://www.reuters.com/article/2011/10/18/us-japan-nuclear-compensation-idUSTRE79H08C20111018

258 http://www.nytimes.com/2012/02/11/business/global/after-fukushima-disaster-a-confused-effort-at-cleanup.html?pagewanted=all

259 http://www.greenpeace.org/international/en/news/features/mayak-nuclear-disaster280907/

260 http://northerntruthseeker.blogspot.com/2011/04/important-history-kyshtym-disaster.html

261 http://www.chernobyl.com.ua/ChernobylFacts.htm

262 http://www.dw.com/en/a-new-cover-for-the-chernobyl-sarcophagus/a-36567348

263 http://www.msnbc.msn.com/id/42219616/ns/business-us_business/t/us-storage-sites-overfilled-spent-nuclear-fuel/

264 http://www.mediamonitors.net/ayazahmedkhan2.html
http://www.jstor.org/discover/10.2307/4313067?uid=2&uid=4&sid=47698754749807

265 http://news.bbc.co.uk/2/hi/6319093.stm

266 http://journeytoforever.org/biodiesel_yield.html

267 http://www.oilgae.com/algae/oil/yield/yield.html

268 The Pinball Effect, James Burke, London Writers LTD, 1996 (p. 26). ISBN 0-316-11602-3

269 http://www.aish.com/h/15sh/i/48965876.html

270 Fruitful, in this context, can be defined as "Producing good or helpful results."

271 http://permaculture.org.au/2008/10/25/learning-from-the-past/

272 http://www.arcworld.org/faiths.asp?pageID=5

273 http://www.ile-madere.com/histoireanglais.htm

274 http://edugreen.teri.res.in/explore/forestry/bisnoi.htm

275 http://scied.ucar.edu/shortcontent/mount-tambora-and-year-without-summer

276 http://www.livescience.com/616-view-easter-island-disaster-wrong-researchers.html

277 http://www.petroleumhistory.org/OilHistory/pages/Whale/whale.html

278 The Pinball Effect, James Burke, London Writers LTD, 1996 (p. 37-38). ISBN 0-316-11602-3

279 The Pinball Effect, James Burke, London Writers LTD, 1996 (p. 222). ISBN 0-316-11602-3

280 The Pinball Effect, James Burke, London Writers LTD, 1996 (p. 43-45). ISBN 0-316-11602-3

281 On average.

282 A People's History of the United States, Howard Zinn, HarperCollins, 2003 (p. 576).

ISBN 0-06-052837-0

[283] This was, fortunately, only temporary. http://blogs.discovermagazine.com/80beats/2009/07/21/obama-admin-rolls-back-bush-era-rules-on-mining-forests/

[284] http://www.wsj.com/articles/obama-lauds-historic-moment-as-paris-climate-agreement-takes-effect-1475701489

[285] http://www.rollingstone.com/politics/news/climate-of-denial-20110622

[286] http://www.climatesciencewatch.org/2010/06/21/new-study-finds-striking-level-of-agreement-among-climate-experts-on-anthropogenic-climate-change/

[287] http://www.noaanews.noaa.gov/stories2011/20110112_globalstats.html

[288] http://www.livescience.com/55469-2016-could-be-hottest-year-on-record.html

[289] https://www3.epa.gov/climatechange/students/impacts/signs/permafrost.html

[290] http://www.livescience.com/3827-125-large-northern-lakes-disappear.html

[291] An Inconvenient Truth, Al Gore, Rodale, Inc., 2006 (p. 116). ISBN 1-59486-567-1

[292] http://earthobservatory.nasa.gov/Features/WorldOfChange/aral_sea.php

[293] https://news.vice.com/article/its-the-worst-drought-in-500-years-and-california-is-draining-its-reservoirs

[294] https://www2.ucar.edu/atmosnews/news/2904/climate-change-drought-may-threaten-much-globe-within-decades

[295] http://ipcc-wg2.gov/SREX/report/

[296] An Inconvenient Truth, Al Gore, Rodale, Inc., 2006 (p. 102). ISBN 1-59486-567-1

[297] http://www.climatesolutions.org/article/1441046075-extreme-weather-and-global-climate-change

[298] http://www.grinningplanet.com/2005/07-26/water-pollution-facts-article.htm

[299] http://www.endangeredspeciesinternational.org/dynamite.html

[300] http://www.anh-usa.org/pesticides-definitively-linked-to-bee-colony-collapse/

[301] An Inconvenient Truth, Al Gore, Rodale, Inc., 2006 (p. 152-157). ISBN 1-59486-567-1

[302] An Inconvenient Truth, Al Gore, Rodale, Inc., 2006 (p. 163). ISBN 1-59486-567-1

[303] http://www.smithsonianmag.com/science-nature/what-is-the-anthropocene-and-are-we-in-it-164801414/?no-ist

[304] http://www.heatisonline.org/contentserver/objecthandlers/index.cfm?id=3591&method=full

[305] http://www.independent.co.uk/environment/climate-change/too-late-to-avoid-global-warming-say-scientists-402800.html
http://arstechnica.com/science/news/2009/01/study-too-late-to-turn-back-the-clock-on-climate-change.ars

[306] While space prohibits my listing all the ways you can fight global climate change, there are many great sites on the Internet that let you know how, including http://climaterealityproject.org/ as well as Al Gore's still-inspiring book (and movie) An Inconvenient Truth.

[307] http://www.sourcewatch.org/index.php?title=Global_Climate_Coalition

[308] http://www.corporatewatch.org/?lid=395/strong/font/pp#antienv

[309] An Inconvenient Truth, Al Gore, Rodale, Inc., 2006 (p. 232-233). ISBN 1-59486-567-1

[310] http://www.synaptic.bc.ca/ejournal/wslibrry.htm

[311] https://priceonomics.com/the-true-story-of-the-crying-indian/

[312] http://www.scj.go.jp/ja/info/kohyo/pdf/kohyo-21-s1.pdf

[313] http://www.climatesciencewatch.org/2010/06/21/new-study-finds-striking-level-of-agreement-among-climate-experts-on-anthropogenic-climate-change/

[314] http://www.guardian.co.uk/environment/2006/sep/19/ethicalliving.g2
http://greenfyre.wordpress.com/2009/08/19/where-theres-smoke-the-climate-change-denial-lobby/

[315] Again, I'm going with Merriam Webster.

[316] Again, Merriam Webster.

[317] And, yes, this includes the ugly ones and the ones who may not be quite so bright.

[318] http://www.bradycampaign.org/risks-of-having-a-gun-in-the-home

[319] This is not to say, however, that they would be Canadian, which I say with no offense meant towards Canadians.

Made in the USA
Las Vegas, NV
29 January 2022